The Rise, Fall, and Resurrection
of Thomas J. Dodd

The Senator from Central Casting

*The Rise, Fall, and Resurrection
of Thomas J. Dodd*

DAVID E. KOSKOFF

N

NEW AMERICAN POLITICAL PRESS

New Haven, Connecticut
2011

New American Political Press, Inc.
Box 207141 Yale Station
New Haven, Connecticut 06520-7141

Koskoff, David E. (1939-   )
The Senator from Central Casting: The Rise, Fall, and
Resurrection of Thomas J. Dodd / David E. Koskoff

Includes bibliographical references and index.

cloth ISBN 978-0-615-41926-8
paperback ISBN 978-0-615-43584-8

1. Dodd, Thomas J. (1907-1971). 2. United States.
Congress. Senate–Biography. 3.United States. Congress. Senate.
Censures. 4. Political Corruption–United States–History–20th
Century.
I. Title [B] E840.8 D6

Designed by Sonia Shannon
Printed in the United States of America

Bronze bust by Norman Legassie.
Photo: Charlie Croom
Drawing by Hans Weiss, Courtesy Weiss Gallery,
Manchester, Connecticut

Contents

Foreword

IN APRIL 2009, I READ AN OBITUARY in the *New York Times* captioned "Michael O'Hare, Figure in Ethics Case, Dies at 73." The name didn't ring a bell to me, but when I read the article, the ethics case (though not O'Hare), came back to me: In 1967, my Senator, Thomas J. Dodd of Connecticut, was censured by his colleagues because of financial improprieties that would never have come to light but for the disloyalty of four of his employees, whistleblowers who revealed Dodd's malfeasance to the press. Michael O'Hare was one of the four. Dodd was the first Senator to be disciplined for financial misconduct; the vote against him was 92 to 5, dwarfing the vote that had brought down Senator Joseph McCarthy. The Dodd case remained the most significant incident of "whistleblowing" to hit Washington until "Deep Throat," W. Mark Felt, blew the whistle on the Nixon administration.

O'Hare was not the ringleader of the four conspirators. Dodd's administrative assistant, James Boyd, was the ringleader, but O'Hare, Dodd's office manager and bookkeeper, played a crucial role in the exposure of Dodd. The strength of the charges against Dodd revolved even more strongly around the word of O'Hare, the bookkeeper, than it did around Boyd's word. For that reason, Dodd focused the brunt of his counterattack on O'Hare rather than Boyd; at a hearing of the Senate Ethics Committee Dodd described him: "Mr. O'Hare is a liar.

It is as simple as that. He is a liar. . . that is exactly the proper language. That is exactly what he is. And I don't know any better term."
Dodd later thought of a better term: "Traitor." Dodd's son Jeremy
promised O'Hare that he would follow O'Hare to the grave.

O'Hare was a deeply sensitive man who had enjoyed a close,
seemingly affectionate relationship with the Dodd family. He appreciated the ethical duty of every public employee to expose wrongdoing in government, yet he was extremely conflicted about his role in
bringing down Dodd and remained so, probably for the remainder
of his life. Whether the shots that Dodd aimed at O'Hare for strategic reasons had their desired effect with the Senators, the electorate,
and the potential prosecutors, the scattershot hit Michael O'Hare and
haunted him, especially the last accusation: Traitor. There was never
any reason for Jeremy Dodd to follow him.

The O'Hare obituary awakened an interest in me about the Dodd
case. I read the book that James Boyd had written about it, *Above the
Law: The Rise and Fall of Senator Thomas J. Dodd,* a suspenseful
crime story as well as a biography, published in 1968, and then read
more. I became engrossed in the relationships among Dodd, Boyd,
and O'Hare, three extraordinarily bright, complex men whom Shakespeare would have woven into a great tragic play. I was also engrossed
by the principal plot line of that tragedy: the transformation of a man
of tremendous promise into a caricature of "The Senator." Dodd became a caricature of a Senator with stirring orations, a caricature of
the highly important Senator well aware of his own importance, and
finally a caricature of a Senator ethically compromised on a dozen
fronts. He was the Senator from Central Casting.

I must acknowledge the invaluable help given to me by James
Boyd, who is neither the hero nor the villain in this book, and his
wife, Marjorie, who 45 years earlier, as Marjorie Carpenter, was Tom
Dodd's personal secretary; to my perceptive editors, Hugh Rawson
and Susan Arensberg, to Sonia Shannon, book designer, to my wife,
Charlotte, to whom I credit the sounder of the insights in this book;

also, to the wonderfully helpful archivists at the Thomas J. Dodd Research Center, the Gelman Library of George Washington University, the Lyndon B. Johnson Presidential Library, and the photo archivists at the Library of Congress. Of course, I blame none of them for the errors that may crop up herein.

David E. Koskoff,
Plainville, Connecticut
January 1, 2011

CHAPTER ONE

The Young Lawyer

THE DEFENDANT IN THE DOCK NOTED the young prosecutor, surrounded by aides and several FBI agents: "I sensed in him a ruthless will to win, and in all of them eagerness of the chase. I noticed how they looked at me, and I felt that I was the evil quarry they were bent on bringing down." The prosecutor arose to make his opening address. When he spoke the defendant's four-part name, he did so in measured beats—"Kurt ... Emil ... Bruno ... Molzahn," so as to emphasize the timbre of the German name.

Kurt Molzahn was charged very shortly after Pearl Harbor with having conspired—prior to America's declaration of war against Germany—with four others to smuggle U. S. military secrets to the Nazis. He knew that he was in for a rough time.

In the days that followed, Molzahn was treated to testimony that seemed to link him to the conspiracy, as well as to other testimony arguably less relevant: One neighbor testified that he had never known Molzahn to display the American flag on national holidays; another, commenting on the fact that a bolt of lightning had struck the spire of the Reverend's church, ascribed the natural disaster to the fact that one could not, simultaneously, "serve God and the devil." Molzahn denied any role in the conspiracy, and denied having Nazi sympathies.

In summations to the jury, Molzahn later wrote in his little-known volume of memoirs, the prosecutor "described the sufferings occasioned by the war in terms so moving that several of the women jurors sobbed quietly, and I heard him cry out, 'This man can never be a citizen of the United States in his heart. Once the fluid of Nazism enters a man, it puckers the soul, and this man is a Nazi.'" In two hours the jury returned its verdict of guilty. Judge J. Joseph Smith sentenced Molzahn to ten years in prison.

Two and a half years later, President Harry S. Truman commuted the sentence to time served, without explanation. Molzahn was restored to another prestigious Lutheran pulpit. Then, in 1956, President Dwight D. Eisenhower granted Molzahn a full pardon, again without comment.

Meanwhile, prosecutor Thomas J. Dodd, Jr., had moved on to other triumphs in a career marked by the familiar rise to great heights followed by the familiar fall into degradation and humiliation.

An off told story, perhaps, but a complex and compelling one.

Thomas J. Dodd was born on May 15, 1907, to a second-generation Irish-American family of modest but growing prosperity. Tom's paternal grandparents had emigrated from County Clare, Ireland, around 1848, to Norwich, Connecticut, where his grandfather established himself as a building contractor. Tom's father, Tom Dodd, Sr., attended Norwich Free Academy, a prototypical magnet school serving Norwich and adjoining communities. His mother, Abigail Margaret Dodd, was also a high school graduate. Tom, Jr., was born when his father was 37 and had taken over his own father's general contracting business.

When Tom was born, the Dodd family was living at 36 Fourth Street, Norwich. Today, 36 Fourth Street is a vacant lot, sandwiched between two poorly maintained residential structures. Nothing about the area suggests that it was ever anything other than humble. Before long, though, Tom Sr. moved his family—his wife Abigail, sisters Catherine and Helen, Tom Jr., Margaret, and Mary—to a house he

Dodd's formative years were passed at 195 Rockwell Avenue, Norwich, CT.

bought at 195 Rockwell Avenue, Norwich. The house was just across the street from a city park, a home and location that attested to the fact that he had attained a certain degree of financial success and status. Tom Jr. spent his formative years in that house.

The young Thomas J. Dodd, Jr., grew up in a household that was much engaged in the civic and religious life of the community. A yellowed news clipping in the Dodd family scrapbook indicates that on January 23, 1903, Tom Sr. had become president of "St Joseph's Literary and Sodality Association." (Sodality: A devotional or charitable society for Catholic laity.) Tom, Sr., also dabbled in local politics. According to "puff" campaign articles issued many years later, the mother schooled Tom Jr. in public speaking.

The Dodd house was a remarkably intellectual environment, full of books and lively discussions of current events. Tom Jr. soaked up this intellectual stimulation.

His kid sister, Mary Dwyer, in a rambling oral history interview done in 1995, when she was about 84 years old, gave telling testimony about her brother:

> My most cherished memory I have of Tom—his personal influence on me—was he was the first one that taught me it was fun to learn. He would say "You have to stop and read this poem. This is a great poem. You have to read this right now." And he'd bring out books. And he was a student not as far as teachers are concerned but an individual student. For ex-

ample, he was born in 1907, so in 1918 he was eleven years old, and he wrote his own history of the First World War. . . . to him there was an excitement about learning things.

When he was 16 or 17, Tom Jr. was sent off to finish high school to a boarding prep school, St. Anselm's (today's Saint Anselm College) in New Hampshire, a Benedictine institution. After two school years at St. Anselm's, he entered Providence College, a Dominican school in Providence, Rhode Island. According to the memoir by his protégé, James Boyd, Dodd seriously considered entering the priesthood and had actually entered a seminary in Buffalo, NY, before deciding that he did not have "a vocation."

Tom Dodd was the big man on the Providence College campus, class president for his last two years there. For predictive value, though, it is equally significant that Dodd was a leader in the Providence College Debating Society. The December 1929 issue of *The Alembic,* a college journal, reports that the society had recently debated "Resolved: That life is worth living." According to *The Alembic's* reporter: "This debate was won, much to the surprise of the local newspapers, by the negative team comprised of Messrs. Dodd, Hafey, and Aylward. Their superb oratory and the sophistry of their presentation swayed the audience, forcing them to return a verdict in favor of the gentlemen who seemed defeated before they started."

From his earliest days, Dodd was imbued with traditional Catholic values by the Dominicans, the Bendictines, and by his mother; throughout life his identification with the Catholic Church was both constant and overriding. He carried rosary beads on his extensive travels and he used them, and from all indications he adhered to traditional Catholic teachings insofar as "family values" were concerned. His political positions were invariably consistent with the public positions of the Church or with its short-term best interests. His later income tax returns show that his annual contribution to his parish church consumed the better part of his total charitable giving, with most of the rest of it going to other entities affiliated with the Church. His mother and the priests were responsible for his world view.

His father was responsible for his temperament. Mary Dwyer said that

> The Dodds were not brought up to compromise. From the time we were this high we were told, "Your independence is your best asset. If you know you're right, and all the world says you're wrong, stand up for what is right. ...." And I think we—including my brother Tom—were brought up more in the art of confrontation, rather than the art of compromise.

He was, therefore, brought up to be traditionally Catholic, with all the reverberations that characterization had during the earlier period of Dodd's life, and to be steadfast to the point of unyielding in his beliefs and opinions about most things. Those characteristics were to mark him throughout life.

By the time Dodd graduated from college in 1930, his mother had died, and the family had left the town in which two generations of Dodds had laid down and nurtured extensive roots. Mary Dwyer said that their father knew everybody in Norwich; his whole life revolved around Norwich. Perhaps the Great Depression struck the Dodds sooner than it struck most people: the father's contracting business was a one-man operation, and he was squeezed both by bigger contractors and by the demands of organized labor. He took things stoically; Mrs. Dwyer quoted him as saying, "If you can't afford to pay your help, you have to get out of business." And he did.

The family relocated to West Haven, Connecticut, in 1928, Mrs. Dwyer said, because the two oldest daughters had become school teachers, and there were more promising opportunities for school teachers in the greater New Haven area. Nobody ever moved from anywhere to West Haven as a step up. Mary Dwyer said: "We had no money growing up because we were Depression kids . . . It was a very

As a young adult, Dodd lived with his family at 551 Savin Avenue, West Haven.

equalizing adventure, but a very difficult one."

Things continued to go downhill for Tom Sr.: He worked as a real estate agent in West Haven with a local broker until around 1935, when he suffered a "serious illness" (according to his obituaries), which caused him to retire, although he lived until the age of 83—long enough to see Tom Jr. enter Congress. Tom Junior's principal material inheritance was his father's watch fob, which one can see in most of the photographs in this book, running from the buttonhole at the top of his jacket's lapel into an upper pocket.

From their unprepossessing rental at 551 Savin Avenue, West Haven, Tom Dodd, Jr., commuted to the Yale Law School, even then perhaps the greatest American law school, and an egalitarian institution that hosted innumerable greater New Haven youth from newer-immigrant backgrounds.[1] His preference would have been to pursue a career in the theater, but his father, a very straight-laced man, wouldn't hear of that. Dodd's sister-in-law, Helen Farley, age 89 at the time of her oral history interview, said that he actually started classes at the Yale Drama School: "he was so good, he was a real actor." A class president, a great debater, and a real actor: a man like that could have a future.

Dodd was at Yale Law School during the presidential election of 1932 and distinguished himself as a member of a group of law stu-

---

1. In later life Dodd would sometimes abbreviate "I went to Yale Law School" to "I went to Yale."

dents that made the rounds speaking at political gatherings as warm-up speakers, to hold the crowd until the "name" speakers should arrive. In that role he was noticed by Homer S. Cummings. Cummings was a Connecticut-based Democratic Party personage of national stature, and he was to become Dodd's mentor.

Dodd graduated from Yale Law School in 1933 and took the Connecticut bar examination in June of that year—but flunked it. Although Dodd became a celebrated trial lawyer, and certainly had a fine mind, he remained gun-shy about the Connecticut bar exam. He applied to take it a second time in 1936 but withdrew that application before the test, and although circumstances and friends later prodded him to take the exam again, he never did.

In the summer of 1933, Cummings, Roosevelt's first Attorney General, found a place for Dodd. Cummings was Attorney General during the golden age of American bank robbery, the mid-1930s. To combat the likes of John Dillinger, Lester "Baby Face" Nelson, George "Machine Gun" Kelly, and their gangs, Cummings vastly increased the manpower of the FBI by adding 230 G-Men to the bureau, under the direction of J. Edgar Hoover. Tom Dodd was one of them. Dodd was sent to St. Paul, Minnesota. St Paul and Chicago were principal centers for crime, and for Hoover's war against it. Dodd was a full-fledged G-Man, deeply involved in the investigation of the famous kidnapping in 1934 of St. Paul banker Edward Bremer, Jr., by Alvin "Creepy" Karpis and his gang. Dodd also participated in one of the most damaging episodes in FBI history, the "Little Bohemia" debacle of April 1934.

On April 20, 1934, John Dillinger and his gang, on the lam, commandeered the Little Bohemia Lodge, a bar and motel in northern Wisconsin. Little Bohemia's proprietors tipped off the FBI as to the robbers' whereabouts, and on April 23 a battalion of FBI men, led by the legendary Melvin Purvis (the man who got "Pretty Boy" Floyd), surrounded the place. When a car with three local revelers left the Lodge, the G-Men mistook them for the Dillinger crowd and opened fire, killing one innocent and wounding the other two.

The gun fire alerted Dillinger that The Law had arrived. In an exchange of gun fire, "Baby Face" Nelson shot and killed a high-ranking FBI man, W. Carter Baum, and all the bad guys got away. Baum was discovered dead in a pool of blood by agent Thomas Dodd. Dodd sometimes made it a little better by claiming that Baum had died in his arms, but as time went on he spoke less and less of his period with the FBI and by the time of his death his glamorous past as a G-Man had faded far into his background.

Purvis's son Alston Purvis told this writer that his father and Dodd kept in infrequent but friendly touch throughout the remainder of Melvin Purvis's life (he died in 1960). Melvin Purvis appreciated the fact that J. Edgar Hoover had "moles" within Purvis's office, who carried back tales to their paranoid chief, but Purvis trusted "Tommy Dodd," the name by which Alston Purvis knew Dodd. At the same time, Dodd managed to remain on good terms with Hoover; decades later Dodd would become Hoover's best friend in Congress.

Dodd was only a year with the FBI, the summer of 1933 to September of 1934, but it was an exciting and eventful year: He was involved in a gangland shootout, he married Grace Murphy, and he was finally admitted to the practice of law.

Grace Murphy, just five months younger than Tom Dodd, grew up in Westerly, Rhode Island, the town of the aristocratic colony at "Watch Hill," where the wealthy of the Gilded Age of the 1890s had summered. Her father had succeeded his brother in a printing and stationery business, although in Grace's obituaries her father was described as having been in the wholesale paper business. She went to Trinity College in Washington, D.C., a Catholic college for women founded by the Sisters of Notre Dame, where she majored in Latin, the language of the Church. Although Tom Dodd worked several summers during school vacations at the resorts at Watch Hill, he does not appear to have known Grace there. Grace's sister, Helen Farley, who may also have been Grace's closest lifetime friend, said that Grace first met Dodd at

Miss Murphy

the Yale-Harvard boat races while Tom was still a student at Providence College. Other accounts say that they met while he was a student at Yale Law School. In any case, they married while he was with the FBI in St. Paul. According to Helen Farley,

Tom could not get away and they had postponed their wedding once before. So that's why Grace and my mother drove out to St. Paul. . .my father didn't go. Grace teased him to go, but he felt at that time he couldn't get away. . .I don't think they were out of Westerly when my father said to me that if they'd only asked him one more time he would have gone. He really felt badly he didn't go.

Tom and Grace were married on May 19, 1934.

Grace was a formal "gentlewoman," a beautiful and graceful lady who (according to her sister) never got excited. Tom, on the other hand, was a somewhat abrupt and high-strung man. He needed a gracious, unflappable spouse.

Being a member of the bar of some state was a prerequisite to actually working as a lawyer, but once a person was admitted to some state bar, he became eligible to practice law both in the state of his admission and also in the federal courts, and he might, after passage of the required number of years of actual practice, be admitted to the bar of another state without having to take that state's bar examination. The elders of South Dakota hoped to fill the prairie of their empty state with educated people by providing an easier route to lawyering than other states did, so Dodd "moved" there, at least on paper. He established an address in tiny Vermillion, South Dakota, at a time when the St. Paul City Directory was showing him as employed by the Department of Justice in St. Paul and residing at 569 Portland Avenue, Apt. 205, St. Paul—305 miles away from Vermillion. In 1934 it might have taken forever to get from the one to the other. No matter. He was officially admitted to the practice of law in South Dakota on July 24, 1934. In a 1966 deposition he testified that he had intended to "stay" in South Dakota but decided that opportunities there were too limited, so "moved" away. There is no reason to suspect that he retained any nostalgia for Vermillion.

Soon after his admission to the bar, Tom Dodd ended his career with law enforcement and his St. Paul period in September 1934. Purvis "got" Dillinger at the Biography Theater in Chicago on July 22, 1934, a fact Dodd sometimes noted in discussing his resignation from the FBI. More likely, Dodd—and his newly wedded bride—had learned the lesson of Little Bohemia: A guy could get hurt in that line of work.[2]

In the mid-1930s, G-Men were veritable heroes to Americans watching the newsreels, and although Dodd was still in his late twenties, he attempted to turn his brief but exciting tenure with the FBI into the basis for a run for Congress for a vacant seat in the New Haven Congressional district. When that didn't work out, Cummings found him a position with the Department of the Interior in Washington, D.C. There Dodd was involved (according to later campaign literature) in combating frauds against American Indians. Helen Farley

---

2. In *Saturday Night Special* (1973) Robert Sherrill writes, "Dodd was honest enough to admit it was during this fight that he first decided the FBI wasn't the place to spend his life 'because I was scared silly.'" This writer hasn't seen this quote elsewhere, so wrote Sherrill asking the source, but got no response.

reported to the oral history interviewer that Dodd had "a great time with the Indians. He visited reservations many times and loved to tell us about them." It wasn't long before something better opened up, which brought him home again to Connecticut.

The National Youth Administration (NYA), established by executive order of Franklin D. Roosevelt in 1935, was a New Deal agency that operated under the umbrella of the important WPA (Works Progress Administration). The NYA was a kid brother, of sorts, to the Civilian Conservation Corps (CCC). The CCC offered full-time work opportunities for unemployed young men (no women) 18 to 25 years old. The NYA offered small stipends for "work study" projects at school and part-time work that included job training for student-aged youth, in this case including young women. Its total national budget was never impressive. The NYA, following New Deal pattern, had 48 State Youth Divisions, one for each of the 48 states, which in turn required the naming of 48 "State Youth Directors," offering 48 patronage positions for worthy young New Dealers, people like Thomas Dodd in Connecticut and Lyndon B. Johnson (born a year later than Dodd) in Texas.

The *New Haven Register* of July 24, 1935, announced that Dodd, 28, of 551 Savin Avenue, West Haven, would head the Connecticut office of the NYA. It indicated that he had been a "strong contender" in the summer/fall of 1934 to be the Democratic Party's nominee for Congressman in the New Haven area, losing the nomination to James A. Schenley (who was elected Congressman and served until 1942). A release in the *New London Day* added that the new director had recently become a Lt. Jr. Grade in the U.S. Naval Reserve, a matter infrequently referenced in later literature and ultimately dropped from Dodd's official resumés. Perhaps it was a "paper" position that was forgotten once more substantial accomplishments could be recited.

From contemporary press clippings, it appears that the NYA did some work in pursuit of its stated goal of offering assistance to young people of school age, while also allowing a lot of networking for its chief, who seems to have made a close to full-time job out of addressing any organization that would hear him, many of them bearing names like The Young Democratic Club of Fill-in-the-Town. He was also given the title of Deputy Administrator of the WPA for Connecticut. In 1936, Dodd was bitterly disappointed to be passed over for head of the State WPA—"when by all the rules of life I was entitled"—in favor of Robert A. Hurley (soon to be Connecticut's first Catholic governor).

In October 1938, Dodd gave up his position with the NYA and began several years with the Justice Department, his first actual legal experience, serving all over the country and under various Attorneys General: first Cummings, then Frank Murphy, then Robert H. Jackson, then Francis Biddle, and last, Tom Clark. His formal title was "Special Assistant to the Attorney General of the United States," although it seems certain that except for his relationship with Cummings, he did not have significant contemporary contact with any of the others. It is likely that "Special Assistant" meant that he was not a regular salaried employee of the Department of Justice but worked as a contract employee—in modern parlance, a "consultant" or a "per diem" man—on specific cases and assignments as demand for his services might arise. Demand, however, was constant. With his South Dakota law license, he could practice in any federal court in the country.

Among his earliest experiences with the Justice Department was one assignment that was both unsuccessful and ominous. In 1939 Dodd worked briefly in Los Angeles with the staff of the Senate's "Committee on Education and Labor, Subcommittee Investigating Violations of Free Speech and the Rights of Labor," more commonly known as the LaFollette Committee, after its chairman, the noted progressive Senator, Robert M. LaFollette, Jr., of Wisconsin. The committee was basically involved in investigating repressive practices by management intent on keeping out labor unions. The head of the Los Angeles office was a lawyer, James P. Hart, Jr. Hart is not a well-known historical figure, but a sketchy image of him can be drawn. He was a southern-gentleman type, the son of a lawyer, born the same year as Dodd. He later served in the Army during War II, fought in the Battle of the Bulge, rose to the rank of colonel and was thereafter known as "Colonel Hart," although after the war he returned to Virginia to build an active law practice in Roanoke, Virginia. He died a distinguished local personage in 2001.

In 1962 Hart wrote Drew Pearson about Dodd's services with the LaFollette Committee. Hart told Pearson that Dodd was often absent, purportedly visiting a sick uncle, who ultimately died, after which, according to Hart's letter

> Dodd pulled a fake breakdown, or at least I think it was a fake. The comic scene after his uncle's funeral was classic—Dodd saying he was going to die, an ex-chiropractor taxi driver trying to give him a chiropractic adjustment, the white coats of the emergency ambulance squad that came to see Dodd, and the blue coats of the police squad car that follows the ambulance, all in our office in the Los Angeles Post Office Building about 9:00 o'clock in the morning.

Dodd had a friend named Hurley who worked just down the hall and, Col. Hart continues, "when he said he was dying he said, 'See Hurley, he knows where to send my body.'" The colonel speculated that pressures of the work, and a fear of failing in it, were responsible for Dodd's crisis. Whatever the reasons, Dodd's situation on that occasion has parallels with later incidents in his life.[3]

Over the next several years, Dodd fell into his role as a Justice Department trial lawyer. A quick learner with a flair for the dramatic,

---

3. This writer would have ignored Hart's otherwise unverified information but for the fact that Dodd had at least two later hospitalizations for what seem to have been nervous breakdowns (both discussed later in this book), which lend credence to the colonel's letter.

Grace and Tom Dodd's first house.

he was soon working as lead counsel in highly important cases, mostly criminal but some of a civil nature, and some involving litmus issues such as the civil rights of black Americans in the South and the rights of labor unions to organize. In a newspaper interview with a *Hartford Times* reporter in July 1942, Dodd said that he had had a hand in at least 250 prosecutions.

Meanwhile, Dodd settled Grace and their growing family, ultimately to number four sons and two daughters, into the first house that the Dodds owned, a five-acre "farm" in the historic center of Lebanon, Connecticut. The residence was a gracious colonial structure immediately next door to the house in which had lived the Revolutionary War hero Jonathan Trumbull, last governor of the Royal Colony of Connecticut and the first governor of the State of Connecticut. The Dodd farm was just down the road from Helen Farley's home. It was a lovely place to raise children, especially with Grace's sister so close for companionship during Tom's regular and frequently prolonged absences from home. And when he was there, Dodd was warmed by the neighborliness of everyone in town and charmed by the natural-born storytellers who hung around the post office.

Dodd kept his eye open for other opportunities. In 1941, for example, Connecticut established a new court for juvenile criminal offenders; this created positions for three new judges to be permanently assigned to the new Juvenile Court. Dodd again enlisted Cummings to try to wangle one of the appointments, providing Cummings with arguments and a resumé. Cummings wrote his friend, Governor Robert A. Hurley, urging "thoughtful consideration to the claims of Thomas J. Dodd, Jr." A letter of this sort to Hurley, who knew Dodd himself and could form his own opinions, probably made little difference to the governor. One of Cummings's correspondents, Democratic State Chairman John T. McCarthy, wrote Cummings with brutal frankness, "With regard to Thomas Dodd, I would like to have you tell me just how sincerely you are interested in him. . . . Unfortunately for Thomas Dodd, he does not seem to be able to supply any strength from a conventional point of view, and it may be necessary to treat this as a requisite before the Governor comes to his final decision." The final decision was "No."

This writer just stumbled on the correspondence relative to Dodd's efforts to become a Juvenile Court judge; Dodd probably angled for other positions during this period.

Dodd was soon thereafter engrossed in one of the two most important litigations of his career, his involvement as lead prosecutor in the matters of five alleged Nazi sympathizers accused of having conspired to give military secrets to the Nazis prior to the American declaration of war against Germany. Investigation of the conspiracy and the trial of one of the alleged conspirators went on for weeks and received national attention and banner headlines in the *Hartford Courant* and *Hartford Times* almost daily. Dodd's photo was run so often that he became a recognizable figure in greater Hartford.

Ultimately four of the five accused pleaded guilty. The fifth, Reverend Kurt Molzahn, insisted upon his innocence, and went to trial.

The key witness against Molzahn was a Rev. Alexei Polypenko, a "suspended" (whatever "suspended" might mean) Roman Catholic priest from the Ukraine. Polypenko had emigrated to Argentina and then had come to the United States in 1941 on a transit visa, ostensibly en route to Canada. He did not continue on his journey north, but instead was recruited as an FBI informant. At trial, Polypenko recited a conversation that Polypenko claimed to have had with Molzahn, which linked Molzahn to the conspiracy to which the other four defendants had pled guilty. Polypenko was the only inculpatory link between the reverend and the other four. Molzahn denied Polypenko's claims and protested his innocence to no avail.

Years later Connecticut's all-time most important political columnist, Jack Zaiman of the *Hartford Courant,* wrote a column about the greatest speeches he had ever heard, among them Tom Dodd's summation in the Molzahn case: "It was really an oration that caught that moment in history, suspended it there for a while in the minds of his audience, and then let it pass on into the archives. . . .The past, present and future of America coursed like a stream in his words. It was an ear-catching, nerve tingling oration, and it goes down in my book as perhaps the best of the few [speeches] that I remember."

Regrettably, the full text of it seems to have been lost: Years later, Dodd looked for his own copy of it but was unable to find it; in February 1962 he wrote to one of his co-counsel on the case, M. Joseph Blumenfeld, asking if perhaps Blumenfeld had a copy of it, but there does not appear to have been a response.

It took the jury two hours to convict Molzahn, and Judge J. Joseph Smith sentenced him to ten years in prison. The *Hartford Times* published a rare "EXTRA" edition reporting the conviction.

Molzahn's later history is interesting, and because it is tangentially related to our story, please excuse a break in chronology. Molzahn entered prison in August 1942. In April 1945, he applied for commutation of his sentence claiming that he was suffering from a serious heart problem; commutation was granted and he was released. Then, in 1956, Eisenhower granted a full pardon, which means not only that the punishment (already having been served) was "vacated," but also that implications of guilt associated with the original conviction were obviated. The pardon attracted little or no attention, and those who did notice probably concluded that the pardon, granted during the Cold War, was given with the hopes that it would promote good will

Rev. Kurt F. B. Molzahn

for America among Germans. In fact, the commutation had nothing to do with any claimed heart problem, and the pardon had nothing to do with Cold War diplomacy.

When the request for commutation was received in 1945, the principal assistant in the Criminal Division of the Department of Justice, James M. McInerney, prepared a lengthy report on the facts in the case. He wrote that there were serious discrepancies between what Polypenko had reported to the FBI, what he later testified to before the grand jury, and what he finally testified to at Molzahn's trial. Although these discrepancies were almost certainly known to Dodd, under court rules of that time Dodd was not clearly obligated to disclose them to Molzahn's attorney or even to the judge, and he did not do so. McInerney concluded,

> The closer one examines the entire facts of this case, the deeper the conviction grows that the judgement of guilt of Molzahn rests on the testimony of one witness; and the more one scrutinizes the background and character of Polypenko, the more one is convinced that he is unworthy of belief and that his testimony cannot be accepted.

Eisenhower's Attorney General, Herbert Brownell, reconsidered McInerney's evaluation in 1956 and summarized:

> Although the petition for clemency was filed by this petitioner in 1945 based on his serious heart condition, the petition was

actually acted upon favorably on the basis of the belief, after careful investigation, that the petitioner was innocent and his sentence was commuted.

After the discrepancies in Polypenko's statements were disclosed to the sentencing judge, Judge Smith wrote to the Justice Department: "The facts set forth in Mr. McInerney's report concerning the witness Polypenko strongly support his conclusion that there is at the very least a serious question as to Molzahn's guilt. I would strongly recommend a full pardon." And it was granted.

It seems certain that Reverend Molzahn, who died in 1979, never knew the real reasons for his redemption by the Truman and Eisenhower administrations, or of the help given to his cause by Judge Smith. From his memoirs, it is clear that Reverend Molzahn had no bitterness within him, and no need for public redemption. He had know from the outset that he was innocent. [4]

Dodd frequently made apologies for not having served in World War II, explaining that he had been disqualified from service because of high blood pressure. He mentioned it so often as to indicate some discomfort about the matter, although he was 34 years old on December 7, 1941, when the Japanese bombed the U. S. Pacific fleet at Pearl Harbor, and had several children, so there was no reason he should have felt particularly uncomfortable about his lack of military service.

---

4. McInerney later became an Assistant Attorney General and enjoyed excellent relations with Dodd and Dodd's staff, such that Dodd arranged to have McInerney's son, Mike McInerney, hired on the staff of the Senate Judiciary Committee's Juvenile Delinquency Subcommittee, which Dodd chaired. The younger Mr. McInerney collected submachine guns and usually carried a revolver, eccentricities that—but for his father's relationship with Dodd—might have been viewed as a disqualification for employment with the Juvenile Delinquency Subcommittee.

At the retirement dinner for the senior Mr. McInerney, Dodd described him as "a man of unimpeachable integrity and ability."

He seems to have suffered from hypertension throughout life—consistent with his mercurial temperament—and as he died of a heart attack at the age of 64, it seems likely that he did have high blood pressure.

Dodd continued with Department of Justice assignments until 1944. At that point he decided that the time had come to go into private practice as a lawyer in Connecticut, but he hit a snag.

Dodd had never been admitted to be a lawyer in the state courts of Connecticut. He made application to be admitted without examination on the basis of his prior experience as a lawyer. His notarized application, preserved in the records of the Connecticut Supreme Court, is dated August 14, 1944. As with most resumés, there is some hyperbole in it: He wrote that he had served as "Chief Counsel" for the federal government in "more than 250 cases." The same number, 250, he had cited in his 1942 interview with the *Hartford Times*. Coupled with a claim of "Chief Counsel," the figure defies belief given Dodd's relatively short career, especially since each of the half-dozen important cases in his professional background would have preoccupied him for periods of months. No matter.

Under the rules of the day he could be admitted to the Connecticut Bar without having passed the bar exam on the basis of prior experience if he had ten years' experience practicing before (in the words of the formal rule) "the highest court of original jurisdiction" of another state—which in Dodd's case meant ten years' experience in the trial courts of the state of South Dakota. The Admissions Committee approved his application, but a gadfly lawyer, William H. Shields, challenged the committee's decision, pointing out that Dodd had never practiced law before the courts of South Dakota. All of Dodd's experience had been in federal court, not in the highest court of original jurisdiction of the state of South Dakota; and, incidentally, there did not appear to have been ten years of federal court practice, either. The unambiguous requirement of the rule had simply been ignored by the Admissions Committee. Shields brought suit over the matter. Dodd won the case in the lower court, but Shields appealed the case to the

Connecticut Supreme Court.

While the case proceeded through the appellate system, Dodd took another federal assignment, one that was to prove to be the highlight of his public career, the keystone for his later political success, and the most positive aspect of his legacy: He joined the American prosecution team in the war crimes trials at Nuremberg. Later, when he appreciated the importance of the Nuremberg trial, and the importance of it in his career, he commented to Grace that the opportunity to be part of it would never have come to him if his admission to the bar had gone unchallenged.

Much if not most of our information about Dodd's role in the Nuremberg trial comes from *Letters from Nuremberg,* a compilation selected from 300-odd letters sent by Dodd to Grace from Nuremberg between July 1945 and September 1946. Although the letters had been discovered in a family basement in 1990, they were put together for publication in 2007 "by Senator Christopher J. Dodd with Lary Bloom," presumably for strategic reasons incidental to Senator Chris Dodd's short-lived presidential candidacy. Notwithstanding the extravagant jacket quotes by celebrated historians/talking heads, *Letters from Nuremberg* adds little to the already well-demarked history of the Nuremberg trials or to any deepening understanding of any of the principal characters in the trial (other, that is, than Thomas Dodd), or to any deepening understanding of the Nuremberg trial's role in world legal or cultural history, or to the mythology of Nuremberg. *Book Review Digest,* the compendium of reviews published in most of the most significant American news, literary, or academic journals, does not include any reviews of *Letters from Nuremberg.*

The selections included in *Letters from Nuremberg* show an elegant writer and a man cultured far beyond the confines of his early background, but they are essentially surface documents and do not hint that his work at Nuremberg evidenced any profound dedication to making the world a better place. Taken as a whole, the selections

Mrs. Thomas J. Dodd

included in *Letters from Nuremberg* do not show Dodd in a particularly flattering light.

Letters consists essentially of love
letters to Dodd's wife, Grace, some
of them tender and poetic, and (at
least until 2007) private; expres-
sions of his loneliness for her and
for his domestic life "back home,"
and pleas that she write more often. There is also some account of
trial happenings, and a considerable amount of discussion of po-
litical infighting among Connecticut Democrats. Dodd was deeply
wounded when the Connecticut Supreme Court ruled unanimously
that "ten years before the state court" meant just that and denied his
request for admission to the Connecticut Bar on the basis of his past
experience. He wrote Grace, "the cheap dishonor of the Supreme
Court decision left me with a hard feeling of pain at the time." After
the Court's decision, *Letters from Nuremberg* contains passages of intemperate denunciation of the Connecticut Supreme Court. *Letters*
also contains complaints about those around him, in such number
and with such regularity as to be numbing.

Most of the American contingent at Nuremberg were military
people, and Dodd had a low opinion of military lawyers. He reminded Grace "how often I have said that I wished no son of mine to enter
Annapolis or West Point. Now I know how right I am. It is a Valhalla
for bums—with a few exceptions." Then there was the touchy matter
of the Jews. No one could seriously maintain that Dodd had anything
against Jews, but there could still be too much of a good thing. Grace
would have strongly disapproved of any kind of ethnic stereotyping,

so Dodd shielded his claws (or semi-shielded them) when he wrote her in September 1945,

> ...this staff is about 75% Jewish. Now my point is that the Jews should stay away from this trial—for their own sake. For—mark this well—the charge "a war for the Jews" is still being made and in the post-war years it will be made again and again. The too large percentage of Jewish men and women here will be cited as proof of this charge. Sometimes it seems that the Jews will never learn about these things. They seem intent on bringing new difficulties down on their own heads. I do not like to write about this matter—it is distasteful to me—but I am disturbed about it. They are pushing and crowding and competing with each other and with everyone else.[5]

In general, he wrote, the American crowd constituted "a maelstrom of incompetence. It is awful." So much for the forest.

The trees were no better. The chief American judge, former Attorney General, Francis Biddle, was "as nasty as he can be—but everyone here knows he is a faker and worse, a man without character." The chief American prosecutor, Robert H. Jackson, a member of the United States Supreme Court who took temporary leave of his judicial duties to serve at Nuremberg, Dodd described as "an administrative impossibility—and worse he compromises at all turns on questions of personnel and personal responsibility"; further, "the justice simply does not have the ability to cross-examine," and finally, Jackson was

---

5. Dodd could honestly declare that many of his best friends were Jewish: Blumenfeld, Judge Irving Kaufman (who presided over the trial of Julius and Ethel Rosenberg), Irving Ferman (more of whom anon), Lewis S. Rosenstiel, boss of Schenley Industries and richest man in Greenwich, Connecticut, General Julius Klein (much more of whom anon), Washington restaurateur Sanford Bomstein. Dodd had no virulent ethnic prejudices, and if he had any low-lying ones (as this writer suspects) they would have been against Yankees.

"inclined to be rash and impetuous." The higher-ranking men around Jackson did not fare as well as did the Justice. Colonel (later General) Robert Gill, executive officer under Jackson, "is such a hypocrite. . . he is a complete faker." He was also a "bigot": "He quietly cuts the heads off of each Irish Catholic in town." Colonel John Harlan Amen, chief of interrogations, is variously described in different letters as "a real fathead," "a gross individual and utterly incapable," and "a real faker." Jackson's "first assistant," Sidney Alderman, probably the man closest to Jackson, was greatly admired by Justice Jackson for the arguments that Alderman had made before the Supreme Court. Dodd was less impressed: "Alderman just isn't on the ball."

The trial participants from the other three Allied nations fared a little better in Dodd's book, but only a little. The head of the British prosecution team, Sir David Maxwell Fyfe, a former United Kingdom Solicitor General and Attorney General, Dodd thought to be "a nice fellow but I am disappointed in him as a lawyer—at least as a man of evidence. He is also a fence straddler." The chief Russian prosecutor, General Roman A. Rudenko, later chief prosecutor of the entire Soviet Union, "was doing a terrible job." An unidentified French prosecutor on one occasion "stalled the proceedings for an hour because of stupidity." In general the Frenchmen on the team were "somewhat stupid. I make allowances for them." After all was said and done, there was really only one strong man in the entire picture: "The whole burden of this case is very much on my shoulders."

The constant jockeying for position and publicity-hounding by the others was such a powerful leitmotif in the correspondence that it must have become wearying even to Grace. Dodd would have no part of that, he repeatedly insisted; he was just going to do his job, or as he put it several times in uncharacteristically inelegant words, he was just "sawing wood." Still . . . the letters do repeatedly mention press coverage of the Thomas J. Dodd participation in the trial; not to complain, but "Apparently I have received little press value from this affair so far and the struggle for whatever may follow in the future is not worth the sacrifices involved." *Letters from Nuremberg* is studded with numerous such comments.

Notwithstanding the above, over the course of the year in Nuremberg, Dodd does seem, in fact, to have become the strongman of the prosecution in the first phase of the Nuremberg trials, the trial of Goering and the other highest-ranking Nazi officials. He started out as one of three lawyers interrogating the Nazi leaders prefatory to the presentation of formal charges against them. He was the lowest man on the professional totem pole, working under Colonel John Harlan Amen (the fathead). In his massive *Anatomy of the Nuremberg Trials* (1992), trial participant Telford Taylor, (later a left-liberal ikon)—who disliked Dodd—writes that he was astonished at Dodd's lack of familiarity with relevant world history and with his general unfitness for the task of interrogating the Nazi officials. In his *Memoirs,* Nazi leader Franz von Papen (who *did* like Dodd) noted that Dodd "had only a very superficial knowledge of events and the internal development of Germany." Even Taylor agrees, however, that Dodd "performed very competently" once the actual trials got underway. A leading British source on the trial, *The Nuremberg Trial* by Ann Tusa and John Tusa (1983), is generally critical of the American prosecution team, but least so as to Dodd's performance.

Dodd brought to the trial considerable prior experience as a trial lawyer, probably unequaled among a group of lawyers composed almost entirely of military lawyers or lawyers distinguished for appellate work. Dodd's confidence about his competence strengthened his competence; everything about the situation brought out the best in him.

Jackson was increasingly impressed with Dodd's ability. To Dodd's own surprise (or at least he claimed surprise in his letter to Grace), Dodd was selected to be one of the actual courtroom lawyers in the trial; then, again to Dodd's own (claimed) surprise, he became "executive counsel" of the American prosecution team, the chief American prosecutor actually working the courtroom. As such he

The deceased was a Pole who had seduced a German maiden.

was the chief lawyer over a huge prosecution staff, working with a warehouse-full of documentary evidence. It was probably not much of an overstatement for Dodd to have claimed that the whole burden of the trial was on his shoulders.

Dodd's personal performance on stage was low-key yet dramatic. Dodd was the prosecutor who presented much of the most horrific (and newsworthy) evidence—the gruesome film depicting the situation within liberated concentration camps; the lampshades made from human skin; the shrunken-head paperweight made from the head of a Nazi victim. From the transcripts of his cross-examinations one concludes that he was a thoroughly prepared and competent advocate, although the Tusas point out a couple of examples in which Dodd forgot the first rule of cross-examination: If a witness hasn't hurt your case, don't cross-examine; you can only make things worse. Trial lawyers' egos sometimes get in the way.

Perhaps the best recommendations for Dodd's trial performance come from the defendants, most of whom were interviewed by Leon Goldensohn, a psychiatrist in the employ of the Allies who reports their comments in *The Nuremberg Interviews* (2004). Baldur von Schirach, head of the Nazi Party's paramilitary youth movement called the Hitlerjugend: "Dodd is the most skillful of the prosecuting attorneys. He really does research and works," and compared Justice Jackson unfavorably with Dodd.[6] Hjalmar Schacht, once head of the

---

6. Punch the name "Baldur von Schirach" into "YouTube" for von Schirach's fascinating interview with David Frost.

Reichsbank, the German national bank (who was one of three defendants to be acquitted) said Dodd was "good. One can see intelligence, clear thinking, in his every word and manner."

Dodd seems to have proceeded against them with uncharacteristic diplomacy, and many of the defendants "liked" him. To Nazi Foreign Minister Joachim von Ribbentrop, Dodd was "the most attractive personality of the prosecution."

Dodd, on his part, could view the Nazi defendants as human beings. His liking for defendant Wilhelm Keitel, Hitler's chief of staff and de facto war minister, approached affection. Keitel was executed for his role in the Third Reich.

In his first interview with Franz von Papen, Dodd took an instinctive dislike to the man. In pre-Nazi Germany Papen had been leader of the conservative wing of the Catholic Center Party, and he had briefly served as chancellor (prime minister equivalent); then, in 1933, he prevailed upon German President Von Hindenberg to name Adolf Hitler as chancellor, on the theory that "We can control Hitler." Dodd wrote Grace that Papen had "made reference to his Roman Catholic faith—and I resented this. . . . He is a politician of the worst type and a professional Catholic—and he is as much responsible for the rise and power of Hitler and the Nazis as any man in the world." With time, though, a mutual respect developed between Dodd and Papen; Dodd would nod his greeting to Papen each morning as they all filed into opposing sides of the courtroom.

In his *Memoirs,* Papen wrote that Dodd was "polite, correct, even kind. . .Mr. Dodd and two admirable Catholic chaplains were a great solace to me during this difficult period." When Papen was acquitted of the charges against him, Dodd sent him a box of cigars.

In his personal relationships, Dodd's relationship with Justice Jackson was the most important. Notwithstanding Dodd's critical comments about the Justice quoted above—with some of which historians agree—the book contains numerous passages of extravagant praise for his chief, some, such as "truly a great advocate," inconsis-

Above left: Dodd's relationship with Wilhelm Keitel, Hitler's Chief of Staff, approached affection. Keitel was hanged for his role in the Third Reich.

Left: Franz von Papen fared better: he was one of three Nuremberg defendants to be acquitted. Dodd would later seek his help in obtaining a Mercedes-Benz distributorship for a friend.

Above right: Justice Robert H. Jackson, seated, was a fine judge of ability and character.

tent with his other characterizations of Jackson. Dodd's overall view of Jackson as it emerges from *Letters* is one of tremendous admiration.[7] Perhaps his opinion of Jackson was influenced in part by the fact that Jackson was a fine judge of the ability and character of others, particularly Dodd's. One of the strongest of Jackson's recognitions of

---

7. Dodd admired very few people and probably idolized nobody with the possible exception of Pius XII.

his top aide was contained in a letter from Jackson to President Truman dated April 24, 1946; in an "oh by the way," Jackson wrote the president

> By the way, I would like to mention a young man borrowed from Tom Clark [then serving as Attorney General] who has done extremely creditable work here. He is Tom Dodd, Assistant United States Attorney in Connecticut, who, I am told, is being looked upon favorably by the Democratic leaders of his State. He has done such excellent work that I should have put him in charge in my absence had I been returning to the States, and I think you are apt to hear of him in the future. In any place for which you are ever in need of a first-class legal mind, enriched by industry and backed by sound character, his name is worth bearing in mind.

Dodd's account of life in Nuremberg, related in *Letters from Nuremberg*, often reads like a novel about life in the British Raj, marked with elaborate parties in grand venues, at which orchestras played and choruses of frauleins would sing, at which officers from the natural aristocracy, such as Colonel Howard Brundage, an important lawyer from Chicago who became Dodd's lifelong friend and benefactor, mingled with scallywags and rogues (those who jockeyed for position). His duties included participating in the entertaining of visiting dignitaries and journalists, including Walter Cronkite and his wife, and Walter Lippman and his wife. Dodd's papers at the University of Connecticut from his time at the trial include innumerable social invitations written in the stilted language of "society" of the 1940s. Meanwhile, just outside the doors, the multitude of German survivors faced severe shortages of food and shelter, like the untouchables of the Raj.

It is apparent from the book that Dodd, notwithstanding his many complaints and his loneliness for his wife and children, enjoyed the milieu. If he accepted the position on the Nuremberg prosecutorial staff only as a time-filler while the Connecticut Supreme Court pondered his application for admission to the Connecticut Bar, he came very much to appreciate the fact that he had become an important player on the stage of history, and that it might later become clear that his period in Nuremberg was the high point in his life, the period to which his children might later point with pride. (And so it came to pass.)

Until the trial actually got underway and Dodd's duties increased, his weekends were frequently taken up with excursions to more beautiful or more interesting parts of Europe, often in the company of Brundage. Such spare time as he had during the working week he spent on his voluminous correspondence with Grace, and also letter-writing to his allies in the Connecticut political scene. Some of his personal correspondence was written during "dull" portions of the courtroom proceedings.

Like so many other Americans in Germany in the immediate post-war period, Dodd delighted in collecting militaria, which he shipped home, items such as Nazi banners or weapons. Special souvenirs were the SS helmets inscribed for "Herr Jeremy Dodd" (then about eight) or "Herr Tom Dodd" (about eleven), that were presented to their pleased father by obsequious POWs hoping for a bigger piece of pie, and perhaps getting a bigger piece of pie for their efforts. Dodd's willingness to accept the perks that went along with his office fore-shadowed ill for him.

His prize souvenir was a set of three detailed drawings prepared by Hitler's chauffeur, Erich Kempka, showing the layout of Hitler's bunker and the location of the Fuhrer's body and that of his wife, Eva Braun, when they were cremated outside the bunker. Kempka had been summoned to the bunker moments after the dual suicide of Hit-ler and Braun, to bring gasoline for the cremation. At a time when a large number of people throughout the world suspected that Hitler had "staged" his death and then secretly escaped, to be hidden by the Nazi underground, Kempka's sketches constituted significant evi-dence for an engrossing and disputed matter of fact, with considerable historical value—and potentially great financial value too. The draw-ings came into Dodd's hands and he sent them to Grace for safe—and secret—keeping.

The letter with which Dodd transmitted the sketches to her does not tell how Dodd came to have them, but the caption to the repro-duction of them in *Letters from Nuremberg* says "Hitler's chauffeur gave Tom Dodd his drawings of Hitler's bunker."

Perhaps the caption is the supposition of the editor of *Letters,* but more likely it reflects oral tradition within the Dodd family going back to Tom Dodd himself. Follow, however, the chronology:

On June 20, 1945, Kempka gave the Allies a lengthy typewrit-ten statement about Hitler's last days and his end, a copy of which is

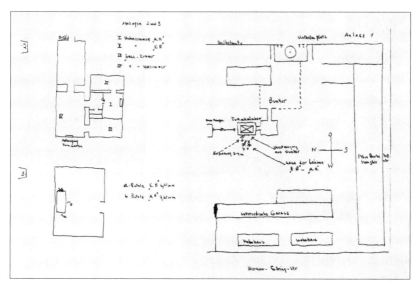

Hitler's chauffeur gave Tom Dodd his drawings of Hitler's bunker, or did he?

included among Dodd's Nuremberg files at the University of Connecticut. In it Kempka discusses, among other things, relative locations within Hitler's bunker and at the cremation, and the statement references annexed drawings—consistent with the recited details, and almost certainly the sketches that Dodd sent to Grace. The sketches are an integral part of the statement, and most likely they would have been given to whomever took the statement, along with the statement itself. There is no hint in Dodd's files, or in his published correspondence with Grace, that Dodd himself ever interrogated Kempka.

Dodd did not arrive in Nuremberg until mid-August 1945, about eight weeks after the interrogation of Kempka that had led to production of the drawings. Dodd sent the drawings to Grace on September 26, six weeks after he arrived. At some time during the six weeks following his arrival (and a significant length of time after Kempka made the drawings) the sketches became Dodd's. Given the chronology, it does not seem likely that Kempka gave the sketches to him. In the note accompanying the sketches, Dodd's second letter to Grace that day, he told her to "put [them] away—in the safest place . . . Do not show them to anyone."

Perhaps it should be noted that immediately after the war, many Americans in liberated Germany were "liberating" all kinds of tangible items, including art objects of greater intrinsic worth than Kempka's drawings. Viewed in that light, taking the drawings (if that is how Dodd acquired them) would signify only that he was unwilling to impose on himself higher moral standards than he believed to be characteristic of Allied life in post-war Germany.

Dodd's children and Lary Bloom, the editorial collaborator on *Letters to Nuremberg,* never imagined that there was anything questionable about Dodd's acquisition of the sketches, and accepted that "Hitler's chauffeur gave Tom Dodd his drawings of Hitler's bunker." They were brought forward in 2007 and reproduced in *Letters*; their inclusion in the book might give weight to the historical significance that Christopher Dodd and Bloom wanted ascribed to *Letters from Nuremberg.* Meanwhile, the passage of six decades might seem to have obviated questions of "rightful ownership."

Jackson doesn't indicate where he got the idea that Dodd was "being looked upon favorably by Democratic leaders," but at the time Jackson wrote the letter, the only Democrat who had much interest in Dodd politically was M. Joseph Blumenfeld, and Blumenfeld, himself a young virtual nobody, could hardly qualify as a party "leader."

Joe Blumenfeld was one of the most important friends in Dodd's life. Blumenfeld was a Harvard Law graduate, Jewish, three years older than Dodd. He shared Dodd's "New Deal" attitudes on domestic policy matters. He also shared Dodd's fierce anti-communist attitudes (either shared them from the outset or was converted to them over time), to the astonished disbelief of most of the liberal Jewish community in which Blumenfeld traveled.

The two met during the Molzahn trial, or possibly slightly before. Blumenfeld was an Assistant U.S. Attorney in Hartford, specializing in eminent domain cases, but he was assigned to work with Dodd on the Molzahn case. While Dodd was a showy courtroom type, Blumenfeld was a more scholarly lawyer, a lawyer's lawyer. One person who knew Blumenfeld as well as anybody knew him told the author that Blumenfeld "glommed onto" Dodd. He apparently had tremendous admiration for traits that he thought Dodd possessed, ones he thought lacking in himself (although Blumenfeld was also highly regarded as a trial lawyer in Hartford County, Connecticut). From 1942 until he became a federal judge in 1961, Blumenfeld remained Dodd's most loyal and constant partisan.

It was Blumenfeld who fought the case over Dodd's admission to the bar. When that cause was lost, he urged Dodd to take the test for admission to the Connecticut Bar a second time, but when Dodd did not pick up on the suggestion, Blumenfeld successfully lobbied to have the bar's rule changed, so that federal service might be held to satisfy the requirement for admission on the basis of past legal experience. Dodd, hard at work in Nuremberg, could not believe that Blumenfeld had succeeded in changing the rules, and he remained grateful for Blumenfeld's loyalty at that time and throughout his later career. When Dodd returned from Nuremberg, he was promptly admitted to the bar on the basis of his prior experience; Shields, having become a civil servant in the meantime, was then clerk of an eastern Connecticut court and let the matter lie.[8] Dodd and Blumenfeld practiced law together, a business relationship (sometimes an informal business relationship) that survived until Dodd's election to the U.S. Senate enabled him to reward his friend with a federal judgeship.

At the time in April 1946 that Justice Jackson wrote Truman that Dodd was being "looked upon favorably by the Democratic leaders

---

8. The second effort to be admitted to the bar without necessity for the exam, however, brought Dodd at least two new good-sized articles in the *Courant*, one in November 1946, and another in February 1947, and possibly press coverage in other Connecticut newspapers, thereby reminding people that the gubernatorial wannabe had failed to pass the Connecticut bar examination.

of his state," Blumenfeld was plumping Dodd—a man who was tied up with heavy responsibilities in Germany—to be the Democratic Party's nominee for Governor of the State of Connecticut. Dodd appreciated from the outset that he was a "longshot" but not necessarily a hopeless one. If the convention should deadlock between the leading candidates, Lt. Governor Wilbert Snow, a Wesleyan professor and poet who was nonetheless a tough politician, and Chester Bowles, a successful businessman then serving as a New Deal administrator, it might turn to a "compromise candidate." There was enough of a hope to justify some effort. A small notice in the *Naugatuck News* dated July 22, 1946, reports

> We don't know who's handling publicity for Thomas Dodd of Lebanon, chief assistant to Justice Robert H. Jackson at Nuremberg—but he's doing a good job . . . Seems that every time the mail man calls he brings in another pose of Mr. Dodd. . . . They come through the public relations office of the U. S. Chief of Counsel . . . Wonder why the buildup."

At the party's state convention later that summer, Dodd did remarkably well. After the first roll call, Snow had 524 delegates, Bowles 454 ½, and Dodd 109 ½ . Then Dodd's delegates began slipping away, for the most part to Snow, who won the convention's nod only to lose the election.

A good part of *Letters from Nuremberg* is taken up with talk about the political situation in Connecticut. Dodd repeatedly wrote Grace that his only ambition was to return home and begin the life of "lawyer Dodd." But he was telling her what he thought she wanted to hear. He was preoccupied with getting into the tussle of the political world, which was dominated by people for whom he either had little respect or outright dislike: "I dislike Mrs Woodhouse [Congresswoman Chase Going Woodhouse], Alfred Bingham, Snow and Bowles running the party in Connecticut. They are all carpetbaggers and opportunists." His biggest dislike, though, was Democratic U.S. Senator Brien McMahon (born James O'Brien McMahon, he changed his name as a young man) and McMahon's sidekicks, the now forgotten Joe Tone, the unsuccessful Democratic candidate for U.S. Senate in 1946, and the almost forgotten John M. Golden, long-time Democratic National Committeeman from Connecticut. Dodd would have known and worked with Tone and Golden, both greater-New Haven people, during Dodd's West Haven/New Haven period, apparently unharmoniously, while McMahon must have given Dodd some offense not discovered by this writer, but sufficiently serious that Dodd vowed repeatedly in *Letters* that he was going to get McMahon. Get McMahon but good: "I do want to knock that bird into a cocked hat and I will do it at the right time. ... I will throw down the gauntlet."

On the Republican side, Claire Boothe Luce especially irked him. A renaissance woman, or at least sometimes characterized as such, Mrs. Luce was the wife of *Time-Life* publisher Henry R. Luce, and represented Fairfield County, Connecticut, in Congress. After suffering the loss of a daughter in an automobile accident, she became engrossed in religion and ultimately turned to the Catholic faith. Legend has it that when Mrs. Luce enthused too extravagantly about her new religion to Pius XII, the pontiff is said to have reminded her that he, too, was a Catholic. Dodd suspected that her conversion was less motivated by spiritual considerations than by political ones. "You know it is an ugly thought," he wrote Grace, "but I think Claire realized that the Catholics in Connecticut are very strong. I hope I am in error. She was flirting with Buddhism a few years ago."

On a national level, he thought President Harry Truman "should be thrown out of office."

Here—politics and the quest for high elective office—was an arena in which Dodd would gladly compete.

CHAPTER TWO

The Rise

WITH THE COMPLETION OF THE FIRST phase of the Nurem-
berg trials, culminating with the conviction and execution of most of
the highest-ranking captured Nazis, Dodd was free to return home to
Connecticut and to his new role as "lawyer Dodd" with the firm of
Pelgrift, Dodd, Blumenfeld and Nair. Lawyering, however, was not
his interest: high elective office was. *Courant* columnist Jack Zaiman,
in possibly his first extensive reference to Dodd, noted in 1947 that
Dodd "would undoubtedly be a candidate for governor in 1948."
Dodd was traversing the state, accepting every speaking invitation,
attending every political affair that came along, always delivering his
"non-political report" on the Nuremberg proceedings. Dodd was to
ride his participation at Nuremberg right into the House of Representatives, and then into the United States Senate.

He became the first Connecticut State Chairman of United World
Federalists and a member of its national board, in the company of notably enlightened people such as Norman Cousins, Mark Van Doren,
Alan Cranston, and Edgar A. Mowrer. He was master of ceremonies
at a banquet in conjunction with the national assembly of the organization in Minneapolis in 1948. It was a seemingly surprising affiliation for one who would later be known as a Cold Warrior, but not by

Justice Jackson (left) presents Dodd with a "Certificate of Merit" while 400 applaud.

any means unique. The first national director of the world federalists, Cord Meyer, made a similar intellectual journey.

Dodd preferred the world to be at peace instead of at war, and he, like almost everybody in the United States, had learned that the isolationism of pre-World War II America had failed the country. The affiliation with the World Federalists, however, probably had as much or more to do with affording Dodd an opportunity to network, make potential political allies, and to get further public recognition, than it did with the goals of the organization. The University of Indiana library, which has 500,000 pieces of archival material from the early files of the United World Federalists, has no name file for Thomas Dodd. This writer consulted Professor Joseph P. Baratta, who has spent much of his long professional life documenting the history of the United World Federalists as to Dodd's role in the organization. Baratta knew the name of Senator Thomas J. Dodd, but he did not connect it with the United World Federalists. Dodd seems, however, to have met Norman Cousins, first president of the organization, during this period, and the two—Cousins the patriotic peacenik and Dodd the civilized anti-communist—became a mutual admiration society that was to prove beneficial to both farther along.

Dodd's chief competitor for the 1948 gubernatorial nomination— that particular nomination and other nominations that might follow— was Chester Bowles. Bowles, a pre-war isolationist, had become a fire-eating internationalist, and Dodd's identification with the World Federalists put him in a position to compete with Bowles for the support of those who wanted to see a meaningful United Nations.

Bowles came from a well-to-do Protestant family, graduated from Yale, and with his partner, William B. Benton, founded Benton & Bowles, an advertising agency. Benton & Bowles is credited with the popularization of the "soap opera" in the 1930s as a vehicle for advertisements. Both grew rich(er) and both became active in liberal Democratic politics. Bowles came to national prominence as the head of the New Deal's Office of Price Administration (the OPA) and its successor agency, the Office of Price Stabilization.

Bowles commanded the loyalty of those who were "New Deal-ers" because of intellectual conviction, as opposed to those who were "New Dealers" because of ethnic or class background. Fancy Demo-crats liked Bowles. Less fancy Democrats were more likely to gravi-tate to Dodd. The chemistry was never right between them. Joseph I. Lieberman, the U.S. Senator, who is also the leading historian of the Connecticut Democratic Party, and who knew both Dodd and Bowles personally, writes in *The Legacy: Connecticut Politics, 1930-1980* (1981) that

> Neither Dodd nor Bowles was a neutral personality. Their clash . . . was a compelling confrontation. Dodd, the ardent Irish Catholic, former FBI man, and vehement anti-fascist and anti-communist, spoke and moved with smoothness; Bowles, the millionaire Yankee and dedicated international-ist, was sometimes exciting, sometimes abrasive. Each left a listener sure that he either liked the candidate very much or not at all.

In April of 1947, the federal "Medal for Merit Board" suggested 32 people for Presidential Certificates of Merit (a lesser honor than the Medal of Merit itself), including Thomas J. Dodd, "in recognition of their contributions to the war effort of the United States." Dodd's contributions, of course, were not to the war effort but to the post-war effort. Perhaps Justice Jackson had a hand in arranging for Dodd to receive some formal award for his service—maybe the actual Medal of Merit, or even the Medal of Freedom, at the time reserved for those whose contributions had been heroic. Any such recognition might be helpful to Dodd politically. Twenty-eight of those recognized have left no footprint on history (as measured by inclusion or omission from Wikipedia); the remaining four were Dodd, two civil-servant scien-tists, and one Harry Crosby, sometimes known as "Bing."

Neither the *New York Times* nor the *Washington Post* noted the matter, but it could still be spun to further Dodd's gubernatorial ambitions. The Connecticut Bar Association, no doubt at the urging of Dodd's partisans, held a dinner at Hartford's leading banquet hall, the Hotel Bond, in September 1947, to celebrate Dodd's recognition. Justice Robert H. Jackson attended, and, according to the *Hartford Courant* "conferred the award on Mr. Dodd, his principal assistant, for President Truman, who signed the certificate." Prior to the dinner subscribers could attend a reception and meet the Justice, which may help explain why—at least according to the *Courant's* head count—400 people showed up.

In later years in his political advertisements, Dodd would run pictures of the presentation of the certificate to himself, identifying his award as the Medal of Freedom (although the parchment illustrated in the photo carries the visible legend, "Certificate of Merit").

At the Democratic National Convention in 1948, Thomas Dodd was one of those who seconded the nomination of Harry Truman for President. It came about this way: When the Connecticut delegation was called upon to cast its votes, delegation chairman John M. Bailey rose on the floor and announced that one of the Connecticut delegates was prepared to second the nomination of President Truman for re-election. Dodd ascended the podium and received a resounding

ovation when he said he would speak for only one minute, rather than the full five minutes allotted to seconding speakers. (Few appreciated that Dodd had difficulty filling even a minute with good words about Truman.) The *Hartford Times* reporter noted that this opportunity to get na-

After one minute, Dodd ran out of nice things to say about Truman.

tional attention "was a big break for Dodd, who tried unsuccessfully earlier in the day to address the convention in favor of a strong civil rights plank in the platform." Then—as now—political people must sometimes do undignified things in the interests of self-promotion.

According to Zaiman, as the State Democratic Party Convention approached, Dodd seemed to be a sure bet. Among Dodd's strengths, he got along well with John Bailey, who had recently succeeded to the role of back-room political powerhouse in Connecticut Democratic politics.

Bailey, like Dodd, was an Irish Catholic, but his background was otherwise very different from Dodd's. Bailey came from wealth and from Harvard. Distinctions such as "Shanty Irish" or "Lace-Curtain Irish" had long ceased to have any relevance to people like the Baileys. In the late 1940s he came to dominate Connecticut Democratic Party politics by listening, negotiating, appeasing, cajoling, and by a refusal to let his ego get in the way of important business. He first played a determining role in the 1946 Democratic State convention that selected Wilbert Snow over Chester Bowles.

In the summer of 1948, the Dodd and Bailey families summered close to one another at the seashore; on one occasion, Dodd spent the night at Bailey's home.[9] Bailey, however, never let personal friendships—or personal dislikes—interfere with important business, and to Bailey, controlling the Governor's office, with all the political patronage positions that were dispensed from it, was important business. 1948 looked to be a tough year for Democrats. It was commonly believed that Truman was a sure loser, whose presumed unpopularity would badly hurt the entire Democratic slate. Worse, a third party,

---

9. This sentence comes directly from a later Zaiman column and invites a question not articulated in Zaiman's column: If the Baileys and the Dodds were living close to one another, Why would Dodd have spent the night at Bailey's home? Was Zaiman telling the reader something without spelling it out?

the "Progressive Party," under the leadership of Roosevelt's former vice-president, Henry A. Wallace, entered the 1948 election and was leaching liberal sympathy from the Democrats. The Progressives nominated a Yale Law School professor, Thomas I. Emerson, for Governor—but made clear that Emerson would withdraw if Bowles were the Democratic Party's gubernatorial nominee. Bailey concluded that the party's best hope of winning the governorship was with Bowles, and he threw his influence behind the Yankee Unitarian, instead of behind one of his own kind. Thereafter Dodd always counted Bailey an enemy.

In the days before the convention, it became clear to Dodd that Bailey—who had seemed to be well-disposed to Dodd's gubernatorial candidacy—had taken the nomination away from him. Bailey and Bowles later claimed that Bailey had negotiated an understanding with Dodd: Bowles would be the candidate, with Dodd running for the second position on the ticket, Lieutenant Governor. If that had been the understanding, Dodd repudiated it. The night before the convention, Dodd withdrew his own candidacy for governor. He denied that he had ever agreed to accept the second slot and made clear that he was not about to accept it. More important, his statement was plainly hostile to the prospective nominee: "My chief concern about the Democratic Party at this time is that it have no arrangements or understandings, open or secret, real or implied, of any kind or character with the Communist-dominated Wallace party." He implied that Bowles's expressed repudiation of a formal endorsement by "any party other than the Democratic Party" was insufficient. The Bowles people were wild; a press release from the left-liberal Americans for Democratic Action was issued attacking Dodd.

Bailey, however, was working. Overnight he patched things up, as best he could. The ADA release was withdrawn. The next day the nomination of Bowles for Governor was seconded by Thomas Dodd. Professor Emerson dutifully withdrew his candidacy.

Dodd, however, was not on the Bowles bandwagon. In the next several weeks he in no way implied any support for the gubernatorial candidate—much to the contrary.

His involvement in the 1948 election (arguably the most important election between 1932 and 1960) was limited to his backing of
Abe Ribicoff, then seeking his first major office, Congressman from
Hartford County.   On October 11, 1948, about three weeks before
election day, a newspaper advertisement announced that that night
Thomas J. Dodd would deliver a radio address in which he would endorse "Judge Abraham A. Ribicoff" (Abe was a part-time police-court
judge) for Congressman.   Dodd's name was in large bold type, Ribicoff's name somewhat less prominent.   The ad included one head-
and-shoulder's photo—of Dodd.   At the bottom of the ad, in small
type, was the "paid for" language: "Paid for by Thomas J. Dodd."   A
copy of the ad is to be found in Dodd's voluminous personal clipping
collection; it was published in the *New Britain Herald*.   New Britain
was Ribicoff's home town.

Dodd's support for Ribicoff, such as it was, was based upon Ribicoff's strength of character, or so Dodd related in his address.   Dodd
assured voters that Ribicoff would be no tool for the communists hiding behind the banner of the Wallace party.   He was critical of other
un-named Democratic Party candidates for not debating the issues
involved in the policies of President Truman, but he did not expressly
endorse those policies, or Truman himself.

To the perceptive eye of locally syndicated political commenta-
tor Alan H. Olmstead, Dodd's selective endorsement of Ribicoff had
been an attack on the rest of the Democratic ticket.   As perceptive an
observer as Olmstead was, however, he failed to note that Dodd had not
really been promoting Ribicoff; Dodd had been promoting Dodd. [10]

A huge Democratic Party dinner held a couple of weeks later at-

---

10. Olmstead did more serious analysis and therefore was probably the better
journalist than Zaiman, whose strong suit lay in political gossip made possible by
Zaiman's status as an "insider."   But because Zaiman was carried in the *Courant,*
the state's leading newspaper, he had much more influence than Olmstead.   Today,
Zaiman's columns can be consulted in the *Courant* archives via the Internet, whereas
Olmstead's have for the most part been lost to history.

tracted over 600 people to the Waverly Inn in Cheshire, Connecticut. According to Zaiman, "Everybody who is anybody in the Democratic Party in Connecticut turned out. . . . The only prominent Democrat who did not show up was Thomas J. Dodd of Lebanon." Then, just a few days before election day, Zaiman predicted that it would take a miracle for Bowles to win the election, but "If, by some miracle he wins the governorship Tuesday, then it would be no surprise to find him being mentioned for President in 1952."

The miracle happened. Bowles beat incumbent Republican Governor James C. Shannon by 2,225 votes. Now Dodd had to face a world in which Chester Bowles and John Bailey (the two had developed a fine relationship over the preceding six months) were firmly in control of the state Democratic Party.

President Truman's victory over Republican Thomas Dewey was an even more stunning upset.

Immediately after Truman's surprise victory, Dodd's friends began lobbying for an important position for him in the new presidential administration. "Pelgrift, Dodd, Blumenfeld and Nair" sounded better than it was; four young lawyers struggling to establish a solid client base, didn't make for a substantial income. Meanwhile, Dodd's family was continuing to grow, ultimately to round out at six children. In his correspondence from Nuremberg he continually inquired about the progress of his children in the enrichment opportunities that he afforded them—piano lessons and the like—and he urged Grace to encourage the older children to take up horseback riding. Also, she should have more help around the house, hired help. There were expectations to be met.

The archives at the Truman Presidential Library contain a letter of extravagant praise for Dodd, written (or at least signed) by Senator Brien McMahon, including a resumé, implicitly suggesting that a place be found for Dodd in the president's administration. Nothing happened. People in the political game, a class that would have included Harry S. Truman, know that such letters are usually drafted by the nominee, and sometimes proffered insincerely.

There is a telegram to General Harry Vaughn, officially Truman's military adviser but really much more, Vaughn having been Truman's intimate from 1917 onward, from a "Commander John Robinson" of West Hartford, Connecticut. Commander Robinson was either a close associate of Vaughn's—or at least assumed a collegial tone in his telegram. The Commander reminded Vaughn of Dodd,

> who seconded the president's nomination in Philadelphia and who single handedly fought for his renomination here in this state and who continued to battle for him against great odd[s] to election day urgently requests that arrangements be made for him to see you and the president at a early date. I am certain the friends of the president in Connecticut will be pleased if such consideration is granted. Dodd is now suffering politically because of his loyalty to the president.

Didn't work.

Bailey, who never held grudges (although he also had a long memory), wrote a laudatory letter specifically recommending Dodd for appointment as Assistant U.S. Attorney in Connecticut. It is unlikely that Bailey would have written if he had not been asked to do so. Notwithstanding the relative modesty of the title, it was a responsible position that carried with it a respectable, steady paycheck, and by virtue of his trial experience Dodd was eminently well suited for the post. By picking cases and courting headlines, the position could be used to keep Dodd's name alive politically, just as the Molzahn case had first brought him national attention. But nothing came of it.

The explanation for the cold-shoulder treatment can be gleaned from a short interoffice memo from Lisa Stiles, secretary to Truman's executive clerk, sent to Roma Lee Klar, secretary to Truman's appointments secretary, dated November 17, 1948, barely two weeks after Truman's astonishing victory. Although the memo is inaccurate as to details (as set forth above), it probably holds the key to the explanation as to why Dodd's entreaties were ignored:

> Mr. Robert Moore, Assistant to Chairman Magrath at the Democratic National Committee, says that Mr. Thomas J. Dodd is something of a "problem child" as far as the committee is concerned. He was formerly assistant to the Attorney General and also was one of Justice Jackson's assistants at the Nuremberg trial of war criminals. He came home to run for Governor and lost to Chester Bowles in the primary. In the campaign he made only one speech (after the primaries) and in that speech he bitterly attacked Chester Bowles. Mr. Moore says he writes letters to the Committee in which he insists that he did a lot for the president but the records do not bear it out.

In short, Dodd was stigmatized as a poseur.

Here was Tom Dodd, having successfully directed the courtroom happenings in what had been (and probably still is) the most important judicial proceeding in the history of the world—in the process winning respect and accolades from a member of the United States Supreme Court—and he couldn't get a job.

Dodd kept his face and name public, attending every political or public function that came along, everywhere delivering his "stump" speech lambasting the "isms"—all of them. It had broad popular appeal.

A more driven man than the other ambitious Democrats cluttering Connecticut's political landscape, Dodd won widespread popular support through more energetic efforts on the grass-roots level than any of the others. And he had one quality that was unequaled by any other Connecticut political personage of his day (quite possibly, unequaled by any other Connecticut political personage since): he had tremendous personal magnetism.

Dodd attracted considerable press attention, and possibly some business support, by becoming chairman of the Connecticut arm of the "National Citizens Committee for the Hoover Report." In 1947, President Truman had named a blue-ribbon committee headed by former president Herbert Hoover to find ways to "streamline" the federal government. In the report of its efforts, the Hoover Commission, as it was known, made 273 recommendations, which spawned the "National Citizens Committee" to help build public support for their implementation. In his capacity as Connecticut chairman, one of Dodd's responsibilities was to name 28 prominent citizens from the ranks of business, labor, education and civic affairs to help. If the chairman had any other duties, they are not apparent.

Dodd preferred efficiency in government to inefficiency in government; furthermore, some of those 28 people might even be useful to himself farther along.

He also attracted considerable press attention because of his involvement in a highly charged case involving claimed corruption at the State Liquor Control Commission. The chairman of the commission, John T. Dunn, Jr., was an insurance agent, and he was also an important man in state Republican Party affairs. Liquor-related business was only a small part of the Dunn firm's portfolio before Dunn went on the Liquor Control Commission, but by 1948 more than half of the policies written by Dunn's agency were written for holders of liquor licenses. It was common knowledge in the liquor business that holders of liquor permits who found themselves in trouble with the commission for sale of liquor to minors, or sale of liquor after hours, or slot machines in their bars or taverns (illegal but quite common in Connecticut of the late 1940s) would get a better deal in disciplinary hearings if they took out an insurance policy with the Dunn Agency. After-the-barn-door clients were always sympathetically welcomed by Mr. Dunn.

When the situation was called to the attention of Bowles, the newly elected Governor, Bowles suspended Dunn pending investigation, and Dunn retained a lawyer, Thomas J. Dodd. The first thing Dodd did in defense of his client was to demand that Bowles recuse himself from his statutory role as hearing officer in the case. In a page-one story in the *Courant,* written by Zaiman, the political columnist, Dodd was quoted as saying that Bowles had already revealed his bias and prejudice against Dunn. There was no percentage in it for Bowles to continue in the case, so he delegated the role of hearing officer to a well-respected Republican judge from the State Supreme Court (who decided against Dunn, leading to Dunn's dismissal).

During this period Dodd moved his family from the small town of Lebanon to West Hartford, which brought him within the Hartford penumbra. Greater Hartford had (and has) the largest single block of delegate votes in Democratic state conventions; before Dodd and since, ambitious politicians have relocated to Hartford County for supposed strategic advantage. At the least, it might make him an obvious choice for the Democratic Congressional nomination for Hartford County if, by chance, Ribicoff should ever vacate it.

The new house was a small mansion, 12 rooms with 4 fireplaces, under a slate roof, and it projected the same appearance as did its owner: impressive, formal, somewhat austere. It was a house for an important man.

In the elections of 1950, Dodd attracted most attention helping U.S. Senator Brien McMahon, running that year for re-election. McMahon ran a campaign independent from the rest of the Democratic Party ticket, headed by Governor Bowles, who was also running for re-election.[11] McMahon, sensing an anti-Democrat temper in the state, did not identify himself in his radio and TV appearances as a Democrat, nor did he urge the election of the Democratic candidates.

---

11. The Connecticut Governor served for a two-year term until the gubernatorial election of 1956, when the term was upped to four years.

West Hartford mansion

Dodd appeared alongside him in television spots, and on the night before election day, Dodd delivered a radio address that had been adver-
tised in the newspapers as "The Truth About McCarthy"—Senator
Joseph McCarthy, the demagogic anti-communist who was publicly
supported by many Catholic priests. McCarthy's specific arrows were
directed against Democratic Party candidates. Dodd's speech was
intended to minimize defections from McMahon by Catholic voters.
A newspaper ad for his speech indicated that it was paid for by the
McMahon campaign. McCarthy, however, was still in the early stages
of his anti-communist crusade, and it would be another several years
before he was at the height of his power and influence. If McCarthy
was of any help to McMahon's Republican challenger, one Joseph E.
Talbot, it wasn't enough; and if Dodd was any help to McMahon, it
probably didn't matter. McMahon handily beat the Republican.

   In the same election, Congressman Ribicoff, candidate in the

Democratic stronghold of Hartford County, walked to re-election, but Bowles was turned out of the Governor's mansion by Republican Congressman John Davis Lodge, who had painted Bowles as a far left-winger. Bowles's former partner, William Benton, whom Bowles had appointed to fill a Senate vacancy a year earlier, barely edged out his Republican challenger, Prescott Bush, of whom more was to be heard.[12]

In 1952, Senator Brien McMahon announced his candidacy for President. Before the convention he became aware that he was terminally ill with cancer, but as a final show of respect, Connecticut Democrats supported him at the convention as its favorite-son candidate—with one exception: delegate Thomas J. Dodd backed Georgia Senator Richard Russell instead.

After McMahon's death on July 28, 1952, one of the first to announce his availability to fill the vacant Senate seat was Thomas Dodd. Like a character out of *The Last Hurrah,* he obscured his personal ambition with alligator tears over the loss of his dear friend. (Dodd was especially eloquent at the ceremony introducing the Brien McMahon Commemorative Postage Stamp ten years later.) Abe Ribicoff was eager for the shot at the Senate as well, and as an incumbent Congressman just completing his second term, Ribicoff could fairly claim to be "next in line." On the train ride out to the Democratic National Convention earlier that year, Dodd had busied himself lobbying the Connecticut delegates to oppose Bailey's choice for Democratic National Committeeman, John Golden, who was elected to that posi-

---

12. All of the biographical literature about Dodd mentions his support in the 1950 election for Brien McMahon, without mention of any Dodd effort in support of Senator Benton, although Benton, not McMahon, was McCarthy's more focused target. McCarthy came into Connecticut three times to campaign against Benton. Because of the absence of documentary evidence, this writer is uncertain what to make of that, but it would undoubtedly be true that any anti-McCarthy statement would rebound to Benton's advantage, at least as much as to McMahon's advantage.

tion by the Connecticut delegates with Dodd casting the only negative vote. Not surprisingly, Bailey seemed to favor Ribicoff over Dodd.

Dodd turned to his long-time counsel, Homer S. Cummings, for advice; after their visit on August 20, 1952, Cummings wrote himself a minute of the meeting: Dodd had

> said that Bailey and Kelly [Hartford Democratic Town Chairman] lean toward Ribicoff and that Bailey had intimated that if Dodd would retire from the Senatorial race, he could have the nomination for Congress for the First District if Ribicoff should be nominated for Senator . . . I told him that I thought the battle for the State at large and for the Senatorship might be hard fought, with dubious outcome. I told him that if we could not carry Hartford County, we could not carry anything in Connecticut and that, therefore, the nomination for Congress from the First District was much more apt to succeed than the nomination for Senator and that if he wanted to get into public life, this would probably be the best route, namely, through the Congressional nomination.

And so it came to pass. Ribicoff, who had previously been nominated to run for re-election as Congressman, withdrew from that nomination and was nominated, instead, to run for McMahon's Senate seat against Prescott Bush. Pursuant to party rules, the vacancy in the Congressional nomination was filled by those Democratic State Central Committee members from the Hartford Congressional district—only 15 people. Bailey delivered 13 of the 15 to Dodd. From Bailey's point of view, he had "rewarded" a man who had been a thorn in his side, but there were pluses to it too: He had headed off a potential confrontation with its inevitable risks, and Dodd's presence on the ticket might blunt Irish Catholic hostility to the Jewish candidate, Ribicoff, or head off McCarthyite attacks on the ticket. Who knows: Unlikely as it seemed, Bailey's intervention on Dodd's behalf might even bring Dodd "back into the fold," or "into the fold," or whatever. For his own part, Dodd was in the unaccustomed position of being the "organization candidate," a role in which he never felt comfortable. Always a lone wolf, he never wanted to be beholden to another political leader, at least not to one of Bailey's rank. And he was not about to be.

Dodd's Republican opponent was a retired corporate secretary of the Phoenix Insurance Company, John Ashmead. Ashmead campaigned against "the steady trend towards socialistic legislation in Washington," a not-too-appealing message in working- class Hartford County. Dodd spoke more of his opposition to corruption, both his opposition to corrupt officer holders (some of whom might have been members of President Truman's administration), and also to those business interests that might attempt to corrupt them.

On election day, Ribicoff and all of the Democratic Congressional candidates except one went down to defeat, smothered in Republican Dwight D. Eisenhower's huge victory over his Democratic Party opponent, Adlai Stevenson. Dodd was the only survivor. Dodd carried the district with a plurality of 23,000 votes. Aubrey Whitelaw, press spokesman for the campaign, said that the victory "exceeded reasonable expectations. Tom Dodd proved in his first try for elective office that he has what it takes even against those surprising odds."

Alan H. Olmstead ascribed Dodd's victory to the fact that Dodd, after years of following public affairs closely, had a fine grasp of the issues and an easy way of handling questions, while he described Ashmead as a weak and faltering candidate. But there was more to it than just the personal attributes of competing candidates: As Olmstead sized up the results, he saw that the victory probably had more to do with the fact that Dodd was blessed with running in overwhelmingly Democratic Hartford County. Dodd came out of the city of Hartford with a plurality of 24,000 votes, and won the seat by 23,000 votes. Ribicoff, though losing his state-wide race to Prescott Bush, had carried the Congressional district by a more impressive 49,000 votes.

Still, Dodd was the sole survivor, and John Bailey and Abe Ribicoff, both with long faces, showed up late at the Dodd victory party at
the Hotel Bond to pay tribute.

After years of battling for recognition, Tom Dodd had at last received a place in the sun; at last he was in a position from which he
could go places. Whitelaw refused comment on whether Dodd would
seek the Governor's office in 1954.

In modern America, the vast majority of people come from a religious
background in which the teachings of Jesus Christ are central, and
therefore most people regard themselves as "Christians," at least for-
malistically so. Only a small percentage of them, however, identify
themselves—to themselves and to others—as "Christians." When
such a one tells you he is a "Christian," he does not mean that he is one
of a group that includes 90% of the country; he means that he is from
a relatively small percentage of the population that is really Christian,
evangelically so. In the late 1940s and the 1950s a very small percentage of people in the United States were sympathetic to communism;
the vast majority of Americans were not sympathetic to communism,
and therefore might properly have been called "anti-communist." But
when somebody proclaimed that he was an anti-communist in 1948
or in 1958, he did not mean that he shared the views of 90% of his fellows; he meant that he was evangelically—aggressively—anti-communist, and willing to sacrifice other values in the interests of opposing
communism. Tom Dodd was proudly anti-communist.

Now that the threat of Soviet-style communism has disappeared,
it is easy to forget the factors that made anti-communism a reasonable
position in the late 1940s and the 1950s:

Josef Stalin was a classical Marxist who believed in spreading
communism. His capacity for brutality cannot be overstated. At the
Yalta Conference between Roosevelt, Churchill, and Stalin, and the
Potsdam conference between Churchill, Stalin, and Harry Truman, at
which the Allied leaders determined the fate of post-war Europe, it

was posited that certain countries in Eastern Europe would be within the Soviet "sphere of influence," but Czechoslovakia was posited to become an "uncommitted" country. In February 1948, a communist coup in that country brought it firmly within the ambit of the Soviet satellite nations. The following year Chiang Kai-Shek and his Nationalist army withdrew from mainland China, leaving the Chinese communists in control of the world's most populous nation. International communism was clearly on the march.

At least a Soviet threat to the United States was remote. On August 6, 1945, the United States exploded an atomic bomb at Hiroshima. With enough A-bombs the United States could obliterate Russia's cities. For four years thereafter, Americans relied on what became known as "A-bomb diplomacy"—the belief that America required no diplomacy because of its monopoly of atomic weapons, which would insure the safety of the country from the Soviets and from Stalin's apparent expansionist policies. Then, in August 1949, the Russians detonated their first atomic bomb. Americans now had to take the Soviet threat seriously and began to prepare for all eventualities—with bomb shelters and air-raid drills although they would be near useless in the event of atomic attack. National security planners began designing the underground bunkers into which the federal government might retreat, and from which the country could continue to function after a Red attack.

Some comfort could still to be taken from the fact that Soviet aircraft did not appear to be sufficiently advanced technologically to deliver an atomic bomb to the U.S. mainland, while the United States had rimmed the Soviet Union with bases from which the U.S. could easily get to the Soviet heartland. But there was bad news too, as when Mao Zedong's Red Chinese Army held its own against the United States—many would say defeated the United States—in the Korean War. Then all comfort for the United States was stripped away in October 1957, when the Soviet Union launched the first man-made satellite, Sputnik I. Sputnik itself was a blow to American national pride, but it was not particularly significant from a strategic point of view. More important, the launching mechanism that put Sputnik into orbit could just as easily be fitted out to deliver a nuclear warhead to the continental United States.

Dodd's dedication to the Catholic faith put his world view in direct conflict with that of Marxist doctrine, with its rejection of organized religion. His hostility to communism, which was to become the hallmark of his political persona, was steeled at the Nuremberg trial. He viewed the Nazis and the Stalinist government as being without significant differences from a moral standpoint. It seemed inappropriate to him that the Russians should sit in judgment of the Nazis; the presence of a Russian seat on the judge's bench tarnished the whole Nuremberg proceedings. His attitudes were reinforced by a longer-than-usual private audience that Pope Pius XII granted exclusively to Dodd and Colonel Brundage. The Pope's abhorrence of Russian communism was second to none, while his abhorrence of Nazism— though sincere and profound—was perhaps second to the abhorrence in which some others held the Nazis. For every murder of a Catholic priest that could be laid at Hitler's doorstep, a dozen were Stalin's responsibility, and at least Hitler was not openly contemptuous of the Catholic Church. The litmus test: Pius XII excommunicated no Nazis for their politics, but threatened excommunication and damnation to those who supported the Italian Communist Party in fiercely contested Italian elections in 1948. Dodd greatly admired Pius XII; after his visit with the Pope in 1945 he wrote Grace, "I resolved yesterday, after talking with the Holy Father, to stand openly and firmly against this menace [communism]. If we fail to do it, who will?"[13]

Long prior to his election to Congress Dodd was publically de-

---

13. Throughout his later life, Dodd remained identified with the highly traditionalist views of Pius XII, resisting the more "liberal," reformist trend identified with the views of Pope John XXIII.

nouncing communism—"a vicious evil far worse than Nazism or fascism"—in his many public appearances and speeches. He accepted a decoration from the Czech government for his services at Nuremberg prior to the Red coup in that country, but with considerable state and national publicity, he rejected the offer of a Polish medal in 1949 because, he said, he saw no difference between the tyranny then operating Poland and the Nazi tyranny. His massive collection of newspaper clippings preserved at the University of Connecticut contains reportage of numerous examples of contemporary rhetoric. In his principal address on the subject during his 1952 campaign for Congress he explained the source of the problem:

> The fundamental thing to remember about Communism is that it is atheistic and anti-God and therefore, utterly without principle in its foundation because, without a belief in God, there is no foundation for morals or principles in the world.
>
> This helps us to understand why Communists lie, why they can swear falsely under oath, can break solemn agreements and treaties, wantonly destroy family life, coldly dispose of human beings by murder, imprisonment, and enslavement and provoke war and civil strife, and confusion across the face of the earth.

In a different address—or rather, in numerous different addresses—he makes clear that the "spiritual and physical survival" of the United States depended on the defeat of communism.

Once elected to Congress in 1952, his statements remained consistently and narrowly hard-line anti-communist, sometimes more tempered and reasoned, sometimes less so, depending in part upon the status of his mercurial mood and partly upon which of his assistants had collaborated with him on the particular speech. He was in something of a position to further his anti-communist agenda as a

member of the House Foreign Relations Committee. His first important statements on foreign policy were issued in 1955, particularly his
widely circulated statement about the Geneva Summit Conference,
to be held in July 1955. At that time, President Eisenhower, Prime
Minister Anthony Eden of Britain, Premier Nikolai Bulganin of the
U.S.S.R., and Prime Minister Edgar Faure of France, all of them accompanied by their foreign ministers, met in Geneva, beginning on
July 18, 1955, with the stated goal of reducing international tensions
and exploring possibilities of arms control and an eye to fostering
trade between the West and the communist block.

Dodd, cognizant that "the communists have never yet kept an
agreement which they have made," was unimpressed with such efforts. In a speech to Congress (or at least reported in the *Congressional Record*, which regularly includes as "delivered" speeches those
that are not) a week before the summit, he emphasized that "the acts
of aggressive Communists are the real and the only cause of tension in
the world. ... There can be no peace in Europe as long as the aggressive occupation of the once free captive nations by Communist Russia
continues." As for arms control, he said: "Essentially, disarmament
is a matter of mutual trust, good faith, a will for peace and national
honor. The communists have none of these qualities. ... We may take
up disarmament when the communists stop aggression and release
the once free but now enslaved and imprisoned people of the world."
Trade: "The Communists are interested in more trade with the free
world because they want to build up strength for use against us."

Dodd weighed in early on the developing situation in Vietnam,
being one of the first Congressional cheerleaders for Ngo Dinh Diem.
Some background history is relevant for an understanding of Dodd's
positions relative to Vietnam, as those positions were to emerge over
the next decade:

Bao Dai, the last in the historic line of Vietnamese emperors, had
come to the throne in 1926 at the age of 13; he was a puppet emperor
for the French. Then, after the Japanese took Indochina during World

War II, he was a puppet emperor for the Japanese. When the Japanese lost the war in 1945, he abdicated rule, turning the country over to Ho Chi Minh, a Tito-esque Marxist who had led Viet resistance to the Japanese. During the French Indochinese War (also known as the "First Indochina War") between Ho's Viet Minh forces and the French over control of Vietnam, Bao sided with the French. That war was settled at a Geneva Conference in 1954, at which Vietnam was "temporarily" divided in two halves at the 17th parallel, the northern half being left in control of Ho, the "Free Vietnamese" (under French guidance) to control the South, with the understanding that unification elections would be held in 1956 aimed at re-unifying the North and the South.

The French installed Bao Dai as "Head of State" in the south, to reprise his role as a French puppet. Bao Dai selected Ngo Dinh Diem, whom Bao had never liked, as Prime Minister because Bao believed that Diem, an impeccably devout Catholic whose older brother was the Archbishop of Hue, would bring powerful backing to South Vietnam from the United States. And indeed, American Catholics, led by Francis Cardinal Spellman of New York, overwhelmingly backed Diem, and thus the government of South Vietnam. In the months that followed, close to one million refugees, most of them Catholics, crossed the open border at the 17th parallel, to settle in South Vietnam.

Although Bao Dai had brought Diem to power, the personal relations between them remained poor, and historians generally agree that Bao Dai worked against Diem's efforts in 1954-55 to institute government control over the private armies maintained by the various religious sects and by organized crime. Friction between Diem and Bao had a destabilizing effect in South Vietnam.

At this point, Dodd made his first public statement about Vietnam: in a speech on May 2, 1955, he blamed the "weak, vacillating and confused" American policy for the civil strife in South Vietnam and opined that the U.S. should disassociate itself from French colonialism and the French-tainted Bao Dai. He said that it "would be a disaster" for the United States to abandon or lessen its support for Diem, whom he regarded as "the best hope for the free world and free Indochina."

In the fall of that year, after a fraudulent referendum, Diem ousted Bao Dai and seized absolute control of the instruments of state. He repudiated the Geneva agreement about the re-unification elections scheduled for 1956. It was true, as he said, that the government of South Vietnam had not signed that agreement. (Also, it seemed certain that Ho would carry any such election.) Diem became increasingly tyrannical and brutal, and increasingly dependent upon the props provided to his government by the United States. Dodd's support for Diem was unflagging. To be continued in the next chapter.

Dodd also took particular interest in events in Guatemala. In the early 1950s, Guatemala's democratically elected president, Jacobo Arbenz Guzman, embarked on a program of agrarian reform that was threatening, mostly to American interests—specifically, to the United Fruit Company. The CIA, headed by Allan Dulles (a stockholder in United Fruit), became satisfied that Arbenz Guzman was a communist or a near-communist, no point to quibbling, and that if he were allowed to remain, Guatemala would become a Soviet foothold in the Americas.

Starting in 1953, the CIA began arming, training, and financing a coup intended to topple Arbenz Guzman and install a reliably pro-American administration in Guatemala. After considering various candidates to become *el jefe,* the CIA settled on Carlos Castillo Armas to lead the insurrection. The operation succeeded without significant resistence. In *Guatemala* (1979), published by the left-oriented North American Congress on Latin America, the escapade is called a showcase for counterrevolution. (Its easy success sent a misleading message to the CIA, which was largely to blame in luring the United

States into sponsoring the unsuccessful invasion of Cuba known as the Bay of Pigs episode.)

Castillo Armas took the presidential office on September 1, 1954. He promptly canceled the law that had facilitated land reform; removed the voting rights of illiterates, thereby reducing the roll of eligible voters by half, and established the National Committee of Defense Against Communism, which is sometimes credited with being the first modern right-wing death squad in Latin America. He was pro-American, reliably. In the 1950s, Latin America was a disfavored part of the world when it came to doling out foreign aid assistance, but Tom Dodd, in 1955, successfully argued in the House Foreign Relations Committee to raise the handout to Guatemala from $5 million to $10 million, and then, on the floor of Congress, succeeded in having it boosted another $5 million to $15 million.

Dodd was also an eager participant in the proceedings of the "Kersten Committee" (more formally, "The House Select Committee to Investigate the Incorporation of the Baltic States into the U.S.S.R.," succeeded in 1954 by "The Select Committee on Communist Aggression"). As a member of the Kersten Committee, Dodd went on study tours abroad to investigate matters, the conclusions of which had been well known at the departure airport. It made for press coverage, not all of which was completely positive. The *Hartford Courant,* never a left-leaning organ, commented that the committee, in its report of a foreign expedition in August 1954, "was traveling in well-beaten paths when it undertook to search out the evidence of Communist crimes." The *Courant* viewed the committee's positions as "extremist," which, if adopted, would commit the United States "to what can only be an endless state of hostility."

Dodd could certainly have joined, as well, the House Un-American Activities Committee (HUAC), but he did not. HUAC suffered an unsavory reputation among a sizable percentage of Connecticut voters, particularly active Democrats, in good part because of its immediate-past chairman (1947-48), J. Parnell Thomas (R, NJ). Thomas had at least one no-show employee on his payroll who kicked all of her salary back to Thomas.   Thomas's secretary turned over incriminating documents to muckraking journalist Drew Pearson; after Pearson publicized the material, Thomas was prosecuted and jailed. Thomas gave HUAC a bad name. Anti-communism, too.

Most of the most prominent anti-communists were Republicans and, like Thomas, Republicans of dour conservative stripe.   Dodd was the exception. On domestic policy he voted down the line with liberals and with organized labor policy. Although he supported efforts to bar candidates who advocated violent overthrow of the government from the election ballot, Dodd's civil liberties record was otherwise acceptable to people who were concerned about matters of that sort. In the ten weeks preceding election day in 1954, he delivered substantially the same speech (probably it was the same speech) to the Adjutant Generals section of the American Bar Association, to a gathering of 150 schoolteachers, and then to 200 members of the Machinists Union, the last on September 26.[14] In it he warned against the danger of losing Democratic institutions and freedoms in the fight against communism, and singled out proposed legislation allowing wiretapping and immunity of witnesses as notable threats to American freedoms, which he therefore opposed.   He was particularly eloquent in his opposition to wiretapping:

> Perhaps the most specious argument . . . is that no innocent person needs to worry about wire tapping. This is probably the worst type of police-power propaganda. . . . Have we become a nation of faceless people, without individual personalities, without privacy, and without individual dignity? Are there no sacred things left? Are we committed to live in

---

14. In a private letter to *Hartford Times* editor Robert Lucas, Dodd frankly acknowledged that he "re-cycled" his speeches, not just "stump speeches" delivered on the campaign trail, but also policy statements issued after election.

a police-state goldfish bowl? God forbid that the nature of America has been thus altered.

As the election season of 1954 warmed up, Dodd made noises that although he was not a candidate for Governor, he "would accept" the gubernatorial nomination if the party wanted him. So too would Chester Bowles. Bowles had spent the prior two years (1951-1953) as President Truman's ambassador to India and then was shunted out of that position by the Eisenhower administration. Dodd and Bowles plus Abe Ribicoff generated a lot of press speculation of the who's-on-first stripe. In the spring of 1954, however, Bowles announced that he would not be running, leaving Dodd and Ribicoff as the contenders for the nod.

The campaign against incumbent Republican Governor John Lodge would be a tough one; if Dodd waited, in another two years, in 1956 Prescott Bush's seat in the U.S. Senate would be open for contest. Yes, that would be a tough race too, but in Connecticut in the 1950s there were only tough races—except, that is, a race for Dodd's Congressional seat: Dodd had re-election to that locked up tightly. And if Dodd would wait until 1956, by then Ribicoff would either have succeeded Lodge in a four-year term as governor, or Ribicoff would be a two-time loser; either way, Dodd would not have to contend with Ribicoff in a contest for the nomination to run against Bush. So Dodd took a pass. That November he walked all over his Republican challenger for the Congressional seat, Wallace Barnes, a Bristol industrialist and state senator, while Abe Ribicoff defeated Lodge by a whisker.

The nomination to run as the Democratic Party's candidate for U. S. Senate in 1956 was Dodd's for the asking. That year Eisenhower was running for re-election. He had been a popular President during his first term and was generally expected to carry Connecticut by a wide margin (as, indeed, he did). Chester Bowles talked about running for

When Dodd ran unsuccessfully for Senate in 1956 against Prescott Bush,
Newsweek wrote that Bush was "warmer" on the hustings than Dodd—and
Prescott, remember, was the least charming of the political Bushes.

Bush's Senate seat, but his heart really wasn't in it. Perhaps he figured
that this was the year for Dodd to be beaten so badly that Bowles
would be able to walk into the next Senate nomination, coming up in
1958, without major competition for the nod. Anyway, Bowles did
not enter the contest, and at the Democratic State Convention, Congressman Dodd was nominated by Governor Abraham Ribicoff to be
the party's nominee to run for U.S. Senate against Bush.

Bush, an aristocratic Yankee and a Wall Street financier, was essentially a New Yorker, who just happened to live in Greenwich,
Connecticut, a wee bit on the Connecticut side of the New York-
Connecticut state line. Though basically conservative, he was not
an unenlightened person. He was involved with the American Birth

Control League as early as 1942 and served as treasurer of the first national fund-raising drive of Planned Parenthood in 1947, at a time when any form of artificial birth control violated the laws of Connecticut. Contraception was fiercely opposed by the Catholic hierarchy (as a state legislator, Ribicoff voted against legalization of condoms), and Bush's well-known position on the subject cost him with Catholic voters, a large segment of the Connecticut electorate.

Bush had become the finance chairman of the Connecticut Republican Party, and from that position he had won the nomination to oppose interim Senator William Benton in 1950, losing to Benton by only a thousand votes. Then, in 1952, he was elected to fill the remaining four years of deceased Senator Brien McMahon's term by defeating Abe Ribicoff. The Democratic Party was lucky to get its only Democratic Congressman, Tom Dodd, to undertake the uphill challenge. Dodd was never afraid of an uphill fight. According to his sidekick on the political hustings, James Boyd (in a 2009 note to this writer), "electioneering satisfied many of his inner needs—the need for combat, for intrigue, for vindication, for excitement, for conquest, for being the center of attention, for being audibly on the stage of history, if only transitorily."

The intense campaign was brutally demanding and brutally fought. Although Ribicoff made the nominating speech for Dodd, he gave Dodd little support during the campaign, and a day of campaigning on Dodd's behalf by first-term Massachusetts Senator John F. Kennedy did not bring anybody to Dodd whom he did not already have. Dodd's back-up ticket was uninspiring, and Dodd himself was generally unknown outside of his Congressional district. He had to carry the whole load, including Adlai Stevenson. He couldn't do it.

Bush later discussed the campaign with an oral history interviewer from Columbia University. An oral history interview, bear in mind, is a tape-recorded statement in which a historian may prod a narrator into airing a lifetime's accumulation of grievances, some perhaps unfounded, against adversaries of times gone by. With that caveat: Bush told the historian "Dodd had already assumed the likeness of the Joe McCarthy in his speeches, and he was referred to as 'Joe McCarthy in a white shirt,' and he spoke constantly on the theme of communism." Dodd frequently became angry during their debates, using words like "lie." Bush was used to what he regarded as civilized campaigns against more restrained opponents (he maintained cordial relations through life with Abe Ribicoff), but Bush came to despise Dodd: "I'm not disposed to get into personalities in campaigns, and have always tried to avoid them, but [Bush made an exception] Dodd was a very difficult opponent, and made it very difficult for me to hold my temper and keep my equilibrium . . . [because of] the rashness of this man. He's willing to make very reckless charges and very reckless statements, and I formed the opinion then, which I haven't changed since, that he's a very unreliable sort of a person." (Regrettably, we don't know what Dodd might have told an oral history interviewer about Bush, as he did not leave tape-recorded reminiscences.)

The election results gave a plurality to Bush over Dodd of major proportions—but the Bush plurality was dwarfed by Ike's Connecticut plurality over Adlai Stevenson! Dodd had acquitted himself nicely. As Bush told it—no doubt correctly—Bush suffered defections from conservatives within his own party but had profited from support from the normally Democratic "intellectual community in our state": "They were afraid of [Dodd]. They felt that he represented something that was spiritually offensive to them, that he was a threat to intellectual freedom."

Bush's comments about an angry Dodd, a reckless Dodd, are given credence by the letter—actually a mimeographed flyer—that Dodd circulated immediately after the election among state and local Democratic Party leaders. In it, Dodd excoriated the state's unidentified Democratic Party leadership, which everyone understood to mean Bailey and the cabal of big-city leaders who together constituted the state party's "smoke-filled room." They were the weak link in the statewide campaign, to which Dodd ascribed his loss of the Senate seat.

The letter would haunt Dodd in his bid for another crack at a Senate seat two years later, not because Bailey was thin-skinned, but because some of the other bosses took the intemperate flyer personally. Joseph Lyford, seeking the Democratic Party nomination for Congressman-at-Large in 1958, wrote in *Candidate,* Lyford's account of that campaign, that when he visited Edward Bergin, sometime mayor and usual party boss in Waterbury, the fourth largest city in the state, Bergin said that the letter had been interpreted as a slur on the Waterbury Democratic Town Committee, and that many members of the committee had been offended. He was talking about himself. We cannot know how many other local party leaders felt the same, nor how many "organization" strongmen worked, or at least teetered, against Dodd because of the letter.

Dodd followed that up by involving himself unnecessarily in an intra-party squabble in Stamford, the fifth largest city in the state, where Democratic Mayor Thomas Quigley was seeking a third term. Quigley was challenged for the nomination by Frank W. LiVolsi. Dodd publically spoke for the challenger, saying that he was "anxious" to have LiVolsi win the mayor's position as well as leadership of the Stamford Democratic Party. When Dodd had run for Senate the year before, he said that he had "had to sit around on the steps of City Hall waiting for the Mayor." Quigley's slate won the primary two to one.

Dodd was invariably picking unnecessary fights. Psychologists might consider whether the etiology of his combative nature lay in the so-called Napoleon syndrome (if such a syndrome is well-founded), the supposed tendency of short men to be extremely competitive or combative in an effort to overcome the presumed handicap arising from short stature. Dodd was 5' 6" tall, the same height as Napoleon. Because his frame was somewhat on the large size, Dodd did not appear small, but perhaps he felt the need to overcompensate for his height. Or perhaps his disposition was simply a matter of his upbringing; recall his sister's comment that "we—including my brother

Tom—were brought up more in the art of confrontation, rather than the art of compromise." Whatever the cause, his unwillingness to wait quietly for an opportunity to get even with the Baileys, the Quigleys, and the Bergins turned his quest for the 1958 Senate nomination from a walk into a tough contest.

With his loss to Bush in 1956, Dodd was returned to private life and to the practice of law. He promptly became involved in another high-profile case, this one involving the Teamsters Union. In 1957, Dave Beck, president of the Teamsters Union, was disgraced (disgraced even by the standards of the Teamsters Union) by U.S. Senator John McClellan and the attorney for McClellan's Senate investigating committee, Robert F. Kennedy, in their investigations of union racketeering. Beck decided not to seek re-election as union president. Jimmy Hoffa, even worse than Beck in the eyes of Bobby Kennedy and Mc-Clellan, stepped forward as a candidate, and despite a campaign by McClellan, Kennedy, and Secretary of Labor James P. Mitchell to help the other guy, or perhaps because of it, Hoffa was elected union president by a huge margin in September 1957. Thirteen union men brought suit, claiming that the election had been "rigged" and asking that it be set aside and held over fresh. The 13 were represented by attorney Godfrey Schmidt, apologist to the grave for Senator Joseph McCarthy and longtime attorney for the National Association of Manufacturers and for Cardinal Spellman. Schmidt brought Tom Dodd/ Joe Blumenfeld in to help with the case for the 13.[15]

The plaintiffs' case was tried for 22 days, whereupon the parties, without the Hoffa side introducing any evidence, stipulated a judgment: Hoffa was to remain as "provisional president" under the watch of three "monitors" (one of them being Schmidt), until a new conven-

---

15 . The thirteen grumbled about Dodd's participation on the theory that his political ambitions might conflict with their interests, but Schmidt insisted that Dodd participate.

tion could be held to elect officers, with the union to bear the legal fees for all parties. When, ultimately, the convention was held, nobody ran against Hoffa, and he ascended to the presidency by acclamation. As for the lawyers' fees: Schmidt and Dodd/Blumenfeld requested $350,000; the judge allowed them $210,000, half for Schmidt and half for Dodd/Blumenfeld. Dodd told the press, "I had always said that I would be satisfied with whatever Judge [F. Dickinson] Letts's decision would be. This was an important case. It showed a way to guarantee democratic processes in large labor organizations. Union members will benefit from this case for many years to come." A less friendly eye might have observed that the union had begun the litigation under President-elect Hoffa and had ended the litigation with Hoffa's hand strengthened; that in hindsight, the litigation should not have been undertaken; and that the only winners were the Schmidt associates.

By way of postscripts: Hoffa's lawyer, Edward Bennett Williams, thereafter negotiated the fee down to $180,000. Dodd wrote Schmidt that Dodd was not a member of the Blumenfeld firm, and that the fee should therefore be divided in three parts, not two. Schmidt was thereafter removed as a monitor when it appeared that he had compromised himself and his position by negotiating on behalf of various employers with the Teamsters Union that he was supposed to be monitoring. According to John Hutchinson, a scholar of industrial relations, in *The Imperfect Union: A History of Corruption in American Trade Unions,* by the end of 1960 the "monitoring" aspect of the settlement "had cost the union $634,026 in direct expenses and probably over $1 million in legal fees." (This writer does not know whether that includes the $180,000, nor what the ultimate split was between Schmidt and Dodd/Blumenfeld, or perhaps we should say, the split between Schmidt and Dodd and Blumenfeld.)

Dodd found other new clients. The government of Guatemala retained him, together with his partner on that particular representation, Washington lawyer Sheldon Z. Kaplan, an old hand in Central

American affairs. According to the left-wing publication *Guatemala,* that country had "the best lobby in Washington." Dodd insisted, however, that he did no lobbying; that his services were limited to rendering legal advice, although he was registered with the U.S. Government as a "foreign agent." When he was elected to the Senate in 1958, he promptly—and publicly—released Guatemala from its contract, thereby purifying himself from any taint of conflict of interest, and waived the balance of $41,666.67, to which he and Kaplan would have been entitled pursuant to the contract. Dodd made it up to Kaplan in other ways.

The practice of law was only a filler for Dodd. From the day after his 1956 defeat he had his sights set on running again for the Senate in 1958. He was not alone in coveting the Democratic Party's Senatorial nomination that year.

Everything looked great for Connecticut Democrats as they approached the 1958 election season. Governor Ribicoff had achieved tremendous popularity. His alertness to photo ops when a disastrous flood inundated many Connecticut towns proved Ribicoff's humanity, while his much publicized "highway safety program," essentially a vigorous crackdown on highway speeders, established his responsibility. Political people believed that whoever was fortunate to appear on his ballot line would be swept to victory (which turned out to be the case). This made men, three in particular, eager to capture the Democratic nomination to run for the Senate against Republican incumbent William A. Purtell. Dodd was joined in the contest by Bowles and by Bowles's one-time partner, William Benton, two men with national reputations as Democratic Party leaders, whose conflicting ambitions signaled the end of what for each of them must have been the friendship of a lifetime.

After their amicable business separation in 1935, Benton became an Assistant Secretary of State (1945-47), and had an important role in the organization of the United Nations. He became publisher of

Encyclopedia Britannica, which in the pre-Internet period was regarded as the premier source of information about everything.

When Republican Raymond Baldwin resigned from the U.S. Senate in 1949 to accept a position on the Connecticut Supreme Court, Governor Bowles appointed Benton to the seat. Benton had only tenuous ties to Connecticut and no local political credit. (He once boasted to Dodd that he had more friends in London than he had in Hartford.) His appointment to the Senate was a highly personal gift, perhaps intended to serve Bowles as well as Benton: Bowles might have considered his friend a place-holder, who would fill the Senate seat only as long as Bowles himself did not claim it, rather than as a potential competitor. If that was Bowles's thinking, however, he was very much mistaken.

Whatever the rationale for the Benton appointment, it could only have given offense to others who wanted it, and who, by the rules of the game, deserved it—at least ahead of Benton—notably John M. Bailey. Bailey never held a grudge over that—he appreciated that the voters might rebel over the appointment of a political boss to the Senate—but some of Bailey's closest friends, such as his political right arm, Katherine Quinn, did. Miss Quinn, as she was known far and wide, was an old maid "Irisher," the secretary of the state Democratic Party, and she idolized Bailey. She would later prove to be an important ally for Dodd.

According to Bowles's memoir, *Promises to Keep: My Years in Public Life* (1971), Bowles's appointment of Benton to the Senate vacancy also irritated Ribicoff, who was at the time in his first term in Congress, a slight (or two slights, counting Bailey) to which Bowles ascribed ambition-destroying consequences for himself.

Benton's appointment was good only until the next general election, at which time a successor would be chosen by the voters to hold the seat until the expiration of the Baldwin term. When the next general election rolled around, in 1950, Benton narrowly beat Prescott Bush, which gave Benton the seat until 1952, when the original

Baldwin term would expire. That year Benton was defeated in the Eisenhower landside by Bill Purtell. According to Sidney Hyman, Benton's biographer (*The Lives of William Benton,* 1970), Purtell was an intimate personal friend of Tom Dodd and other prominent Irish Catholic Democrats, a matter that had helped Purtell turn Benton out of office in 1952. Benton's happiest years were those he had spent in the United State Senate, and he longed to return to it.

According to Sidney Hyman, the day before Dodd announced his own candidacy for the Senate seat, Dodd called Benton and urged him to announce also, telling Benton that if Dodd himself did not get the nomination, Benton would be Dodd's choice.[16] Benton tried to reach Bowles to pass this news along, without success. When he did reach Bowles, Bowles was nonplussed about it (claimed Benton in self-defense) and did not indicate that Bowles himself had wanted to run.

One wouldn't guess any of that from Bowles's account. Bowles says that Dodd's motive in tipping off Benton was simply to get Benton into the race in order to split the liberal vote between Benton and Bowles. Bowles was known to be an all-but-certain contender. Chester Bowles viewed a seat in the U.S. Senate as the culmination of his career; this was his opportunity. He refused to believe that Benton, his dear friend—his creation—would be so manipulated, would be such an ingrate as to deprive him of his time in the sun. When it became clear that Benton would and was, Bowles remained certain that at the end Benton would withdraw from the contest in Bowles's favor; that Benton could never face the liberal community—or even

---

16. In later years Dodd and Benton had correspondence marked with effusive good will, but privately Dodd told his protégé James Boyd that Benton was "a complete fool," citing Benton's boast about knowing more people in London than in Hartford as an example of Benton's ineptitude. Notwithstanding the updated editions of *Encyclopedia Britannica* with which Benton periodically gifted Dodd, his frank opinion of Dodd was no doubt scarcely kinder.

himself—if he were to bring about a situation that delivered a Senate seat to Dodd. Wrong again.

Benton knew from the outset that he would start out third in the field, but he believed that a stalemate might develop between Dodd and Bowles, and that at that point Bailey and Ribicoff would throw decisive weight behind Benton as a compromise candidate.

From the outset, Bowles felt confident, as he writes in *Promises,* "that when the chips were down neither Governor Ribicoff nor John Bailey would support Dodd, who had vehemently opposed Bailey, Ribicoff, and the organization on many occasions. Dodd's principal strength in the party had always been rooted in dissident groups whose major objective was to throw Bailey out." Bailey's Boswell, Joseph I. Lieberman, writes that Bailey certainly preferred Bowles; he had forgiven Bowles, whereas "You just never know about Tommy." What Bowles failed to appreciate was that Bailey's overriding interest was in controlling the Governor's mansion, not in winning

Dodd and Party Chairman John M. Bailey (center) shared begrudging respect for each other. Dodd and Governor/Senator Abe Ribicoff (right) did not.

Senate seats, in boosting the chances of people he liked or in settling old scores—at least not if doing so would jeopardize control of the Governor's mansion.

Historically, the state conventions of the Connecticut Republican and Democratic Parties had nominated the candidates for statewide office, and losing candidates had no avenue to appeal the convention's choice in a primary. The Connecticut legislature changed that in 1955, when it adopted the Connecticut primary law, allowing any candidate who obtained 20% of the vote in a convention to force a primary to select the party's candidate. Conventional wisdom at the time held that primaries would drain off too many resources, create too much intra-party animus, and lead to the party's loss in the general election. Primaries also threatened to undercut the traditional role and power of the party boss. Bailey and his like-minded counterparts in the Republican Party believed that primaries were to be avoided at all cost—even if the cost was allowing a thorn like Tom Dodd to have a Senate seat. The policy positions of competing candidates were no more important to Bailey than the possibility of settling old scores, but avoiding a primary that might threaten the Governor's mansion—that was important.

Early in the 1958 season Bailey and Ribicoff announced that they would not attempt to swing the convention either way—they would keep "hands off"—but they hoped that a primary could be avoided, and to that end they announced that they would vote for whichever contender had a majority at the end of the first ballot. That said, Dodd, Bowles, and Benton and their backers spent much of the spring in vigorous campaigning at local Democratic town committee meetings, courting stronger and lesser satraps, seeking delegates, jockeying for position. It seemed pretty clear to Bowles that he had the upper hand, that he was getting stronger still—which, Bowles thought, had prompted Dodd's people to turn dirty. And Dodd himself. In his oral history interview, Bowles claimed that Dodd played up Dodd's advantage as a Catholic in an overwhelmingly Catholic Party:

BOWLES: I knew that Dodd was getting very bitter and that there was an awful lot of anti-Protestant stuff coming out of Dodd's office

Q: From Dodd himself?

BOWLES: Oh yes. He totally promotes himself on the Catholic issue. I was a Unitarian. And he had the idea that Unitarians do not believe in God, I remember that. It was very nasty.

Bowles does not mention that his side also fought "hard," spreading the word that Dodd had received a "payoff" from Guatemala for having gotten that country extra millions of dollars, plus rumors that Dodd was near bankruptcy (which was not entirely untrue) and that Dodd was a chronic drunk (which had not yet become true).

Joseph Lyford, in his memoir, *Candidate,* says that as of 3:30 a.m. on the day of the convention the Senate race was still in doubt, although Dodd's chances seemed to be improving and Bowles's deteriorating.

Dawn brought light as to where "the organization" was going to be: Katherine Quinn had set up a table in the lobby of the convention hotel and was openly urging delegates to vote for Dodd, a clear signal as to what Bailey and Ribicoff had decided. According to Bowles, Miss Quinn threatened delegates that there would be retribution against those who failed to follow the line when patronage was being passed out. Bowles continued to believe, however, that Benton would withdraw in his favor, and that with the resulting boost in his delegate count, and the psychological impact of the development, he could go over the top, never mind Bailey and Ribicoff. It never happened.

When the roll call began, the first two names called were the names of the Governor and of the Party Chairman. Each answered "I pass." When the West Hartford delegation was reached, home of

At the moment of crunch, Miss Quinn was to be Dodd's timely ally.

both Dodd and Katherine Quinn, all of that delegation except for James Kennelly, Bailey's son-in-law, voted for Dodd. (Bowles took that as a mark of Kennelly's character, but it was more likely the result of direction from his father-in-law, in the interest of maintaining an appearance of Bailey-family neutrality.) When the Windsor Locks delegation was called, Bailey's new sidekick, Ella T. Grasso (later Connecticut's first woman Governor), thought to be generally liberal and therefore one who might have been expected to be for Bowles or Benton, delivered that delegation for Dodd. At the close of the first roll call, the tally was 469 for Dodd, 312 for Bowles, and 98 for Benton. Then the convention chairman called for passed votes and changed votes, and began: "Abraham A. Ribicoff," with the response, "Thomas J. Dodd"; "John M. Bailey," with the response, "Thomas J. Dodd." That was it.

Bowles's explanation (at least his public explanation) as to why the organization had gone with Dodd was that a Bowles-Purtell battle would have pitted liberal against conservative and taken the focus away from the less-charged gubernatorial contest between Ribicoff and Republican gubernatorial candidate Fred Zeller, a colorless man from the right flank of Connecticut's Republican Party. Ethnic considerations probably had more to do with it. Many left-oriented Democrats believed that Ribicoff had thrown his weight to Dodd over Benton or Bowles on the theory that, as a Jew running for office in a Catholic state, Ribicoff preferred the "safety" that went along with having a Catholic running mate.[17] Benton and Bowles were Protes-

---

17. Interesting that Bowles did not subscribe to such thinking, or at least he did not admit to subscribing to it.

tants at best, probably covert deists. Then there was the matter of the primary. Even without Katherine Quinn, Dodd had powerful support, maybe majority support, and should Dodd have lost the convention's designation, he would probably have taken the matter to a primary, thereby threatening to upset the whole plum cart. Dodd didn't give a damn about "splitting the party" or risking Abe Ribicoff's re-election, or the patronage that flowed from the Governor's mansion: What was any of that to him? Bailey and Ribicoff knew that if they shut out Tom Dodd this time, they would have to be prepared to go all the way at a primary, with terrible risks involved. Bowles, however, if denied the nomination, would very likely accept the convention decision and move off. If that was the thinking of Bailey and Ribicoff, they were right on point: Midway through the second roll call, Bowles ascended to the podium and moved that the nomination of Thomas J. Dodd be made unanimous. The convention went wild.

Bowles was not bitter about it, not insofar as Ribicoff and Bailey were concerned. To the Columbia interviewer he even delivered a tribute to Ribicoff, sort of: "I always had a good deal of respect for Ribicoff, considering he was not a person of great depth or any great liberalism. But he was shrewd and very much on the make."[18] Other Democrats coming from the same vantage point as Bowles took it less well. Writing in *The New Republic* of September 15, 1958, Arthur M. Schlesinger, Jr., the most prominent intellectual in the upper reaches of the Democratic Party, was both despondent and furious that men of the caliber of Bowles and Benton had gone down to defeat, not just in Connecticut but in several other states, at the hands of men like Tom Dodd—"mediocre party hacks." "What leadership can we ex-

---

18. Ribicoff was one of the few topics on which Dodd and Bowles agreed: Again to protégé Boyd, Dodd said that Ribicoff was "a faker, he has no depth." Otherwise, as to Bowles: "he's been fooling people for years, but he's nothing; he's been wrong on every major issue since the days when he was an apologist for the Nazis, and it's high time that he was exposed for the fraud that he is."

pect from Tom Dodd, with his purple rhetoric about 'liberation' and his ambiguous relations with the Teamsters?'"

Bowles saved all of his bitterness for Benton. As of his 1963 oral history interview, Bowles still had no doubt but that "if Bill had gotten out, or had come over to my side, there's no doubt we could have easily beaten Dodd. . . . I thought it was unfair in a sense. Of course he had a right to do whatever he wanted to do, but you don't conceive in politics of creating a life for a person and then he turns around and . . . " In her oral history interview, Mrs. Bowles said that Benton had effectually sent Dodd to the U.S. Senate: "To send Tom Dodd to the Senate? What worse could you do?"

After the battle for the nomination, the general election was anti-climactic. Dodd's opponent, Republican Senator William Purtell, was a self-made man who had made a lot of himself. Born into poverty in 1897, he dropped out of school, entered the army in 1917, then worked as a salesman for ten years until 1929, when he and a few friends organized Holo-Krome Corp., a company that produced high-quality screws. Although Holo-Krome started at an inauspicious time, it persevered, then prospered, and Purtell became a wealthy man. He was one of the 28 state leaders to be appointed by Chairman Dodd to serve on the Citizens Committee for the Hoover Report.

In 1950 the Republican Party bosses offered Purtell the chance to run for Governor against Chester Bowles, but he refused. Then, after the Republican organization had dragged the unwilling Congressman John D. Lodge into the gubernatorial contest, Purtell changed his mind and entered the convention as a contender for the nomination against Lodge. He lost that year, and Lodge went on to defeat Bowles. But Purtell had gotten enough of a taste of politics to find that he liked it. In 1952 he challenged the Republican Party organization, won the nomination to run against Senator Bill Benton, and beat him in the Eisenhower landslide.

In a reminiscence published at the time of Purtell's death in 1978,

Jack Zaiman described him as "an industrialist with a vibrant, pep-pery, glad-handing approach." That described Purtell in his prime, in 1952; much of that had faded by the time Purtell had to face Thomas Dodd in 1958. He had served one term as an unspectacular but apparently hard-working Senator, a faithful servant of the Eisenhower administration. Then he had to run for re-election against Dodd, a tireless campaigner and an inspired orator, who only two years earlier had crisscrossed the state running against Bush. With his silver hair highlighted against a black background—as often seen on television—Dodd looked particularly handsome. Purtell was not a good-looking man. And this time, instead of running on a ticket with Dwight D. Eisenhower, as he had in 1952, he was running on a ticket with Fred Zeller. The influential Washington pundit Joseph Alsop, whose brother John Alsop was a major player in Connecticut Republican politics, predicted several months before election day that there would be a Democratic landslide in Connecticut of unprecedented proportions.

Dodd never took any election for granted; he always campaigned tirelessly, but this campaign was devoid of the bitterness that had characterized the one against Prescott Bush. Purtell was also from West Hartford, was a member of the same Catholic parish as the Dodds, and if they were not "intimate friends," as reported in Hyman's Bill Benton biography, they at least got along well personally.

Purtell was remarkably good-natured after his inevitable loss to Dodd, and made efforts to shore up the spirits of his fellow Republican loser, Edwin H. May, who had succeeded Dodd as Hartford County's Congressman, only to be turned out of the seat on that unhappy day (unhappy for Ed May) by Emelio Q. Daddario. Purtell had wakened on election day with a sniffle that had gotten worse over the day, and he was clutching a wad of handkerchiefs when the reporters asked him for a post-mortem. His first comment was that the handkerchiefs were for the cold, not to wipe away any tears. The *Courant* editorialized that Purtell had "carried out his committee assignments faithfully. But unsung labors do not substitute in the public mind for the political fame that attaches to an outspoken advocate. ... Mr. Purtell can retire to private life satisfied that he did a workmanlike job."

Dodd beat Purtell by an impressive margin of 116,000 votes, a margin that would have been even more impressive but for the fact that Ribicoff beat Zeller by a whopping 246,000. Among other things, the *Courant* quoted Dodd as saying, "I am going to put an end to the Democratic radicals in the Democratic Party"—people like Arthur Schlesinger. He could control himself only for so long—and to Tom Dodd, it was something that really did have to be said!

CHAPTER THREE

The Senator

CONTEMPORARY ARTICLES ABOUT Dodd regularly described him, his appearance, and his personal style by reference to the Roman Senator of antiquity, an image that almost certainly traces back to Jack Zaiman's *Courant* columns. With his noble features, classic profile, and flowing white hair, he was easy to picture in a toga speaking in the Roman Forum, or in his earlier days (he was prematurely gray), as destined for the Forum. Nobody ever looked more like The Senator than Tom Dodd. He carried himself like an actor from the cast of Julius Caesar.

Nobody ever sounded more like The Senator than Tom Dodd. Even his ordinary speech tended to consist of speeches; his sentences, aphorisms. His oratory was inspiring, often extravagant. Continuing the Roman Senator analogy, Zaiman described Dodd's speaking style:

> Representative Dodd has a speaking style that goes with his features. When he is hot, there is a sweep and majesty to his words that make them sing. He starts off low and subdued, then gradually picks up steam. By the time he has arrived at fourteen minutes, or twenty-eight-and-a-half minutes, as the radio or TV case may be, he has the flag waving in all direc-

The new Senator is sworn in by Vice-President Richard M. Nixon.

tions. He's an orator of the old school, one whose voice could
be heard for three blocks without the benefit of amplifiers.

Zaiman's words do not do justice to Dodd the orator (nor can this
writer's words do justice to Dodd the orator). One must look at the
old Tom Dodd videos available at the University of Connnecticut to
see a great classic orator. Every inflection, every jesture, the facial ex-
pressions, the cadence and volume—all were perfect. When he said
the word "evil" (as in "the evil plans of the Soviets") one could feel
the hot breath of the devil close by. His deep conviction in the truth
of his message, his total absence of doubt, was obvious and impressive—even when it might have been less than entirely sincere.

When Dodd addressed a local Democratic town committee, assembled in a Grange Hall, one sensed being in the presence of great-
ness. His adulatory sidekick, James Boyd, or sometimes a young
lawyer, John J. Daly (later a respected Connecticut judge), or Alvin
Goodin, a young man and one of many who genuinely admired Dodd,
would drive him to his engagements and would have one duty even
more important than chauffeuring—getting Dodd out of the hall right
after the speech, before he had one drink too many, got into an argument with a local poobah, and broke the fantasy.

The image of the Roman Senator was the flip side of qualities that
some might have considered shortcomings in a candidate: Dodd was
aloof; there was a stiffness about him. When he ran against Prescott
Bush in 1956, *Newsweek's* reporter commented that Dodd was a
more accomplished orator than Bush, but that in hand-shaking, the
reporter credited Bush with "a little more warmth and fervor than
Dodd." Dodd appreciated that his chilliness was an aspect of the for-
mality that was part of his public persona; he viewed a touch of "un-
approachability" as part and parcel of his political appeal. When he
was elected to the Senate in 1958, the *Courant* photographer asked
for a picture of him with Grace and Dodd's sister Mary Dwyer, both
kissing him. Dodd was always very conscious of the image that news
photos might project of him; the requested photograph would not

have been consistent with his desired message. According to the *Courant's* report, "Dodd smiled a little uncomfortably. 'No,' he said, 'I'm known as the icicle.'" It is cold on Olympus.

It was easy and inviting to imagine Dodd as the Senator from Ostia Antica–but it would have been just as appropriate to describe him as the Senator from Central Casting.

Lyndon B. Johnson, who conferred with staff and other "regulars" while seated on the toilet, had a very different personal style.

The relationship between the new Senator from Connecticut, Thomas Dodd, and the domineering larger-than-life Senate Majority leader, Lyndon B. Johnson, went back a long, long way, to 1935, when both had been state directors for the National Youth Administration. Or so recites standard biographical material on Dodd. In politics, people (even if only recent acquaintances) are prone to claim a we-go-back-a-long-way status; it implies that those who might have waved to each other across a crowded room had a genuine relationship, makes the lesser of them appear more important than he is, and sounds good in yarn weaving. Johnson and Dodd may have seen each other at national meetings of NYA administrators, if such meetings were ever held, but this writer has seen no evidence that the two knew each other prior to the day Dodd showed up at his new job at the Senate, and in any case it is a certainty that they had no genuine relationship.

No matter: Circumstances made the two natural allies, potentially tremendously useful to each other. Johnson was already eyeing a run for the presidency in 1960, and his likely competition for the Democratic nomination was an Irish Catholic Senator from New England (ICSNE). In a contest of that sort, Johnson could have no more valuable ally than another ICSNE, particularly if that other ICSNE was also a handsome, articulate Kennedyesque figure. From Dodd's vantage point, Bailey and Ribicoff, Kennedy's earliest promoters, had already locked up the Kennedy franchise in Connecticut; the best Dodd could hope for from backing Kennedy would be to be a third fiddle in a Kennedy symphony. If the Massachusetts

If the President was to be a young Irish Catholic Senator from New England,
"Kennedy" was not the first name to spring to the mind of Thomas J. Dodd.

Senator should become President, Bailey and Ribicoff could never
be toppled as Connecticut's "top dogs." However, if Dodd should
back Johnson, a southern Protestant, and Johnson should become the
party nominee, it was probable that he would want to have a Catholic
as his vice-presidential running mate (who better than Dodd?), and
even if that did not happen, if there was a "President Johnson" in the
White House, Dodd would ascend to unsurpassed power and stature
in Connecticut. And last, or maybe not last, if the President was going
to be a young Irish Catholic Senator from New England, "Kennedy"
was not the first name to spring to Dodd's mind.[19]

---

19. If all of this were not enough, Dodd also despised Kennedy's closest friend
and confidant, brother Bobby— "a fresh arrogant kid," he told Boyd. "When I was a
Congressman he once came to my office in Hartford and asked me when I was planning to leave the House, because he was thinking of moving to Hartford and running
for my seat."

All the way with LBJ.

There was never any need for Dodd and Johnson to make a formal alliance: they gravitated to each other like magnets.

Johnson took the freshman Senator and gave him choice committee assignments: Appropriations, with its obviously powerful role;
Aeronautical and Space Sciences Committee, a very important corner in which to be during the cold-war period dominated by Sputnik
and the "missile gap"; and the Judiciary Committee, along with the
effective chairmanship of Judiciary's Internal Security Subcommittee,
which carried with it tremendous headline-garnering potential.[20] He
was also assured of the next vacancy on the Foreign Relations Committee (which Dodd was awarded in 1960, over higher-ranking Sena-

---

20. Dodd's actual title was vice-chairman, but the chairman, Senator James
Eastland, yielded control of the subcommittee to Dodd.

tor Joseph Clark). These assignments gave Dodd almost unprecedented springboards to Senate importance, which, as things turned
out, he did not utilize.

Dodd repaid Johnson's courtesies with solicitous attention to
Johnson's wishes, beginning, immediately after the swearing in, with
a vote consistent with Johnson's direction, not to change the traditional rules about filibustering, notwithstanding Dodd's earlier promises to the contrary. (Dodd was not alone among the freshmen Senators to appreciate that Johnson was no one to "cross" on the first days
of one's Senatorial career.) In a June 1959 letter to Blumenfeld, he
passed along a request that had originated with Johnson for a summer job for somebody in the Hartford-based insurance field: "It is of
utmost importance that I get this girl a summer job. I have been asked
to do this by the Majority Leader. This I must do." More important,
Dodd gave Johnson reliable votes in support of the Majority Leader's
positions—with one notable exception, on a matter of deep principle
involving Lewis Strauss and, peripherally, scientist J. Robert Oppenheimer.

Oppenheimer was the scientific director of the Manhattan Project
in the 1940s, which developed the atomic bomb, and he is sometimes
identified as the bomb's father. After Hiroshima, heated internal dis-
putes within and between the scientific community and the highest-
ranking officials of the Eisenhower administration over the proposed
development of a hydrogen bomb pitted "left-wing" scientists, who
opposed development of the H-bomb, against "right-wing" ones,
who favored it. Oppenheimer had numerous left-wing associates and
affiliations he proudly identified with, and he was a key opponent of
the H-bomb. Was his opposition to the bomb, perhaps, motivated by
an active or passive loyalty to some foreign power?

Strauss, usually called "Admiral Strauss" (he achieved the rank
in a non-combat position as assistant to Secretary of the Navy James
Forrestal), was the activist chairman of the Atomic Energy Commission during the period 1953-1958. He predicted that the day would

come when nuclear power would make electricity so cheap that there would be no point to metering consumption. He also subscribed to the Eisenhower/Dulles policy of "A-bomb diplomacy." So did Tom Dodd. Albert Einstein is said to have quipped (this writer doubts the authenticity of the comment, but, still, it makes good telling) that under Strauss's leadership "AEC" had to be translated as "Atomic Extermination Conspiracy."

In 1954, Strauss was the driving force to revoke the security clearance that allowed Oppenheimer to function in his work. Many publicized hearings were held on the matter before the personnel security board of the Atomic Energy Commission, dividing politically aware people between the anti-communists, who supported Strauss's position and Oppenheimer's backers, who might be called anti-anti-communists (if not pro-communist). Where one stood on Strauss/Oppenheimer was a litmus issue. The anti-Oppenheimer people prevailed. Oppenheimer was later publically rehabilitated, Soviet-style, when he was designated by Presidents Kennedy/Johnson (Kennedy announced the award, and Johnson delivered it post-assassination) as recipient of the Enrico Fermi Award for lifetime scientific achievements in the field of energy. The award carried with it a purse of $375,000 and a gold medal featuring Fermi's likeness, and more significant to the independently wealthy Oppenheimer, the award carried with it implicit political respectability. But in 1958 Oppenheimer was still disrespectable.

In 1958, Eisenhower nominated Strauss to be Secretary of Commerce. The Democratic majority, corralled by Majority Leader Lyndon Johnson, rallied to reject the nomination by a Senate vote of 49 to 46. Dodd, a man of principle, was one of the few Democrats to go down to defeat with Strauss and his sponsor, President Eisenhower. Never mind claims of party loyalty; certain things are more important than petty partisan opposition. But wait:

Throughout his career, Dodd had a habit of hanging behind and positioning himself so as to be able to cast votes of seeming principle that he could privately justify to key players like Johnson as having been dictated by political considerations—and which ought to be forgiven inasmuch as his vote would not have made any difference anyway. A practical wheeler and dealer such as Lyndon Johnson could understand that, and give the "courageous independent" a pass.

As the presidential season of 1960 heated up, Dodd drew notice with his loud public identification of himself as a Johnson backer. He was especially noisy in the press in opposing the Connecticut "unit rule," under which the entire state delegation to the Democratic National Convention would be committed to vote for whichever candidate had the majority of the Connecticut delegate votes.   When state National Committeeman John Golden criticized Dodd's refusal to go along with Kennedy peacefully, Dodd took the opportunity to decry "bossism." That said, at the convention, the unit rule was enforced, and pursuant to it the Dodd vote was cast for Kennedy—but not until after Dodd had placed the name of Lyndon B. Johnson in nomination for the presidency, with what James Boyd, by then Dodd's key Senate employee, described as "blazing platform oratory." At the close of the convention, Boyd later recalled,

> I remember being driven with Dodd in a chauffeured limousine to the great ballpark where Kennedy was about to make his acceptance speech, an event comparable to FDR's 1932 appearance in Chicago, a moment to remember for a lifetime. When our car pulled up to the entrance and I exited and held the door open, Dodd wouldn't get out. 'I'm not going in,' he said, handing me a chocolate bar he had been unwrapping. 'I'll see you later at the hotel.' He had no interest in someone else's coronation.

Chester Bowles was the chairman of the Democratic National Convention's platform committee that year. Right after the election, Dodd issued a statement formally divorcing himself from support for any section of the Democratic platform "merely because it was adopted by our party convention." Indeed, party platforms should be abolished, he said, "except for a general statement of goals and attitudes." If there was one guy who was not going to tell Tom Dodd what to do, it was Chester Bowles. (Actually, there were many such guys.)

After Johnson left the Senate Majority Leader's position to become vice-president to President John F. Kennedy, things didn't seem the same in the Senate, not for anyone: The gargantuan Johnson was succeeded as Democratic majority leader by Senator Mike Mansfield, a mild man with a very different personality and a very different leadership style. Johnson, capable of personal pettiness, privately belittled his successor, or semi-privately belittled him.

In November 1963, with Senate business piling up, Mansfield canceled a Senate junket to Paris in which Tom and Grace had planned to participate. In one of the frequent evening sessions of the Senate, Dodd, after considerable tippling in the office of the Senate secretary, took to the Senate floor and succumbed to his lifelong predisposition to say whatever he goddamn pleased.

In his biography of Mansfield, Francis Valeo, the clerk of the Senate, writes that Dodd, "With tears forming in his eyes, expressed a watery nostalgia for the days under the leadership of Lyndon Johnson." Dodd delivered a rambling off-the-cuff statement in what the *Baltimore Sun's* reporter, Joseph Sterne, later described as a "boozy voice," complaining that the Senate did not work hard enough; that it should keep in session for longer hours—24 hours a day if necessary (the speech was being delivered in an evening session)—to attend to the important work that was languishing, and mostly, that the Senate craved leadership:

> If we are to accomplish the business of the Senate [the majority leader] must behave like a leader. Because a leader is one who leads. He must say "No" at times, he must say "Yes" at times. But he must be a leader. I remember when the pres-

To Dodd, Mike Mansfield was "mild Mike, a weak leader and a mush-head in foreign affairs."

ent Vice President, Lyndon Johnson, stood there. I used to tell my friends in Connecticut when they asked me, 'What kind of leader is he?' that he reminded me of an orchestra leader. He stood up and blended into a wonderful production all the discordant notes of the Senate.

As for Mansfield, "I wish the majority leader were present, because I know this will be construed as a criticism of him. It is meant to be. It is a criticism of him. I do not think he is leading the Senate as he should, and I believe we should have leadership."

Dodd had comments on the Republicans too. According to the *New York Times* account, Dodd said: "The opposition is so weak, so decadent, so fallen, so anxious to curry public opinion, that it does not say what it should be saying."[21] When Dodd returned to his office that night, he told Boyd, "I may have gotten myself in trouble."

It was not in Mike Mansfield's nature to respond in kind; when he did reply, he thanked Dodd for what Mansfield pretended to have been a constructive addition to Senate discussion. The Republican Minority Leader, Everett Dirksen, implicitly on the receiving end of Dodd's comments about the opposition, was less indulgent:

> I shall say very little about the incoherence that I have found, this morning, set out in the *Congressional Record*. The brave crusader from the Nutmeg State on his white charger has

---

21. Most of the discussion on the floor of the Senate about this matter is omitted from the *Congressional Record*. This account is based on newspaper reports of the proceedings and on biographies of Mansfield.

great zeal for being here and getting on with business, and he is not here [now]. If he does not know that the Senate is in session, he ought to know. So I will be prepared to suggest the absence of a quorum and see if he can find his way to the Senate chamber where the business is done.

Dodd showed up late—"I was at a meeting"—after which Dirksen resumed:

When I read the Senator's comments in the *Record* this morning, I thought it was a bundle of incoherence . . . The Senator is not around enough. I can prove it with the Senator's Committee record and with his record of attendance on the floor. . . . I will not come to the floor with a twenty-page effusion first having delivered it to the press, to make it appear what a great crusader the Senator from Connecticut purports to be, emotionalizing on a 24-hour Senate day. . ."

According to the *New York Times* account, Dirksen "described Mr. Dodd's performance as the product of 'cerebral incoherence' and 'emotional inconsistency.'" Still other accounts quoted him as saying, "Quite a number of things can induce cerebral incoherence." Dodd shouted back at him that Dirksen "does not frighten me with his menacing words and implications."

Later the same day, Dodd took the Senate floor again and delivered apology-ish remarks: "I felt this morning somewhat like a skunk at a lawn party . . . I fear I was harsher than I meant to be last night toward [Mansfield] and, I might add, toward my friend, Everett Dirksen, whom I really like and for whom I have affection." From the heat of Dirksen's above comments, it seems unlikely that Dirksen reciprocated the feeling.

Later that month, John F. Kennedy was assassinated, and the orchestra leader, Lyndon Johnson, became President. The *Hartford*

Courant's Washington correspondent, Robert D. Byrnes, noted that "Johnson has the reputation at the Capitol of a man with a long memory for both praise and criticism." He reported that the change in administrations effectually meant a transfer of power from the Kennedy man, Ribicoff, from being the most powerful Connecticut Democrat in Washington to the Johnson man, Dodd. Dodd himself had no doubt that the change in administrations spelled a sea change in his political fortunes.

LBJ's every minute, plus all of his telephone calls, appointments, and visitors, was meticulously logged by secretaries. Their records make clear that Dodd had no fuller personal access to the President than any of the other hundred Senators. Dodd was a peripheral figure among the hundred—maybe thousands—of people in Johnson's grand scheme of things, perhaps most significant for the attention he required. The files of correspondence and memoranda of President Johnson and his aides at the LBJ Library are cluttered with copies of correspondence from Dodd containing laudatory news clippings, speeches that Dodd was preparing to deliver supporting the President's positions, recommendations (some obviously perfunctory) for innumerable job seekers. The volume of requests that Dodd generated for signed presidential photographs inscribed to this or that Connecticut personage (one even to be inscribed to his enemy Democratic National Committeeman John Golden), was so overwhelming that presidential aide Ivan Sinclair had to write Dodd's people to the effect that the Dodd office had to cut down substantially on requests for photographs inscribed with anything more than just the President's signature.

The weight of detritus and relative lack of substantive material in the LBJ archives, together with the minimal personal contact between Johnson and Dodd, make clear that Dodd never approached being in Johnson's inner circle. Not that he didn't try.

One of Johnson's calendar entries indicates that the Johnsons attended the Dodds' 30th anniversary party at the University Club on

May 19, 1964, for precisely 12 minutes, from 8:34 p.m. to 8:46 p.m. This brought the President a thank you letter from Dodd that was extravagant to the point of obsequiousness.

When Clare Boothe Luce, the conservative Catholic wife of *Time-Life* publisher, Henry Luce, was about to begin her tenure as a Washington columnist, Dodd called aide Mike Manatos at the White House to report that Dodd had "elicited from her a promise of support for the President in the next campaign and feels that it might not be a bad investment of time if the President could see her for a few minutes. The Senator would like to bring her in." By hand, another of Johnson's aides, Bill Moyers, told Manatos "The President told Mrs. Luce on the phone last week to come in. I don't think Senator Dodd, therefore, should be bringing her in."

A mid-July 1964 memorandum from Johnson aide Jack Valenti to Walter Jenkins, the President's closest assistant, reports that "Senator Dodd's man, Jim Boyd, called me. Dodd thinks he could be useful to the President and the Party in the role of the firm anti-communist (particularly since the Republicans seem to be attacking us on being soft on communism). He would like to be useful in some role in the Convention." Could Dodd, perhaps, have had in mind some particular convention-related service that he might render to President and party?

In a later telephone conversation with Attorney General Nicholas Katzenbach, Johnson told Katzenbach that Dodd had asked to be on the President's ticket as the vice-presidential candidate, telling Johnson that he could be useful as "a Catholic candidate."[22] If so, Dodd does not appear to have told his staff of his overtures, as it is apparent from James Boyd's book about his life with Dodd that Boyd was un-

---

22. Based on a recorded but not transcribed telephone conversation between the two on April 1, 1966, and apparently not noted by any of the historians of the Johnson presidency. There are literally thousands of such conversations out there and available to researchers, but unless one were specifically researching Dodd, one would be unlikely to pick up this particular conversation.

aware of any such conversation between his boss and the President. Perhaps Dodd wanted to insulate himself against loss of face, or his staff against disappointment, in the event the President should reach an adverse decision. Johnson told Dodd that he would let him know when he had decided.

Meanwhile, Johnson encouraged press speculation as to whom he would anoint. The Democrtic Party's nomination of President Johnson for his own run for the presidency was a conclusion so foregone as to deprive the convention of any excitement whatsoever, which meant that the press was unlikely to pay much attention to it either. Historians now agree that it was to give the press and the public some incentive to follow the convention that Johnson manufactured a phony contest for the vice-presidential nomination by pitting the commonly believed front-runner for the nod, Minnesota Senator Hubert Humphrey, against Senator Thomas J. Dodd of Connecticut. A second reason for Johnson's ploy was a sadistic one: To keep Humphrey dangling, which necessarily required that he keep Dodd dangling as well. In reflecting on "Conventions I Have Known" in a 1988 *Washington Post Magazine* article, the celebrated journalist David Broder described Dodd as a cat's-paw, used by Johnson to torment Humphrey. Johnson did not reveal his hand to anyone, knowing that to do so would have punctured the ploy.

The President was staying in Washington until the right moment for his own appearance at the convention in Atlantic City, but he had both Dodd and Humphrey flown from the convention to Washington, for "visits," and in telephone calls to people he knew would blab things around, he said that he was "visiting" with Dodd and Humphrey and weighing his options—although, the President said, he doubted that Dodd would accept the vice-presidential nomination if it should be offered to him. Johnson built in a face-saver for the man he intended to disappoint. As Johnson recounted it to Katzenbach, when they got to the White House, Johnson told Dodd that it "wouldn't work," and gave his assurances to Humphrey that the nomination was his.

Whom would Johnson anoint as his vice-presidential running mate?
This photograph is also interesting because it shows Dodd with eyeglasses.
Dodd's eyeglasses were a constant in his hour-to-hour life, yet the above is the only
photograph the writer has seen of Dodd wearing glasses. Note the telltale marks
on the bridge of the nose shown in the photos on pages 117 and 222.

It was Dodd's habit to write a daily minute of his activities of the day, frequently extensive, sometimes very brief. None is shorter than his minute of that particular day, which gives no hint whatsoever as to why he had been summoned to the White House or what had transpired, so we will never know his account of the visit. The minutes were typed every day by an office secretary, and Dodd knew that any account he might relate in the minute would promptly be bandied around the office and beyond.

After it was all over, with Humphrey nominated for vice-president, a wistful Dodd had this exchange with Boyd:

"Some of those people out there are disappointed," he said, motioning toward the sitting room, now jammed with friends and supporters. "They thought I was going to be vice-president, but you know I had never even considered it, don't you Jim. It was never in the cards."

I kept a judicious silence.

"I'm not Presidential material, and I've never fooled myself. If he had offered it to me, I would have run a mile. The Senate is my cup of tea."

Then he brightened and speculated that he might, however, be tempted to accept an offer to succeed J. Edgar Hoover at the FBI, or perhaps John McCone, then serving as head of the CIA. "Naturally, I would want to take you with me," he assured Boyd. "We've got great things ahead of us."

Among those great things was the election campaign in the months following the convention. The Republicans nominated Barry Goldwater for President; in the political climate of that time, Goldwater was regarded as a right-wing extremist. The inevitable result was that Johnson clobbered him, with beneficial runoff for Dodd.

In his race for re-election to the Senate that year, Dodd faced former Governor John D. Lodge. Lodge's political views stood about where they had been at the time that Lodge had defeated Chester Bowles in 1950, although the Connecticut electorate as a whole had moved to a more liberal position. Lodge was handicapped by that change in the political climate; by Goldwater; by the fact that he personally liked Tom Dodd (privately Dodd made fun of Lodge's over-refinement); and also by the presence of a "mole" in the Lodge campaign, who leaked advance warning to the Dodd forces of some of Lodge's expected moves, thereby enabling Dodd to outflank his opponent. Although the *New York Times* and most "important" newspapers endorsed Lodge, Dodd's anti-communism brought him the public backing of Young Americans for Freedom and most of the right-wing columnists, while his down-the-line support for the Kennedy-Johnson domestic agenda brought him the public admiration (or at least the endorsement) of Americans for Democratic Action, of Dean Eugene Rostow of the Yale Law School, and other known names "on the left." [23] The letterhead of the "National Non-Partisan Committee for the Re-Election of Senator Thomas J. Dodd" included on the list of committee members the names of Dean Acheson, Steve Allen, A. A. Berle, Jr., Victor Borge, Taylor Caldwell, Prof. Sidney Hook, Admiral Arthur Redford, Elmo Roper, Danny Thomas, Gene Tunny, and many more whose names probably meant a lot more in 1964 than they do today. Both candidates campaigned as if it were a live race, but probably neither really believed it was: Dodd rolled to an easy victory, 341,652 votes ahead of Lodge.

Dodd told the press that his victory was "humbling." Boyd had been upset that in 1958 Dodd had acknowledged his first Senate victory by vowing to "get" the "Democratic Party radicals," so he drafted Dodd's victory speech with an emphasis on humility. But you couldn't keep a muzzle on Tom Dodd: In responding to a journalist's question, he took a gratuitous swipe at Abe Ribicoff. Dodd rejected suggestions that he might accept a Cabinet post in the President's administration. "I didn't run for that thing. I would never do such a thing to the people of Connecticut." It may have occurred to some people, maybe even to Abraham Ribicoff, that Ribicoff had run for, and had been elected to be, Governor of the State of Connecticut in 1958, yet had abjured his responsibilities as such to the people of Connecticut midterm to accept a Cabinet post in 1960 in the Kennedy administration. Ribicoff would do such a thing. (And so, it seems, would Dodd if the offer had been to head the FBI or the CIA.)

Most of Johnson's telephone calls were recorded on "dictabelt,"

---

23. In his minute of February 5, 1964, Dodd records: "Walter Jenkins called from the White House and said that the President had asked him to call me about how I felt regarding Eugene Rostow for the Second Circuit Court of Appeals. I told him that Rostow would do us no good at all in Connecticut, and in a few days I would give him a name."

and today anyone can eavesdrop on these 1960s conversations, most of which the National Archives has "digitalized" and made available to the general public over the Internet. Lyndon loved the telephone, and there are thousands of available conversations, one of the more charming of them being the four-way conversation between Johnson, Dodd, Lady Bird, and Grace, held on election night, 1964, in which four ecstatic people—or two ecstatic women and two calculating men—congratulate one another. Johnson commented on how "The ole' National Youth administrators, you can't hold 'em down," and mentioned how pleased he was that he had gone to Connecticut in order "to raise the money to go 'round, and doggone it paid off." While he was at it, he committed Dodd to future support in the Senate for the President's positions. That was never in doubt.

Johnson was now free to embark on his plans for his "Great Society," except, that is, for the fact that he and the country at large became permanently distracted from the Great Society by the most significant issue of the later 1960s: the United States's ill-conceived crusade in Vietnam.

As for domestic needs and issues, Dodd compiled a voting record scarcely different from the record that Bowles or Benton would have had (except for civil liberties, discussed below). On issues involving civil rights for blacks, Dodd's record paralleled that of Harlem's Congressman Adam Clayton Powell, Jr. It was in the realm of foreign policy that Dodd's positions distanced him from the policies of the "liberals." Those of the outlook of Chester Bowles, or of Senator J. William Fulbright, chairman of the Senate Foreign Relations Committee, operated on the theory that accommodation with the Soviets could and should be worked out. Dodd and his fellows of the anti-communist stripe regarded such thinking as wishful, and argued that accommodation with the communists was impossible consistent with honor because the communists themselves were wholly without honor.

As might have been expected, Dodd denounced people like

Owen Lattimore, possibly America's leading scholar of the Far East, who had been labeled by Joseph McCarthy as the country's "top Soviet agent"; and Cyrus Eaton, the multimillionaire peacenik known as "the Kremlin's favorite capitalist"—people whose demonhood was widely accepted and whose status as certified pinkos dated back even prior to McCarthy. More emblematic of Dodd's positions, however, was his attack on Dr. Ralph K. White, chief of the Soviet Bloc Division of the United States Information Agency's Office of Research and Analysis. Dr. White, a scholar of the psychological causes of war, was among the first to promulgate the theory that misunderstandings can lead nations to war. He was best known (or as best known as this little-known man was) for his theory of distinguishing between empathy and sympathy for one's adversaries.

In a speech to the American Psychological Association in September 1961 reported in the *New York Times*, Dr. White said that both the U.S. and the U.S.S.R., shared three common delusions about the other that threatened world peace: Each had a mental image of evil leadership on the other side; each believed that everything the leaders on the other side said was a lie; and each believed the other was not afraid. He developed these thoughts at some length. In the process, White took the position, publicly, that the U.S. had erred in sending U-2 spy flights over the Soviet Union, one of which was shot down, thereby proving that President Dwight D. Eisenhower and the United States had lied in denying that the United States undertook air reconnaissance. White also criticized the United States for having sponsored the invasion of Cuba by counter-revolutionaries at the Bay of Pigs in April 1961, a Soviet-style "liberation" of Cuba that was the proximate cause of the Cuban missile crisis that came close to annihilating the world.

White might have had Dodd in mind when he formulated the three delusions. Little wonder that the Senator regarded White's positions to be the "wrong-headed" kind of talk that, if given credence, would lead to Soviet world domination. He called not only for the ouster of Dr. White, but also for an investigation of the USIA, parent agency of the Voice of America, to be certain that there were no other such apples in the barrel.[24]

Dodd's image in history will be controlled by the jingoistic rhetoric he regularly delivered, both in the Senate (or at least in the *Congressional Record*), and with less restraint outside the Senate—to American Legion conventions, Holy Name societies, and meetings of ad hoc "educational" institutions like The Southern California School of Anti-Communism. He was continually inserting laudatory material in the *Congressional Record* about the heros of the anti-communist right, people like General Douglas MacArthur or Whittaker Chambers. His suggestions that American diplomatic blundering had delivered Cuba to Fidel and the Reds, just as American blundering had delivered China to Mao; that there were perjurers in the State Department; and that the State Department was muzzling anti-communist analysts, all had a decided McCarthy-ish sound to them. Although Dodd was unambiguously left of center on domestic issues, his reliable support of the anti-communist right on things foreign, and his adoption of much of the right-wing rhetoric, gave him a free pass in right-wing circles and the undying support of the American right.

He opposed inviting Nikita Kruschev to the United States in 1959, suggesting that the U.S. acknowledge the visit of the Russian leader with a period of mourning, and with the exception of the partial nuclear test ban treaty of 1963, he opposed efforts to limit nuclear testing—or pretty much anything that might lead to the easing of tensions with the U.S.S.R. He warned that talk about "peaceful coexistence" was intended to lull the West into letting down its guard and would lead only to "peaceful coexistence as the Kremlin practices it." He engaged in debates on the pages of the newspapers over nuclear

---

24. White died at the age of 100 in 2008. His obituary in the *Washington Post* referenced a 2001 article in *World Policy Journal* in which Robert S. McNamara had called White "the foremost advocate of realistic empathy in foreign affairs."

"One of the most impressive men in all of history." Who else but Moise Tshombe?

testing and the general approach to the Soviet Union not only with spokesmen who might be tarred as "left" but also with such "realists" as John Kenneth Galbraith and George F. Kennan.

He was the principal Congressional spokesman for the breakaway state of Katanga and its leader, Moise Tshombe. When Belgium gave up its colony in central Africa, Belgium Congo, the central government of the liberated Congo fell under the control of Patrice Lumumba, a leftist. Most of Congo's richest natural resources were within its Katanga Province, and Moise Tshombe, a right-wing Christian, led the province to secede. The United Nations and the United States officially supported the central government in the civil war that followed. Reactionary elements in Belgium—and Tom Dodd—sided with Tshombe. According to a "Washington Merry-Go-Round" column by Drew Pearson, Dodd's initial Senate speech attacking American support for Congo's central government was published in the Katangese capital, Elisabeth, before it was delivered in the Senate. He speculated that it had actually been ghosted by Katanga's well-connected Belgian lobbyist in Washington.

Dodd and Grace made a visit to the Congo in 1961 ostensibly to study the situation first hand; as a member of the Senate Foreign Relations Committee, and of its Subcommittee on African Affairs, Dodd had "standing" for such an expedition. The press reported that the visit was an effort to dramatize Dodd's support for Katanga and undercut the position of the Kennedy administration. Dodd probably did not believe that Tshombe was "one of the most impressive men in all of history," but he permitted himself to say it anyway. During the visit a dinner in Dodd's honor was disrupted by Katangese troops who dragged away two senior United Nations officials and beat them severely.

Dodd opposed Fidel Castro while Fidel was still a ragtag guerrilla hiding out in the mountains of the Cuban interior, and Dodd continued to oppose him before, during, and long after the abortive invasion of Cuba at the Bay of Pigs. Even after the Bay of Pigs (and after Robert Kennedy's secret assurances to the Soviet ambassador to the United States, Anatoly Dobrynin, that there would be no repeat of the Bay of Pigs), Dodd continued to criticize the passive acceptance by the Kennedy and Johnson administrations of the status quo in Cuba, and advocated "open and increased assistance" in support of another invasion. He criticized capitol police for "overreaction" when an anti-Castro march in Washington briefly broke into a riot.

He opposed proposals to admit the People's Republic of China to the United Nations–either in addition to the Republic of China headquartered on Taiwan, or in place of it. Along with the conservatives in Congress—and those Catholic Congressmen who identified with the "traditionalist" wing of the Church—Dodd was dismayed when Pope Paul VI called for the United Nations to admit "all nations." He was probably the only one, however, who had a remonstrance hand-delivered to the Papal Nuncio in Washington:

> I am worried by the implications of your Holiness's proposal that the United Nations should study the right method of opening its doors to all countries now excluded from its roster. I gravely fear that, in the context of the present world situation, this statement will be construed by certain people as

Dodd was a staunch ally of Nationalist China (or at least a dedicated foe of Red China). Here the Dodds greet Chiang Kai-Shek and Mde. Chiang.

a plea for the admission of Red China to the United Nations. . . . Red China's admission would rob the United Nations of all moral significance, and would paralyze whatever capacity for peaceful action the United Nations still retains. It would exacerbate rather than reduce the conflict between the free world and the Communist world.

He was less delicate in the admonition that he issued to Rev. Martin Luther King, Jr., whose position on the admission of Red China to the U.N. paralleled that of the Pope, warning King that his "intemperate alignment with the forces of appeasement" was alienating King's Congressional supporters.

He joined the periodic criticisms of UNESCO (United Nations Educational, Scientific and Cultural Organization) mounted every so often by the American right on the theory that UNESCO was too sympathetic to the communists.

Dodd's most important foreign policy stands, however, pertained to his unflagging support for the war in Vietnam. With time it became apparent to the Kennedy administration that it had been betting on the wrong horse in backing Ngo Dihn Diem. While the corruption of Diem's government was a constant, the discriminatory measures of his regime against the country's Buddhist majority became more aggravated; unrest and self-immolations by several Buddhist monks hinted at the possibility of civil war between Buddhists and Catholics.

David Martin, a reformed Trotsky-ite, ghosted Dodd's anti-communist messages. Here, Martin greets South Vietnamese President Diem.

Ultimately a coup that had the tacit approval of the United States (if not the active involvement of the United States) deposed Diem in early November 1963. Diem and his chief confidant, his younger brother Ngo Dinh Nhu, were promptly executed, an act that came as a complete surprise to the people in Washington.

Dodd protested that the coup, and America's refusal to intervene on Diem's behalf, had been based upon misinformation; that the persecution of the Buddhists was either nonexistent or vastly exaggerated, and that the agitation was essentially political. History sides against his position. However, the misfortune that befell Diem and his brother did not lessen Dodd's enthusiastic support for continuation of the war alongside Diem's successors.

Long before it became the majority position, Dodd was urging that the United States assist South Vietnam in extending the war into the territory of North Vietnam. Until the summer of 1964, this was a comparatively lonely position. That changed in August of 1964, when "skirmishes" (the extent and nature of which are still much contested) in the Vietnamese Gulf of Tonkin between U.S. and North Vietnamese vessels led to enactment of the "Gulf of Tonkin Resolution," adopted by the Senate with only two dissenting votes. The resolution vested in the President the authority to assist any Southeast Asian country whose government was considered to be jeopardized by communist aggression. The escalation of the war started almost immediately and then (with occasional pausing of the bombings) was intensified until Johnson left office.

As American involvement in the war deepened, opposition to American involvement increased, first on the theory that "we cannot win the war in Vietnam," later with the argument that the United States should not win it—that the American position was immoral. Dodd's response was to heighten the volume of his warnings about "appeasement." His positions become more fiercely pro-war, more narrowly "patriotic."

As early as October 1965, Dodd told the Senate in a report of the Internal Security Subcommittee that "control of the anti-Vietnam movement [in the United States] has clearly passed from the hands of the moderate elements who may have controlled it, at one time, into the hands of the communists and extremist elements who are openly sympathetic to the Vietcong and openly hostile to the United States." Later, when the atrocities perpetrated by American troops in the village of My Lai became undeniable, Dodd suggested that the misconduct might have been linked to marijuana usage. He reported at the Waterbury, Connecticut, Kiwanis Club (and no doubt at other forums) that the massive peace rallies and protests in the United States in the fall of 1969 were dominated by "hard-core communists" and "hippies looking for a piece of the action." Dodd observed that ten times as many Americans were attending Saturday football games in college stadiums as were involved in the anti-war protests—a fact that had been ignored by "stuffed shirt television news commentators." Dodd long believed that a presumed minority of defeatists and appeasers, "by dint of their incessant clamor . . . and the apparently limitless funds which fanaticism always generates, have had an impact that is out of all proportions to their actual number." He was prescient, however, when he predicted as early as 1965 that the outcome of the war in Vietnam might be determined not on the battlefields of Southeast Asia but on the domestic front in the United States. Cold War historian John Lewis Gaddis says that that is exactly what happened.

None of this, of course, meant that any of Dodd's sons should respond to patriotic call. His oldest son, First Lieutenant Thomas J.

Dodd, Jr., was promoted to captain, apparently with a little help from his father's office, but did not see active duty in Vietnam.[25] The Dodd office staff had the task of regularly arranging student deferments from the military draft for Dodd's second son, Jeremy. Jeremy, the gray sheep of the family, drifted from one academic institution to the next, each change requiring that his student deferment be put back in order. Jeremy was tough to keep in school. Ultimately he took refuge in the National Guard. In that period, members of the National Guard were never "called up" for active duty, or sent to the battlefields of Southeast Asia, and the Guard became a common refuge for privileged young men such as Jeremy Dodd and George W. Bush. The third son, Christopher, received a deferment from the military draft while serving in the Peace Corps, and then he, too, joined the National Guard.

Dodd's positions on matters of foreign policy brought him into constant conflict with Senator J. William Fulbright, chairman of the Senate Foreign Relations Committee, and principal spokesman for those Senators who believed that peace with the Soviet Union was both essential and feasible. In his first speech in the Senate, on the Berlin crisis of 1959, delivered less than two months after his arrival in the Senate, Dodd was openly critical of the positions associated with Fulbright, who was advocating a more flexible policy designed to avert confrontation with the Soviets. Dodd said that "flexibility is not only without virtue; it becomes vice." Dodd urged inflexibility, saying that the United States should back down on nothing. The speech attracted national attention, and was featured in *Time* magazine as being the point of departure for national debate. Boyd wrote in his later

---

25. James Gartland, Dodd staff member, to Tom Jr., July 10, 1962: "Thank you for your letter of July 7, concerning your interest in promotion to Captain. I have discussed the matter with Colonels Vandervort and Ramsey and they will check out this entire situation and notify me accordingly. I will keep you informed."

memoir that the episode "set the tone for Dodd's first term—bold, vigorous, controversial, and independent."[26]

With time, the friction between Dodd and Fulbright became more pointed. Their dislike for each other approached obsession, and although Dodd was almost invariably courtly in his relations with Senators—as required by the traditions of the Senate—he lapsed where Fulbright was concerned. Their exchanges became openly hostile, particularly during debate over United States intervention in the Dominican Republic.

In 1963, Juan Bosch was elected President of the Dominican Republic and set about outraging the oligarchy with programs to break up the large plantations and grant organizational rights to labor unions. His attempts to secularize the country offended the Catholic clergy. After only seven months in office, Bosch was ousted in a coup. Two years later Bosch's partisans in the Dominican military removed the governing junta and were about to restore Bosch when the United States invaded the country. At first President Johnson explained that the U.S. had proceeded in order to protect foreign nationals residing there. Then he spoke more freely and acknowledged that his real concern was to make sure that the Dominican Republic did not become the second Soviet foothold in the Western hemisphere. There was never any good reason to believe that Bosch was a Marxist or that his

---

26. At later hearings of the Senate Ethics Committee held in 1966, Dodd became agitated at Boyd's claim to have ghosted the speech— "It is an absolute lie to say he wrote that speech." In a sense, Dodd was correct: As Boyd recounted it to this writer in November 2009, Dodd assigned to him the task of ghosting the speech, but Boyd did not have a lot of experience at ghosting, had even less experience at foreign policy, and was bewildered as to how to proceed. A few days before the due date, while filling in for the Senator at a "freedom dinner" for one of the captive nations, Boyd heard an eloquent address delivered by a leading anti-communist, Dr. Walter Judd, the Republican physician and Congressman from Minnesota. Boyd borrowed Judd's narrative, aped Judd's form and build-up, and to the extent possible recreated Judd's sense of drama, the end product becoming Dodd's maiden speech in the Senate. The splash that "Judd's" speech made for Dodd in the national press, and the favorable publicity that it generated, led the Senator to ascribe greater strengths to Boyd than Boyd knew to be deserved.

support was principally communist, but Johnson wasn't taking any chances. Fulbright spoke out against the invasion:

> We cannot successfully advance the cause of popular democracy and at the same time align ourselves with corrupt and reactionary oligarchies; yet that is what we seem to be trying to do. The movement of the future in Latin America is social revolution. The question is whether it is to be Communist or Democratic revolution, and the choice which Latin America makes will depend in part on how the United States uses its influence ... In their panic lest the Dominican Republic become another Cuba, some of our officials seem to have forgotten that virtually all reform movements attract some Communist support. ... it is quite possible to compete with the Communists for influence in a reform movement rather than abandon it to them. ... economic development and social justice are themselves the primary and most reliable security against Communist subversion.

Dodd delivered the rebuttal, characterized by Fulbright biographer Eugene Brown as "a vituperative barrage of personal invective." Fulbright, said Dodd, "suffers from an indiscriminate infatuation with revolutions of all kinds, national, Democratic, or Communist." He had a general "tolerance of communism." Fulbright had "shut out from his mind all facts which failed to harmonize with the preconceived thesis that the rebels were right and the administration was wrong." He was giving aid and comfort to the enemy: "I am certain that his speech will be picked up and played heavily by every Communist and crypto-Communist and fellow traveler and anti-American leftist who wields a pen in the Latin American press."

The *Washington Post*'s editorial decried Dodd's "tawdry if familiar tactic of depicting those who differed with him as being soft on communism." Perhaps more significant to Dodd than what the *Post* had to say, his attack on Fulbright disrespected the Senate's unspoken but well-established rule requiring politeness and civility in debate. Dodd committed an offense to Senate culture that carried a price tag liable to be paid at some later date.

Civil liberties issues involved the all-out fight against communism (as Dodd viewed it to be), and so one's attitude on civil liberties issues was likely to run along the same lines as one's attitude on foreign policy issues. Dodd supported expansion of the 1940 Smith Act, which had outlawed the Communist Party, in order to reverse a Supreme Court interpretation that the act did not outlaw advocacy of forcible over-throw "as an abstract doctrine." He supported measures to widen the definition of illegal espionage, as well as legislation to allow denial of passports to communists "and communist sympathizers" if grant of a passport might "endanger U.S. security." Dodd also retreated from his earlier civil libertarian position on restricting wiretapping, adopt-ing the position of traditional war-on-crime advocates. Increased ability of federal police to tap wires, of course, would assist the crime fighters not only in battling the mafia and the drug dealers, but also in fighting activities deemed to be politically subversive.

Dodd was one the Senate's most consistent and vocal proponents of the Freedom Academy, envisioned to be a facility that would train Americans to counter the tempting but false doctrines of Marxism in its various flavors—that is, to propagate "pro-American" talking points. Dodd and other proponents of the Freedom Academy said that it could be as significant as the Army, Navy, or Marines in the bat-tle to win the cold war, and Dodd envisioned it as having status equal to West Point or Annapolis. Dodd touted the Freedom Academy in many of his foreign-policy pronouncements.

The Orwellian implications of the Freedom Academy as an instru-ment for domestic indoctrination did not alarm its proponents—after all, the Academy would stand for good arrayed against evil rather than the reverse—but the Academy did prompt opposition from the State

Department and from the Justice Department. The bill to establish it passed the Senate in 1960, but it never got anywhere in the House because its most influential opponent bottled it up in committee. The opponent was no civil libertarian, but the opposite, Representative Francis Walter, the Pennsylvania Democrat who headed the House Un-American Activities Committee. Professor Stacey Cone, of the University of Iowa, the only academic known to this writer to have published on the Freedom Academy, wrote in *American Journalism* that Congressman Walter was miffed because the intellectual father of the Freedom Academy had rejected HUAC's help.

Dodd's conduct of Senate Internal Security Subcommittee hearings certainly had the effect, and probably the intention, of helping to discredit the peace movement by casting doubt on the loyalty of peace activists. The hearings also had the familiar effect, if not the purpose, of chilling left-liberal and peacenik activists from furthering their political goals through meetings, protests, and petitions. One of the longer-running of his Internal Security confrontations was that between his committee and scientist Linus Pauling. Pauling had received a Presidential Medal of Merit in 1948, and then, in 1954, he was awarded the Nobel Prize in Chemistry. Thereafter he increasingly devoted his energies to the world peace movement. In 1957 he organized a massive petition drive among scientists against nuclear proliferation, urging a ban on further testing of nuclear weapons that was signed by over 11,000 scientists from 49 countries. The petition was submitted to the United Nations in 1958.

Dodd subpoenaed Pauling before the committee to inquire into the background of the petition, beginning the proceedings with the observation that "some of the propaganda activities against nuclear testing is Communist-inspired or directed." He stopped midway through his long prepared statement and suggested that, instead, it be incorporated in the record. Among the parts published in the record but not read aloud in Pauling's presence, was the statement, "Furthermore, our interest in Pauling's petition is justified by Dr. Pauling's long record of service to Communist causes and objectives, many of them related in no way to his special field of science." That sentence wasn't material Dodd wanted to read in the presence of the feisty scientist: Pauling would have seized the moment for protestations that would command the front pages, giving a public-relations victory to the peace crowd. Committee counsel Julien Goode Sourwine—Jay Sourwine—took over the questioning. Sourwine was an anti-communist from the pages of Mad comics.[27]

Sourwine got right to the point, demanding that Pauling provide the committee with a list of the names of those who had helped circulate the petition. Pauling refused. The proceedings were adjourned to give Pauling an opportunity to reconsider his position. He was ordered to return to the committee with a copy of the petition and the list of names of those who had helped him round up the 11,000 signers.

The criminal status of a refusal to name names before a Congressional committee was well-traveled ground; others before Pauling had been jailed for refusing to implicate others by revealing names. Pauling believed that his circulators, if identified, might be subjected to reprisals, and make others less likely to help in the peace movement in the future, thereby setting back the cause, thereby increasing the possibility of nuclear Armageddon. He was not intimidated by fears that his refusal to disgorge the names of his "accomplices" might lead to imprisonment.

---

27. Occasionally Sourwine's enthusiasm for the anti-communist cause was too much even for Dodd to bear. When a printed subcommittee draft of a report on "The Techniques of Soviet Propaganda," for which Sourwine was responsible, became public, Dodd had to publicly chastise Sourwine over a line that the respected Quaker organization, the American Friends Service Committee, was "a well-known transmission belt for the Communist apparatus."

Spourwine was a compulsive gambler, and once had to call on Dodd to guarantee a $2,500 check for him (that Dodd was later forced to cover when Sourwine defaulted on it), in order to cover a gambling debt. His gambling problem would seem to have made him a security risk.

When the hearings reopened on October 11, 1960, all the players were aware of the position that Pauling would take if pressed.

At the outset of the October 11 session, Pauling turned over to the committee a copy of the petition, 11,000 names taking up, with translations, some 12,000 pages, all packaged into three gigantic leather-bound volumes, the pages of which Pauling himself had hand-numbered. Pauling dragged out his presentation of the books, with details and digressions probably intended to tweak the impatience of the Senators. He had discovered a couple more signatures, raising the number of represented countries to 50. As a preliminary, before getting into the names of the circulators, he had some testy exchanges with Dodd, and then, as to the main question, he politely said no, he would not reveal the names of the circulators.

Sourwine's questioning resumed: Did Pauling know that among the signers from the U.S.S.R. were known communists? That did not surprise Pauling. Was Pauling aware that Professor Yakawa of Japan had been awarded the Lenin Peace Prize? No, Pauling did not know that, but Pauling did know that Professor Yakawa had been awarded the Nobel Prize. Did Pauling know that Martin Kamen, an American signer, had been accused by the House Un-American Activities Committee of passing classified information to Soviet agents in Bernstein's Fish Grotto in San Francisco during World War II? Pauling wasn't sure about that, but he did know that Kamen had won a libel suit against a Chicago paper that had printed the story. He delighted the audience--peace activists had packed the hearing room—by insisting that he did not follow the communist line; that the communists were following the Pauling line. Patience was never Dodd's strong suit. As impatient as he was with Pauling, he was equally impatient with Sourwine, protesting that some of Sourwine's evidence was irrelevant. But nobody pressed Pauling to reveal the names.

It is sometimes suggested that Norman Cousins, whose association with Dodd went back a long way, to the United World Federalists, and who continued as a national leader in the peace movement until his death, intervened on Pauling's behalf and convinced Dodd not to press the matter. More likely, a refusal to press relentlessly in such confrontations was about all that distinguished Dodd from Joe McCarthy. He appreciated the fact that once he forced people to name names—or caused those who might refuse, to be jailed—his own fate would then rise or fall on the same strengths and weaknesses that had brought down Joe McCarthy. McCarthy's overreaching had led to his disgrace and condemnation by the Senate in 1954; no one should invite such a fate.[28]

Pauling was awarded his second Nobel, the Nobel Peace Prize, in 1962, and in 1968 he joined the ranks of Professor Yakawa when he was given the Lenin Peace Prize. His political rehabilitation in the United States was solemnicized in 2008, when his face was put on a U.S. Commemorative postage stamp—oh no, not for his dedication to world peace, but in recognition of his work on sickle cell anemia. J. Robert Oppenheimer never got his own postage stamp.

Dodd had similar if less entertaining face-downs with SANE, the Committee for a Sane Nuclear Policy, which was headed by Cousins, and with the British theater critic Kenneth Tynan, who was affiliated with the "Fair Play for Cuba Committee," an entity that Dodd always regarded as no more than a Castroite propaganda unit. (Dodd scolded CBS in the *New York Times* for having employed as its correspondent in Cuba during the last years of the Batista regime a man who later became the first executive secretary of the Fair Play for Cuba Committee.)

The many stresses associated with being a United States Senator occasionally became too great, requiring that Dodd take a good breather. On February 27, 1960, he was attending a $100-a-plate dinner at a

---

28. Although people generally use the word "censure" in describing what happened to McCarthy, the word "censure" was removed from the text of the final draft of the censure resolution and the word "condemn" substituted in its place. McCarthy's backers regarded *condemned* to be less of a censure than the condemnation that would attach to "censure," with the end result that the condemned McCarthy was never censured.

Jefferson-Jackson Day function at the Hotel Fontainbleau in Miami Beach, seated at the head table with three other Senators, the Governor of Florida, and the guest of honor, former President Harry S. Truman. A thousand people were in attendance. Florida Senator George Smathers was addressing the gathering when Dodd became ill. He was removed to an outer parlor, where he was given emergency treatment by physicians and then taken to the Mt. Sinai Hospital. Dr. Paul Unger, the treating physician, told Zaiman at the *Hartford Courant* that "He has been chasing around the country quite a bit. When he came down here he had no sleep in about 48 hours. He just collapsed from fatigue. . . . I don't want him bothered for three or four days. I want him to have a good rest." No, Dodd had not had a stroke or a heart attack, and there was nothing organically wrong with him; he was just suffering from "extreme fatigue."

For fatigue, one might think that an overnight at the hospital and then Unger's "three or four days" at a beach resort would have sufficed, but Dodd was kept at Mt. Sinai for ten days, until March 7, after which Unger advised an extended rest. Dodd canceled all of his speaking engagements, and he and Grace remained in Florida at an undisclosed location, reportedly a small resort on Marathon Key. In April they returned to Washington, where Dodd underwent several days of in-patient evaluation at the National Institutes of Health before returning to the Senate floor on April 19, seven weeks after the crisis over his extreme fatigue.

One newspaper used the word "breakdown" in its reportage, but nobody coupled "breakdown" with the "N" word (nervous). Those were the times when "everybody" who was "anybody" in Washington knew that John F. Kennedy was a philanderer—some of them on the basis of personal experience. But nobody outside of "the beltway" knew, and most would have found it hard to believe that the idealistic and elegant young President had a degenerate side to him. Similarly, most would have found it hard to believe that Thomas J. Dodd, an American-eagle of a man, was emotionally fragile.

The Dodds congratulate Betty and Joe Blumenfeld
at Joe's swearing in as a federal judge.

Still, it was good to be a Senator. A lot of prerogatives went along with being a Senator—most obvious of them being that a Senator had the chance to reward loyal friends. The most important of those to be remembered was Joe Blumenfeld, who, with Dodd's sponsorship, was given a seat on the federal bench in 1961. He remained an active and highly respected judge for 27 years and was considered to be one of the most liberal federal judges in Connecticut.

There were many other perks too, most of them unknown to the population at large. Dodd took advantage of all of them—and why not? He had fought for them, he had earned them, and, in any case, he had won them.

When he traveled abroad, the State Department would make "counterpart funds"—foreign currencies paid to the United States by those nations receiving foreign aid from America—available to Dodd for investigatory expenses. Dodd's staff pushed local embassies to be generous in the allocation of counterpart monies to the Senator. Dodd's then-aide Charles Hamel, later a Washington lobbyist, delighted in telling this anecdote to fellow insiders back at the office: Upon leaving one European city for home, Dodd asked Hamel what was in the bag his aide was carrying. Leftover counterpart currency, said Hamel, which he would bring back to the embassy. "Never mind returning anything," Dodd said, taking the leftovers. He proceeded to the airport gift shop, and left it with the counterpart currency replaced by an armful of presents.

Dodd's staff always made certain that the Senator was rushed through U.S. Customs at his destination airport in the United States without the necessity of turning in the usual customs declaration forms.

Dodd often took commercial flights on his incessant travels, and usually did so on his long-distance trips, but for "commuting" he more often imposed on the private planes owned by various corporations that did business with the government—United Aircraft; Kaman, the helicopter maker; Avco-Lycoming, an aerospace contractor, the drug company McKesson & Robbins (then involved in investigations before the Senate Anti-Monopoly subcommittee, of which Dodd was a member); Travelers Insurance Company (off-and-on involved in ongoing investigations of the insurance industry before the same subcommittee), or on the plane of any one of a number of private citizens, such as Thomas J. O'Neill, head of General Tire and Aerojet, major government contractors. O'Neill also headed R.K.O., the filmmaker, whose doings were being investigated by Dodd's Juvenile Delinquency Subcommittee. In a pinch, Dodd might use the plane of Connecticut contractor Frank D'Addario, although the builder's plane, he said, had "no class." On the other hand, it also did not have visible, identifiable corporate markings on it. That appealed to Dodd. To a Dodd staff person, D'Addario commented, "We are not interested in having people know who owns the plane as long as Dodd knows who owns it."

Frank D'Addario didn't care if people knew who owned his airplane, so long as Dodd knew who owned it.

At other times the Connecticut National Guard's plane, or an Air Force plane, would meet Dodd's needs. At his destination, frequently agents of the federal Immigration Service, or the Connecticut State Police, would meet the Senator to do the chauffeuring.

Dodd often stayed in hotels, but in many cities there were wealthy patrons who could put him up in style: In New York it might be courtesy of General Julius Klein (much more about him anon); in Miami, Robert Harris, an old, eccentric millionaire (one of the few who seem to have had no motive for his kindness to Dodd more sinister than a need to feel important); in California, any one of a number of entertainment moguls who were indebted to him. In Hartford he would frequently overnight at the mansion of Charles McDonough, head and namesake of Charles H. McDonough Sons, Insurance, one of the (if not the) leading insurance agencies in the state. In the morning, McDonough's butler would drive Dodd to the airport.

Cynics might say that there were hidden pricetags attached to most of these courtesies and prerogatives, but if so, the pricetags were hidden beneath the vision of Tom Dodd, and if the prices were paid, they weren't by way of quid pro quo. These were just harmless courtesies, or simply the perks of office, and if all Senators did not enjoy them, they should have.

The social pace was dizzying, sometimes exhilarating, crowded with "must attend" functions hosted by—or in honor of—various high-ranking officials, or state affairs at which an important visiting dignitary might be the guest of honor. Occasionally the guest of honor might be Senator Dodd himself. Or Senator and Mrs. Dodd. Perhaps even more to his liking were the private soirees at the homes of legendary Washingtonians: Alice Roosevelt Longworth, the brilliant, acerbic daughter of TR ("If you can't say something nice about somebody, come sit next to me"); or Pearl Mesta of "Call Me Madame" fame; or Thomas G. "Tommy the Cork" Corcoran, FDR's favorite young man in the 1930s, who spent the rest of his life as the Washington peddler with the most influence to rent.

After angling for significant committee assignments, Dodd found that committee meetings were not really to his liking, and he took to skipping most of them. His attendance record at the Foreign Relations Committee, presided over by his nemesis, Senator William Fulbright, approached never. He rarely showed up at the work sessions of any committee, the sessions where the real business of Congress is undertaken, and he suffered bad-mouthing from the mouths of Senators whom he had offended by word, by deed, or by shortcomings in the work-ethic department. Senator Steven Young (D, OH) permitted himself to be publically quoted as saying that in 1963 the only meeting of the Aeronautical and Space Sciences Committee that Dodd had attended was the one at which astronaut John Glenn would be appearing for photo shoots. Dodd was not a willing listener, and although he had once been a prodigious worker, he no longer demonstrated an appetite for the level of work that had characterized him on his rise upward.

Like all Congressmen, he delegated most constituent contacts to staff members, but even scheduled appointments with the Senator himself were regularly ignored or postponed at the last minute "until tomorrow," due to pressing demands "elsewhere." Elsewhere frequently meant the sanctuary of Dodd's inner office, where Dodd was preoccupied with sharing a bottle of scotch with his admiring cronies.

Claimed urgent business in the capitol would sometimes force him to make appearances or deliver scheduled speeches at functions

Dodd was usually enveloped in a cloud of cigar smoke, but he avoided photographs of himself with a cigar. When he was on a health kick, he would switch to a pipe.

in Connecticut via telephone. In his memoir, Boyd explained how it worked:

A huge, blown-up photograph of the Senator would be dispatched from the Hartford office and placed on the platform, and at the appointed moment the voice of the Honorable Thomas J. Dodd, larger than life, came booming over the amplifier. All he had to do was sit in his Washington office and read. Of course, there was an element of inconvenience in having to wait in his office, so we arranged for him to broadcast from wherever he happened to be. One night, unknown to several hundred Connecticut listeners who had been told that important action on the Senate floor was preventing him from being with them in person, the familiar voice behind the smiling photograph originated from the living room of Thomas G. Corcoran, the Washington lobbyist, Dodd's host at dinner that night.

Some of Dodd's letters from Nuremberg are both eloquent and elegant; he could be a fine writer and, as a representative in Congress, Dodd had drafted the greater part of his own speeches. But at the Senate he was much busier, no time for that, and it wasn't necessary, either: Dodd had an office budget for things like editorial assistance, and people like Boyd, or David Martin, a reformed Trotskyite who handled most of Dodd's foreign policy and "anti-communist" positions, understood Dodd's views, and learned to echo Dodd's style.

Increasingly, Dodd relied upon Boyd and Martin, and infrequently Sourwine, to prepare the speeches, articles, and presentations for his regular radio broadcasts (he had a wonderful radio voice) sponsored by the American Security Council. With the zeal of his Marxist youth redirected, Martin, author of books about the Balkans, turned out a great volume of hawkish verbiage that would attract the most public attention, appeal to well-heeled right-wing political contributors, and maybe also put some income directly into Dodd's personal checkbook from the Senator's public appearances at anti-communist events, from publications, or from his broadcasts. Dodd's own input declined to insignificance.

The delivery of many of the speeches was also not what it might have seemed: According to Boyd's memoir, most of Dodd's speeches that appear in the *Congressional Record* as having been delivered on the floor of the Senate were not, but were inserted into the record after the day's adjournment by obliging clerks, who, at least since the 1800s, have always been willing—eager—to compromise the public record at the behest of one of the powerful. Dodd thus ceased to be significantly involved not only in the creation of his policy statements, but also in the delivery of them as well. His part in the Dodd operation increasingly became a matter of role-playing: He was the star in a continuing soap-opera, "The Senator."

In Washington, Boyd wrote in his memoir,

> The office into which Dodd entered was the focus of his existence. From his arrival at ten in the morning, he would often remain without leaving until nine at night. Comfortable in a slightly elevated swivel chair, he would direct his activities on many fronts, hatch his projects, plan his investigations, receive his courtiers, and let soar his imagination. Here, life was ordered exactly to suit him. .... All eyes and ears were bent in his direction. Anticipating his needs and fancies was with us a continuous preoccupation. By pressing the right button, he could have a want or a whim attended, produce a staff mem-

ber or a boon companion, set in motion a furious march of events, or suspend all action or intrusion.

He could spend hours on end on the telephone. Dodd loved the telephone. He invariably ate up his own Senate allocation of long-distance calls (they cost a lot of money in the 1960s) and then used up the calls allocated to the Juvenile Delinquency Subcommittee and the Internal Security Subcommittee—and then, with help from the Senate's paid staff, he hacked into the allocations of less talkative Senators.

After the close of regular office hours, his evening companions would appear, a group of political hangers-on and sycophants, mostly never-beens but sometimes including a former Republican Congressman, Al Morano, from Fairfield County, to express their agreement with the Senator's positions and laugh at his jokes—which was easy to do inasmuch as Dodd was a great raconteur—while Michael O'Hare, the office manager, made certain that the glasses were never empty. The happy hour would often extend into the late hours.

Back in Connecticut, the Dodds sold their West Hartford home in 1959 for about $31,500 (the 1959 sales price has no significance except as a benchmark for other dollar figures recited in this book). With Dodd's elevation to the Senate in November 1958, West Hartford had served its purpose, and the Dodds moved full-time into their "summer" home, in North Stonington, Connecticut. It had never been a grand house, there were no impressive facades, and it wasn't much more than an abandoned farm when the Dodds bought it for $12,000 in 1952, but with a substantial investment and the help of some contractor friends, it could be restored and fitted out for luxury living, and it was.[29] The main house dated back to the Revolutionary War,

---

29. One of the contractor friends was Sydney Symon, New London carpet dealer, who provided new carpets for the home. Symon later called on Dodd for help in getting a Presidential pardon for one of Symon's friends who had done time in prison for income tax evasion. Notwithstanding the high-handed attitude with which Symon pressed his demand, Dodd stressed to his staff that Symon's request should be made high priority; it was, and the pardon was granted.

A Senator requires an appropriate house.

and there was a separate guest house, a stable (Dodd continued to encourage his children to ride), a vast manicured lawn, and a pond stocked with trout; the grounds totaled 180 acres in all. The paved road ended at the beginning of the long driveway into the Dodd parcel, with the public way continuing farther along to the next town as a dirt track. All in all, it was an appropriate estate for a United States Senator. Much as southern gentlefolk lived in named estates, the Dodds' North Stonington retreat became "Laurel Glen," the address engraved on the formal stationery used by Grace for her correspondence.

Dodd so loved the trappings of office, the trappings of his physical office in the nation's capitol, that he planned to duplicate the office on the North Stonington property. He discovered a cave in a hillside on the estate, and envisioned digging it out further, and turning it into a "rath," a living space enclosed within a cave or earth walls, that could be fitted out to replicate the Senator's Washington office. To that end he assembled detailed scale drawings and photographs of his capitol refuge and its furnishings for use in the planned re-creation. His staff called the boss's fantasy "the rath of Dodd."

The Dodds also maintained a proper and well-staffed "Senator's house" at 1407 31st Street in Georgetown, a brick house of three or four stories (depending on how one counts the stories), in the most elegant and expensive quarter of Washington (though for Georgetown, Dodd's was not an "imposing" home). The purchase was made possible by a $25,000 loan for the down payment, advanced by the powerful New York lawyer Mathew (not "Matthew") Manes, name partner in the firm of Manes, Sturim & Laufer, who generously helped out the Senator by making the loan free of interest. The house was big enough to accommodate the children, but there was no need to scrimp, so the Dodds' high school-aged son, Christopher, was a boarding student rather than a "commuter" at Georgetown Preparatory Academy, an exclusive Jesuit high school spun off years earlier from Georgetown University, located nine miles up Wisconsin Avenue.

Both the North Stonington estate and the Georgetown house were stage sets for a man who was living a fantasy life.

Grace took to writing a regular newspaper column, variously titled "This Week in Washington," or "Last Week in Washington." She was not a political wife, like, say, "Stebbie" (Mrs. Chester) Bowles; she had no real interest in current events except insofar as current events might impact Tom. When her columns did venture into the issues of the day, she echoed Tom's views, but she conveyed them without the stridency injected into Tom's pronouncements by David Martin or James Boyd, with which Dodd himself felt perfectly comfortable. More often, Grace's articles consisted of chitchat about goings on among the wives of Senators and of Senatorial equals: "We went to a delightful party the other evening at the home of General and Mrs. . . ." She was one of Pearl Mesta's favorite people. Grace's articles were carried in numerous smaller-town Connecticut weeklies and a few dailies during the idyllic period of the Dodds' stay in Washington, 1963 to 1965. The column reported upon and represented the good life that was about to end.

CHAPTER FOUR

The Weakness

LIVING FAR BEYOND HIS MEANS was a habit deeply ingrained in Tom Dodd. From his Nuremberg reputation, Dodd was a well-known lawyer in the early 1950s, and he maintained a home and a truly impressive office suitable for a leader of the bar. Because of his illustrious prior career, he was entitled to be a leader of the bar, but he was not, at least not a leader of the Connecticut Bar, and he never had a personal clientele that could support the lifestyle he demanded.

When it became necessary to reveal his embarrassed financial circumstances, Dodd dated the onset of his money problems with his run for the Senate in 1956. As he later explained to the Senate Ethics Committee, he could never catch up with the debts that he incurred running unsuccessfully for the Senate against Prescott Bush in 1956, and then running successfully in 1958 against Bill Purtell—"once you get behind, it is almost impossible to get out." His debt problems became "a revolving thing": "I had no help from the State Democratic organization in any of my campaigns. . . . Other candidates were financed in a different way, but I never was, because the organization was unfriendly to me then and it is now, and consequently I had to row my own boat."

Dodd had self-discipline about almost nothing. He would sometimes consume gluttonous portions of food, and then subject himself to tortuous fasts.

The evidence does not indicate that Dodd came out of either the 1956 or 1958 campaign with significant campaign-related debts. The 1956 debt got rolled over into the financial structure of the 1958 campaign, and Dodd appears to have come out of the successful run in 1958 with an "on paper" debt of perhaps $20,000—not much in the bigger picture.

What is clear is that Dodd insisted on living in a grand manner befitting his station as a United States Senator. The position of United State Senator invites an ostentatious lifestyle; Senators who are not wealthy when they enter the Senate should content themselves with being the chamber's poor relations. Plenty of them did in the 1960s, and some may still. But Dodd was not about to be anybody's poor relation. Boyd recently recalled an outing for freshman Democratic Senators to which he drove Dodd shortly after Dodd's arrival in the Senate: "When we pulled up at the home of the host, Vance Hartke [D, IN]—a modest pleasant house on a modest, pleasant lot, in what appeared to be a new development—Dodd sat in the car for a moment looking around, quizzically. Then he said: 'Why would a United States Senator live in a house like that? In a place like this?'"

There was neither reason nor need to do so. And Dodd was not about to do so. A Senator enjoyed such flexibility in financial matters that it really shouldn't be necessary to live as a poor relation. Senators' reports on fund-raising were essentially un-audited, as were a Senator's claims for expenses incidental to his "official business" as a U.S. Senator or subcommittee chairman. The Senator's private business affairs were—by tradition—"off limits" to Senate inquiry. The Senate had never purported to render a judgment on a Senator's financial conduct, and there was no reason for it to begin rendering such judgments: after all, the Senate—almost by definition—was composed of honorable men. Looking back half a century, in 2010 Boyd characterized the Senate's practical code of ethics as "a code difficult to run afoul of."

For years Dodd had been making excuses and promises to creditors, rolling over notes with lenders, and imposing on people who for whatever reasons were not in a position to say no, or who for reasons of their own were not inclined to do so. Numerous people in and out of Washington belonged to "the $5,000 Club" (so named by Sanford Bomstein, a Washington restaurateur who was himself a club member), people to whom Dodd owed a personal debt in that amount, frequently not evidenced by written notes. Apparently none of them pressed him for repayment.[30] Many of them enjoyed indirect benefits from the overall relationship with the Senator. Manes, who had kindly advanced the $25,000 down payment for the Georgetown house, for example, was boosted by Dodd (successfully) for a highly sought-after seat on the board of directors of General Aniline and Film Corporation, a German firm with U.S. factories that had been taken over by the U.S. government during the war. During all the time that Michael O'Hare was in charge of Dodd's books, no payment was ever made to Manes toward this debt (although Dodd later testified that he paid back the loan out of the proceeds from testimonial dinners). Others were put on the public payroll, either as members of Dodd's office staff, or as staff members of the Juvenile Delinquency Subcommittee or of the Internal Security Subcommittee. As a United States Senator, Dodd was in a position to relieve his personal financial pressures and live in the style to which he was entitled with a little help from his friends, and from people who might want to become his friends.

Probably Dodd's only confidant (not to say co-conspirator) where financial matters were concerned was his crony Ed Sullivan, the only person Dodd ever trusted with the full picture of his financial operations. Sullivan was a former beer-truck driver with a graduate degree in street smarts, a raspy-voiced old man to whom personal loyalty to Tom Dodd was the highest virtue. He would have been seated right next to Joe Blumenfeld as Dodd's best friend, and when Blumenfeld

---

30. The Internal Revenue Service was less indulgent. At least by 1963 Dodd was being pressed by the IRS for back payments calculated on the basis of his declared income.

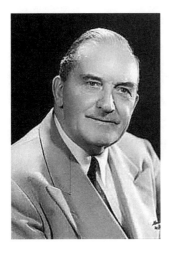

Ed Sullivan was concerned about Dodd's money problems, and flexible in his approach to their solution.

moved to the relative isolation of the federal judiciary, Sullivan was left unrivaled for standing in the Senator's inner circle. He and Dodd would occasionally disappear on two-day retreats, from which Dodd would always return refreshed.

Sullivan was as dedicated to the solution of Dodd's money problems—and as flexible in his approaches to them— as was the Senator himself. Probably more so. In an affectionate reminiscence of Sullivan, Boyd wrote, "He thought that financial affluence should flow from political power and was frank to voice his determination that Dodd should emerge from the Senate a wealthy man. ... Patronage, favors, franchises, and government largess represented to him the essence of involvement in public affairs." Sullivan reinforced Dodd's determination to take the course that a man of Dodd's personal and characterological makeup would have taken anyway.

From his desk in Dodd's Hartford office, Sullivan wrote Dodd regular lengthy hand-written letters that attest to Sullivan's concern about Dodd's financial situation, and he addressed it with concrete proposals. The letters might have been marked "Burn This Letter" but were not, with the result that they ultimately fell into the hands of Dodd's enemies and were preserved, to end up before this writer 50 years later. The first of them, dated February 4, 1959, immediately after Dodd took his Senate seat, gives a good introduction to Sullivan's approach:

> Frank Kelly is interested in a S.B.L [loan from the federal Small Business Administration]. He has not applied and intended to talk with us before making a move. He plans to give

me a preview of the situation Mon., Feb. 9—according to the papers, you will be here Feb. 10—Maybe on the plane you could think this over:

1. Fee for procurement work.

2. Getting a share of stock, plus an agreement that would bring a steady income. This is a good business and a lot can be done for him, he knows the business, appreciates the value of spending money in the right places and has never had enough capital to handle his growth.

   This, of course, are my ideas. I will only try to promote them after you tell me to.

The same letter discusses the interests of a Harold Eckert, described by Sullivan as "financially very well off" and as well-established in the liquor business:

Harold wanted help in getting a name scotch. They also are looking for a warehouse in Htfd and will have New Britain.

They have no attorney in this area. On this deal, I have these thoughts:

Help get a scotch.

Take a fee or become their local atty (not you I know) on a retainer basis. Or

Rent them a warehouse. Or

Take a share of the operation in this branch with a steady income. (If possible).

An awful lot of good could come to the branch—to be considered besides scotch is the top line of National [National Distillers] which would mean a lot of business.

Again these are my ideas. I hope you can agree and let me know when you are in. Money can and will be made.

In a later letter of March 14, 1960:

This morning I spent an hour with Jack Kelly [John J. Kelly, the political boss of Hartford, a very wealthy man with powerful commercial as well as political muscle], we had a real good talk. I know there is nothing Jack wouldn't do for you and also I know that he can steer things your way that would easily solve all your problems. I am to see him again Thurs. We agreed that when you are around we will get together, maybe at the shore or at least at a place where we will not be bothered, and Jack promises he will come up with something. I am sure he will, believe me he is a good friend of yours.

I am sure Tom this is the right move, your Washington income must be added to and you must agree on a plan that will do this. You spoke for an Engineering outfit, some little atty came to Jack for them, they got what you asked for, this is fine if you are "in" [quote marks added], but no good otherwise. This is enough to let you know we covered all bases and I hope you approve. I know such a thing can work if done right, it cannot work unless handled right. I have no intention of reporting back to Joe [identified as "Joe B," presumably Blumenfeld] or Bill [presumably Bill Curry, a leading Hartford politician], I can always say I have not been able to catch up with Jack. Only 3 of us know of this move.

Kelly's insurance agency was "Agent of Record" for all the insurance policies issued to the State of Connecticut or any of its entities, which brought to Kelly both wealth and power—and which indicated that he knew all about how the game was played.

Still later, either from June 22, 1961, or from November 30, 1961 (which of the two dates is unclear from the documents) Sullivan wrote:

The big question now is, what to do to continue some extra income. I bet you have ideas, I hope so, we must talk over on first chance.

A long time back, we talked about an S.B.A.[Small Business Administration] Finance concern, then dropped it, to me it seems this must have merit. A new license has just been is-sued in Stamford—in the country as of now there is 419 con-cerns. The amount of money required is $150,000. This to you would not be tough—Mortenson, Jack Kelly, Hogan, Al Donahue to name a few that have the money and might be interested, Matt Moriarity on the board of both Manchester banks, a set up such as this you need, it is permanent.

His letters regularly mention money making opportunities for people in Dodd's circle: "I see where the G.S.A. [General Services Administration] is seeking bids in Arizona, Cal., Nevada, for Car and Truck Rental service—I remember you had a talk with Henry Neils-en [a greater Hartford auto dealer] awhile back on such business—chances are [the G.S.A. will be seeking rental services] all over." And, "Have you heard any more on the proposed Airports & Heliports in Conn? Bill Doyle has an option on 300 acres in Goshen." What was good for Henry Neilsen or for Bill Doyle could only be good for Tom Dodd.

The closest Dodd ever came to finding the Holy Grail about which he and Sullivan dreamed involved Dodd's efforts on behalf of the "Marincello" project, contemplated by his associate Thomas Frouge. Frouge, with offices in Bridgeport, Connecticut, and Manhattan, was a major New York City builder/developer in the 1960s. His Frouge Corporation had functioned as the general contractor on seven major developments for the New York City Housing Authority and Board of Higher Education, and he had built large apartment houses in the city on his own account. As a Papal Knight of the Equestrian Order of the Holy Sepulchre of Jerusalem, he and Dodd shared a common interest in Church activities.

"Marincello," as envisioned by Frouge, was to be a gigantic multi-use development on 2,138 acres on the "Marin headlands," just north of the Golden Gate Bridge, ultimately to constitute, he wrote Dodd, "a satellite city to San Francisco." Formally, Dodd acted as one of Frouge's hired attorneys involved in the project, but he was almost certainly promised an equity interest in Marincello, as well, for his influence: Frouge wrote Dodd "Tom, I think this is a great opportunity for you and me." For you and me.

Frouge flew Dodd to Sacramento in an effort to influence California Governor Pat Brown to speed along the Marincello project. Dodd wrote Frouge after the trip that he had "had a long, very pleasant and interesting chat with Governor Brown. Afterward his chauffeur drove me to San Francisco and I had an enjoyable visit with Mr. and Mrs. Grant [Henry M. Grant, the vice-President of the Frouge entity overseeing the Marincello project]. I feel I did some good, but I think there is more to be done." There followed further letters to Governor Brown, and intervention by Dodd, in personal visits and in correspondence, with Secretary of the Interior Stewart Udall, intended to head off the creation of a National Park on the site contemplated for Marincello. Dodd also had contacts with the Department of the Army, which controls vast tracts on the San Francisco side of the Golden Gate Bridge and which was Frouge's predecessor-in-title to the Marincello site. He opened discussion with the General Services Administration about possible federal government rental of space at Marincello.

Dodd never used the word "client" in discussing Frouge or the Marincello project with his contacts, nor did he give any indication that he was speaking as a paid advocate or that he expected to gain financially in any way from the project. Frouge was identified simply as Dodd's constituent and friend.

Ultimately Marincello became hog-tied in litigations; Frouge and his principal financial backer, Gulf Oil Company, fell out; and the dreams of a lot of people, particularly Frouge and Dodd, died, while those of Marin County preservationists flowered.[31]

As things developed, neither Marincello nor any of Ed Sullivan's above suggestions turned out, or at least not sufficiently as to give Dodd permanent relief from the problems borne of Dodd's refusal to discipline his spending. The principal, though not exclusive, route to Dodd's financial relief came via Dodd's personal use of "political contributions," particularly his use of the proceeds of testimonial dinners. It would plainly be corrupt for a political figure to accept payoffs for use of his official position to further anybody's private interests, but it is accepted within the culture of American politics—and completely "legal"—for individuals or business entities that may have received assistance from an office holder, or who may want to receive assistance from an office holder, to make contributions toward the election or re-election of that official. And if the money donated as a political contribution should somehow find its way into the candidate's personal pocket . . . oh, what the hell . . . Who's gonna know?

Today (2011) campaign income and expenditures can be and are closely scrutinized by one's political opponents, and if a contributor makes a cash contribution of size, both giver and recipient are implicitly aware that something corrupt is going down. In the 1960s it was easier for all concerned to ignore the realities of the situation.

Dodd supported an extravagant lifestyle largely by dipping into political funds, scarcely audited, for high-styled support of himself and his family. Along with contributions from people who genuinely admired the Senator were "contributions" that disguised other than altruistic motives. An example from the record of the Senate Ethics Committee can serve for illustrative purposes:

A. N. [Abram Nathaniel] Spanel was a quirky and imaginative in-

---

31. Frouge died of a cerebral hemorrhage in 1969 at the age of 54, and his family gave his heart for transplant surgery.

ventor, a Jew born in Russia, a colorful and charming if self-absorbed fellow. He was highly successful in business as founder and chairman of International Latex Corportation, manufacturer of girdles, brassieres, and infant underpants, best known for its "Playtex" line. Once Spanel had one of his vice-presidents get the bust measurements of all the women in the Dodd office and then sent each of them a deluxe bra, thereby winning friends and influencing people.

Spanel was a wannabe in American political life, who published myriad paid advertisements in the *New York Times* and countless other newspapers promoting his political views.[32] He had his eyes set on an ambassadorship. Spanel was a Francophile; he had been honored as a Commander in the French Legion of Honor, and his first choice would have been to be ambassador to France. In a memorandum to Dodd, Spanel sent tips intended for President Johnson on how to handle the imperious strongman of France, General Charles de Gaulle. The advice does not appear to have gone any farther than Dodd's file cabinets.

Spanel employed Irving Ferman, a vice-president of International Latex, as his Washington handyman. Ferman was a well-known man about the capitol. In the 1950s he had been head of the Washington, D.C. office of the American Civil Liberties Union, but he was a Dodd-styled civil libertarian: He despised totalitarianism so much that he appreciated the need to keep domestic "fellow-travelers" under a watchful eye. He therefore maintained an irregular but ongoing covert relationship with Louis B. Nichols, the #3 man in the FBI, keeping Nichols abreast of ACLU happenings, running the names of prospective ACLU hires or board members before Nichols, tipping him off as to the names of two people who were attempting to involve the ACLU in a campaign against the House Committee on Un-American Activities. He shared with Dodd an admiration for J. Edgar Hoover,

---

32. David Martin to Spanel, May 27, 1960: "Would it be possible for International Latex to print the complete text of Senator Dodd's speech as a paid public service advertisement in the *New York Times*? My off hand estimate is that it would require one page and a half which would cost approximately $5,000 to $6,000"?

and once proposed that the Director be given a civil-libertarian award. Little wonder, therefore, that he traveled in the same circles as Dodd. He and his wife socialized regularly with the Dodds.

Ferman later testified that Dodd's aide David Martin had asked Ferman to raise $10,000 toward Dodd's 1964 re-election campaign. According to official filings, Spanel and/or Ferman (the actual donor is unclear) contributed a total of $2,150 "over the table" to two re-elect Dodd campaign committees prior to the 1964 election. Shortly after the election, Ferman delivered $8,000 in cash to the Senator personally, to be used to pay for tickets to an upcoming Dodd testimonial dinner, tickets that Dodd might distribute to whomever at his unfettered discretion. Dodd later testified: "I did not ask who [the money] was from. I probably should have, but I just thought it was from a group of his friends." Mr. Ferman had said these friends would rather not have their contributions made public, so the $8,000 was not listed in any way on any public filings, whether incidental to the dinner or to any past or prospective election. As far as any paperwork might disclose, the payment had never been made, no money had ever changed hands.

Actually the money came from the petty cash box of International Latex Corporation, from which Ferman, with the approval of corporate President W. O. Heinze, had taken it. Ferman left behind a voucher attesting that the cash had been taken, not for political dinner tickets, but for "Industrial Relations Expense."

Dodd turned the $8,000 over to Ed Sullivan, who handled all the money raised by dinners. Sullivan said he used $1,000 or $1,500 of the money toward dinner expenses (there was no paper trail from which details might be reconstructed), and he returned the balance of the eight thousand to Dodd for the Senator's personal use. For all anybody could tell, maybe Sullivan himself had a piece of the action.

Allegations and denials revolved around whether David Martin had promised Ferman that Dodd would push Spanel for an ambassadorship in exchange for raising $10,000. There was testimony from Boyd and two others that Martin had boasted of his success in getting a pledge of $10,000 from Ferman, and that all the Senator had to do for the money was recommend Spanel for the ambassadorship. A secretary, Terry Golden, testified that she had typed a letter to the President for Dodd's signature, dictated by Martin, recommending that Spanel be appointed ambassador to France. (Martin does not seem to have testified on this matter.) Both Dodd and Ferman acknowledged that there had been some discussion of no moment between them about an ambassadorship for Spanel at some time in the distant past, but neither acknowledged any kind of talk about a quid pro quo. Moreover, there was no evidence that Dodd had ever signed or sent the letter that Golden had typed—or that Dodd had ever lifted a finger to obtain an ambassadorship for Spanel. We will never know whether the $10,150 was given in response to a promise of a recommendation of an ambassadorship for Spanel, or whether Dodd (or Martin in Dodd's name) ever made effort, either genuine or faux, to fulfill such a promise. In view of what we do know, however, none of that has much significance: The possibility that Dodd might have "sold" an endorsement for a political appointment for cash-money is the most-nearly innocent reconciliation of the facts.

What is undeniable is that Dodd was not terribly concerned as to the identities of Ferman's "friends"; that he was not squeamish about the accuracy of official accountings of Dodd-related entities; that he did not mind taking cash of uncertain origin and simply putting it into his pocket. He never indicated any discomfort about being handed eight thousand dollars in cash—a quarter of the price of an elegant home in West Hartford. Here is a man who would have been an easy mark for an FBI "sting." Least important: the $8,000 for "dinner tickets" either constituted an illegal campaign contribution by a corporation or it involved a personal gift of sufficient size (under the tax code of that period) that it should have been reported on the donor's required tax returns.

More arguable would be questions like: What interest did International Latex have in moving a large amount of cash into a Senator's pocket, disguising the gift with a phony voucher? (Alternately, Was the voucher phony? Or was the corporation trying to influence improperly the vote of a United States Senator on legislation pertaining to industrial relations?) Was it simple good will that had moved the corporate heart? It is difficult to come up with a reasonable and honorable explanation as to why somebody, whether Spanel, Ferman, or International Latex, would give a U.S. Senator a sum of impressive size–in cash–accompanied by a "please don't mention it" request. On the other side of the coin, Did Dodd believe that Ferman's effort on his behalf, and the delivery of eight thousand dollars in greenbacks, represented nothing more sinister than a spontaneous expression of admiration and warm feeling? Could an ethical public servant have honorably accepted a gift (Dodd later insisted that the dinner proceeds were exempt from income taxes because they were "gifts" to him), of such size in such form?

We cannot know how regularly large sums of undocumented cash were passed into Dodd's pocket by way of "dinner tickets"—or not pretending to be for dinner tickets—or the circumstances of any such transactions. Was this particular transaction an isolated incident, wholly unrepresentative of the man Thomas Dodd? Or is receiving undocumented cash by a public official the kind of offense to cultural norms that is prone to recidivism?

Generally, envelopes of cash given to a political person do not become public, but in Dodd's case there were certainly other envelopes. Another of those "others" was one formally admitted by Dodd before the Ethics Committee:

Dodd regularly intervened with branches of the government on behalf of a Mite Corporation, whose President, Robert J. Blinken, was a frequent visitor to the Senator's office. Next to his name on a list of potential contributors, Dodd noted in hand that Blinken had already been "more than generous." How so? Blinken's name never showed up next to impressive dollar amounts on any official fund-raising reports.

According to Marjorie Carpenter, Dodd's one-time personal secretary who became part of the conspiracy against Dodd, envelopes of cash were frequently given to the Senator, or dropped off at the office for him, particular in the several months before the 1964 election. She reported an occasion when Blinken brought by an envelope while Dodd was in Connecticut; she called Dodd and told him that Blinken had left an envelope for him. She was about to leave for Connecticut to take part in the re-election campaign, and Dodd told her to bring the envelope along with her. When she got there, Dodd opened the envelope in her presence. Inside was cash. "Campaign contribution," he muttered. He offered her some of it for her expenses, but she declined. Later, when the Ethics Committee pressed its inquiries, among the facts stipulated by the Senator was that "Mr. Robert J. Blinken, a businessman of New Haven, Connecticut gave Senator Dodd the sum of not more than $2,100 in cash on or about September 17, 1964 for Senator Dodd's use in his 1964 election campaign. This money was not deposited in any bank account." If the money was not deposited in any bank account, what, then, came of that money?[33]

To a great extent, political contributions are—and have always been—linked to "constituent service." Constituent service, everyone understands, involves the assistance that an elected official renders to a citizen to unclog a bureaucratic pipeline. (Type "A" constituent service.) The official performs Type A constituent service out of a sense of duty. But "constituent service" also covers the efforts that an elected official might make to ease the path of a citizen, maybe a corporate citizen, in seeking a favor, or perhaps a lucrative contact, outside of established channels, or by using the influence of office in a manner that compromises "the system." (Type "B.") Type B services are not performed out of a sense of duty but with the expectation that hands

---

33. International Latex was later prosecuted for making a political contribution, illegal under federal law. It pleaded "no contest" to the misdemeanor, was fined $5,000, and that was the end of the matter. Either half-hearted investigation or good lawyering must have been involved.

There is no indication in the record that there were ever any repercussions from Blinken's cash contribution—or contributions (according to Carpenter, there were other "envelopes" from Blinken).

will wash hands. In that sense, Tom Dodd's were among the cleanest hands in the District of Columbia.

As an example: In March 1965 Dodd wrote President Johnson in an attempt to influence the award of a military contract to Avco-Lycoming, which was competing for the contract with General Electric. The letter stressed the positive effect that the award of the contract would have on employment levels in Fairfield County, Connecticut. The award of a government contract inevitably affects employment levels in both the "winning" community and the "losing" community. His letter to the President closed: "I am vitally interested and concerned about the pending award, and for this reason I have taken the liberty of enumerating the important considerations which should affect the final decision." In an inter-office memo, secretary Doreen Moloney wrote to Gerry Zeiller, who handled "constituent service" matters, "The Senator wants to know if this letter was sent to Valenti [Jack Valenti, a special assistant to Johnson and a "Johnson person"]. He doesn't want it handled by Larry O'Brien [another special assistant, but a Kennedy holdover]." It was too late. Zeiller had already transmitted the letter via O'Brien, who responded, "Your comments will be called to the attention of the Department of the Army and you may be sure that they will be given all appropriate consideration." That's not what Dodd wanted to hear. But he heard even more discordant notes:

Copies of the letter to O'Brien had been sent, as well, both to Valenti and to McGeorge Bundy, Johnson's National Security Adviser. Bundy acknowledged the letter with a response that came as close to a rebuke as a presidential aide might send to a Senator:

> Your office has sent me a copy of your letter of March 25 to the President on the subject of a pending contract. Simply to avoid misunderstanding, I think I should inform you that there are standing instructions here in the White House which forbid staff members to concern themselves with business of this sort which is pending in any of the great departments.

Dodd understood that the message was a rebuke—from a presidential aide to a United States Senator. In a minute prepared for the files, Zeiller noted "Just before the Senator left, he received a letter from McGeorge Bundy which he took violent exception to. . . . First the Senator wanted to write a rather sharp letter to McGeorge Bundy, but after some discussion, he accepted my recommendation that it would be better to look into the matter informally rather than put anything more in writing relative to Bundy's attitude."

Earl "Red" Blaik, West Point's legendary football coach (ret.) was employed in the 1960s as a vice-president at Avco-Lycoming. He was the featured speaker at one of Dodd's fund-raising dinners, a regular contributor to Dodd's campaigns, and frequently arranged to have an Avco plane made available to Dodd for the Senator's needs or convenience. Ultimately, Avco-Lycoming got the contract.

Dodd's office generated a mountain of correspondence involving type B constituent service—efforts to secure contracts or permissions for one or another constituent, sometimes for non-constituents, not only contracts from the federal government but also contracts from governmental or private entities in Connecticut—and in other states too, anywhere that his contacts might bring a favor. Even abroad: A letter to Dodd from his friend General Julius Klein, a man who enjoyed an endless web of business and personal contacts in Germany, chides Dodd for having attempted (unsuccessfully) to obtain a Mercedes-Benz distributorship for somebody through onetime Nuremberg defendant Franz von Papen—rather than through Klein himself.

Sullivan was provided with lists of names of corporations and individuals Dodd had helped in business dealings, and other lists of those who had received no more than "Type A" services, all of them being people or entities that could be solicited for contributions or for dinner tickets regularly on whatever pretext. No contributor needed to know to what specific use his contribution might be put. Much of this money could be funneled off to support a better lifestyle for the Dodds than was enjoyed by, say, the Hartkes.

Tainted contributions, such as the cash from International Latex, or from Mite's Blinken, were not factored into any official filings at all, but simply disappeared. According to Carpenter, the personal secretary, lots of cash seems to have come into the Dodd office.

During the 1964 re-election campaign, Dodd kept a tight rein on expenditures while continually stressing the urgency of raising still more money to build up the war chest, a war chest that might support a more-than-appropriate lifestyle until the next election cycle would refill the till. Official financial reports relative to the 1964 campaign gave no responsible indication of contributions received, while the recitation of campaign expenditures included some purely personal outlays. On balance, the reports were not simply erroneous on specifics; they were fraudulent on the whole.

John D. LaBelle, Connecticut's Chief State's Attorney at the time, and the man (if anyone was the man) charged with rooting out corruption in state government, was an honorable man but a realistic man. He refused to be distracted from his truly important work—keeping murderers, rapists, and arsonist off the streets—by being dragged into some Quixotic crusade against America's national tolerance for gray-area influence peddling. When it became necessary for him to do so in 1967, LaBelle ruled that claimed shortcomings in Dodd's official filings were outside the purview of the Connecticut Corrupt Practices Act.

Beside using political funds for his personal use, Dodd was not above taking presents that a friendly eye would say represented poor judgment but no worse, and that a less friendly eye would view with less tolerance. Another example from the record of the Ethics Committee:

From July 1964 to March 1966, Dodd made regular use of automobiles owned by David P. Dunbar. Dodd later stipulated that Dunbar and one of the corporations controlled by him paid the installment payments on the cars, and the insurance and registration costs. Dodd made very clear that there was nothing "corrupt" about it. He later explained how the arrangement had come about:

I knew Dave Dunbar's father, actually. He was a very fine man. I do not mean that young Dave is not. He is too. So there was a background of that kind. And he was quite a successful young businessman.

In conversation one day he said, "Listen you know I have several cars. I would be glad to make one available to you." I think I was driving kind of a shabby looking car, probably to him. And I thought that was a generous thing to do, and I used it particularly in that year when I was hurrying around a lot for the campaign. And I remember very well afterward saying, "Dave take that car back. I do not need it any more," and he said "No, you know it is something you can use and I would like to have you use it."

I wish now I had made him take it back, but I continued to use it. I did not have the money to buy a new car with.

Actually, three different new Oldsmobiles were involved: Dunbar annually updated "Dodd's" vehicle to the current model, each successive edition sporting Connecticut license plate "USS1." Meanwhile, Dodd urged the Atomic Energy Commission and the Government Printing Office to throw government contracts to the Dunbar businesses, Dunbar Transfer Company and Dunbar Associates, Inc., both engaged in plant relocation, equipment installation, heavy hauling, and related engineering. At least one such contract, to close down the Connecticut Advanced Nuclear Engineering Laboratory, fell Dunbar's way. Dunbar, after all, operated a Connecticut-domiciled enterprise; Dodd would have done the same for any Connecticut business. (Indeed, for non-Connecticut businesses too.) But he later acknowledged: "If I were living it all over again, I guess I would have said 'no.'"

Other similar lapses of judgment dot (if they do not dominate) Dodd's career in the Senate. While a member of various Senate investigating committees, Dodd repeatedly accepted gifts or "campaign contributions" funneled off for personal use, from the people or entities whose activities were under investigation.

An investigation at the Juvenile Delinquency Subcommittee into the effect that the heavy diet of violence on the television might have on American culture and American youth fizzled after John W. Kluge, CEO of Metromedia, the TV outlet most addicted to airing violent television programs, and his PR people, plied Dodd with entertainment, contributions, flattery, and gifts. Dodd's official files, available to scholars at the University of Connecticut, have been purged of most traces of "Kluge, John W.," but a few thank-you notes were left behind: " Many thanks for arranging for Jeremy [and a group of his friends] to attend the Ice Capades . . . "; thank you "for your lovely flowers . . ."; thank you "for the lovely gift of Elizabeth Arden cosmetics" (Grace to Mrs. Kluge).

Kluge is an interesting and surprisingly little-known man who would play a vital role in the resurrection of Dodd's good name, so we will digress for brief biographical information about him. Born in Chemnitz, Germany, in 1914, Kluge emigrated to the United States at the age of eight, reportedly worked on an assembly line job at Ford Motors (although it is not clear from the sketchy materials seen by this writer whether Kluge is a truly a self-made man). He started college at Wayne State University in Detroit and graduated from Columbia University in New York in 1937 with a bachelor's degree in economics. He then worked in sales until he entered United States Army intelligence during World War II. Immediately after the war he began acquiring radio stations, then television stations, notably a string of TV stations called Metropolitan Broadcasting Corporation. His dabbling in other advertising ventures prompted him to rename his combined holdings as Metromedia, Inc.

By the early 1960s Metromedia was "fourth" among major TV networks, but number one in violent programming. The Juvenile Delinquency Subcommittee determined to investigate the general subject. Then Kluge and his PR person, Florence Lowe, began their

courtship of Dodd, principally involving numerous social engagements topped off with a fancy dinner party in the Virginia horse country, at which the guest of honor was the chairman of the subcommittee
investigating violence in television programming. Kluge had a "party
bus," equipped with a bartender, bring the dinner guests, including
Supreme Court Justice Tom Clark, Johnson's closest adviser, Walter
Jenkins, Secretary of the Treasury Henry Fowler, Liz Carpenter (Lady
Bird Johnson's staff director), Senator George Aiken, Senator Gale
McGee (D, Nebraska), Senator Vance Hartke, along with a grabbag
of columnists and celebrities. Talk about a nice gesture! The Metromedia effort was so effective that the investigation not only died, but
Dodd placed Mrs. Lowe's son, Roger Lowe, on the staff of the delinquency subcommittee, thus discouraging later re-consideration of
Metromedia's programming policy.[34] According to Boyd's memoir,
no doubt relying on Carl Perian, staff director of the Juvenile Delinquency Subcommittee, Dodd also insulated NBC—and particularly
its higher-ranking officials—from the searching eyes of the subcommittee staff.

Investigations into salacious motion pictures met a fate similar
to the investigations of TV violence. Another investigation led by
Dodd at the Juvenile Delinquency Subcommittee into high-powered
fireworks fizzled after a delegation of fireworks producers visited the
Senator; they later boasted that they had "fixed things." Dodd's critic
Drew Pearson commented that Dodd had "a disturbing, documented
habit of consorting with the people he is investigating, then permit-
ting the investigations to peter out." There may have been exceptions,
however: Boyd and Carl Perian, of the Juvenile Delinquency Subcommittee, believed that Dodd prolonged his investigatory efforts apro-
pos the insurance industry and also gun control in order to milk those
being investigated.

Dodd's longstanding and aggressive hostility toward Teamsters

---

34. Drew Pearson quipped (in his column) that Roger Lowe's sole qualification
for work on the Juvenile Delinquency Subcommittee was that he was a high school
dropout.

Union Boss Jimmy Hoffa was replaced by condemnation of the Javert, Robert F. Kennedy, who made a career out of haunting Hoffa, after the Connecticut Teamsters became valuable and prized financial support- ers for Dodd. (The Teamsters contributions were laundered through the treasury of the Democratic Senate Campaign Committee, which returned its own check to Dodd, so that reportings would not disclose Dodd's association with a "dirty" entity such as the Teamsters.)

The examples were so numerous and so regular that they smelled of extortion, although certainly Dodd never viewed his conduct in that light. Dodd was never troubled by introspection, and his confidence in his own integrity remained unshaken to the day that he died.

It is hard to know the extent to which alcohol abuse helped ease Dodd into abuse of office. From Nuremberg he wrote Grace that he was living as a "teetotaler"—perhaps just telling her what he thought she wanted to hear—but if indeed he was then an abstainer, that might explain (to compound the speculation) why his Nuremberg period was the most personally rewarding period of his entire career. Except in Nuremberg, though, Dodd's life was marked with heavy drinking. His excessive drinking was an expression of his lack of self-discipline and indulgence of his sense of entitlement.

There were occasions in the later 1950s when his sidekick, Boyd, thought that Dodd's drinking was sabotaging good judgment, but the problem became more serious after his election to the Senate. "The Club" atmosphere of the Senate exposed those with a propensity to overindulge to constant temptations at the bar in the Senate cloak- room, especially during the long evening sessions of the Senate that were common at the time. Senator Wayne Morse (variously I, R, or D, OR) from 1945 to 1969, once said, "There has never been one night session of the Senate in all my experience that hasn't witnessed at least one Senator making a fool of himself and disgracing the Sen- ate." Then, the three-wise-monkeys ethos of The Club protected those who gave in to temptation, shielding them as much as possible from public exposure for lapses of decorum. It was a rare breach of

Senate culture for Dirksen to talk on the floor of the Senate about Dodd's "cerebral incoherence." The media, as well, turned blind eyes to Senatorial drunkenness; it was—like the promiscuity of Presidents—something that "responsible" journalists did not report.[35]

Dodd understood that a reputation for drunkenness would be very damaging to him. With what might be called paranoia (but for the circumstances of his ultimate downfall) Dodd suspected that potentially unfriendly eyes were noting the declining level in each of his bottles of liquor. It was commonly believed among Washington insiders that J. Edgar Hoover documented the personal shortcomings of every public official for potential blackmailing value, even the shortcomings of those such as Dodd with whom Hoover enjoyed cordial relations. Times and alliances change; Dodd could be Hoover's foe tomorrow. Hoover prepared for such eventualities; Dodd knew he should guard against them too. Boyd reports in his memoir that Dodd suspected that the FBI was monitoring the scotch, and that he devised needless, bizarre stratagems to defeat the snoops. But the real threat was much closer to home.

In *The Case Against Congress* (1968) Drew Pearson and Jack Anderson describe humiliating episodes of Dodd's drunkenness too painful to recount, and others are set forth in their "Washington Merry-Go-Round" columns of 1966-1967. Repeating the outline of one of those incidents, however, is essential to understanding the downfall of Thomas J. Dodd because it had a tremendous effect upon his most important aides and was important in turning them against him. The particular incident pertains to Dodd's reaction to the death of Kennedy.

Dodd was in Connecticut on November 22, 1963, when John F. Kennedy was assassinated. He was having lunch at Frank's, a down-

---

35. Occasionally a newspaper item might mention that a Senator was in "high spirits," which insiders, but not the general public, understood to be code words meaning "drunk." Hugh Rawson, *Rawson's Dictionary of Euphemisms and Other Doubletalk*, rev. ed., 1995, entry for "high."

town Hartford restaurant frequented by the political crowd, with Bill Curry, a local political powerhouse, who was also probably Dodd's closest Connecticut crony other than Sullivan. Dodd commandeered a plane from United Aircraft Corporation with the claim that Johnson needed him in Washington immediately. United Aircraft ferried Dodd and Curry to Washington, while a secretary from United Aircraft notified Dodd's Washington office that the Senator was en route and that he had asked that his staff meet him at the airport. He invariably commanded that he be greeted by an entourage, and that he be trailed by a retinue.

Boyd, O'Hare, and Carpenter were waiting when the plane touched down and a lubricated, rumpled Dodd emerged from the aircraft. United Aircraft flew Curry back to Hartford.

Mrs. Carpenter told Dodd that Florida Senator George Smathers had just arrived, and that he was wearing a black armband. Dodd explained why: "Smathers was a friend of the old administration. I am a friend of the new administration." As they drove to Dodd's Georgetown residence, it became clear to the highest-ranking members of Dodd's staff that their boss saw the day as one of triumph, rather than of grief. When they arrived at the Georgetown residence and joined Tom Jr. and a friend before the television set, the Senator mimicked the world leaders who paid tribute to Kennedy. His most-nearly reflective comment was, "I'll say of John Kennedy what I said of Pope John the day he died. It will take us fifty years to undo the damage he did to us in three years."

Alcohol abuse must be at least part of the explanation for the stark and tragic contrast between the respected, highly competent, and disciplined prosecutor, who had directed the most important trial in the history of the world, and the tragic figure considered in the rest of this book.

CHAPTER FIVE

The Conspiracy

JAMES BOYD ENGINEERED AND orchestrated the downfall of Thomas J. Dodd. Dodd spoke sorrowfully of him: "I had taken him out of, I almost say, the basement of the Aetna Insurance Company. . . . I had a genuine fondness for him and I thought he was a mighty decent young man. . . . Mrs. Dodd and I treated him almost like a fifth son." Boyd was brought into the Dodd family by Grace's nephew, Helen Farley's son John, and Boyd and his wife Gloria became godparents to John's children. In her oral history, Helen Farley reports that when her daughter overheard a Boyd telephone conversation that she thought might be threatening to the Dodds, she reported it to Grace, who wouldn't hear of it: "You mustn't talk that way about Jimmy. Jimmy's a wonderful person." Mrs Farley trailed off. ". . . They were so fond of him . . ." Later Dodd confessed on the floor of the Senate that as far as insofar as Boyd was concerned, "I was guilty of a profound misreading of character."

From the spring of 1964 through 1965, Boyd, the administrative assistant, joined with three others to bring Dodd down. The others were Marjorie Carpenter, Dodd's office favorite; his office manager and bookkeeper, Michael O'Hare; and O'Hare's girlfriend,

Dodd confessed on the floor of the Senate that as far as James Boyd was concerned, "I was guilty of a profound misreading of character." Left: James Boyd.

Terry Golden. The most trusted people in Dodd's office conspired against him and were assisted by still others on Dodd's staff or within his inside circle. Carl Perian was both the highest-ranking and the most useful of these "others," but there were still more, most of whose identities have never been revealed.[36] What must Dodd have done to poison against himself so many of his staff, led by the three who knew him the best and who owed him the most?

Boyd was born in 1928. His grandparents had emigrated to the U.S. from County Clare, Ireland, and his father ran a grocery store in Portland, Maine. A sister was a Catholic nun, a brother was a baker. Boyd left South Portland High School before graduation, joined the Marines, was discharged in 1948, and then went to Boston University on the G.I. Bill. He graduated after three years. One did not have to see his Phi Beta Kappa key to know that Boyd was very bright. In 1952, aged twenty-four, he was working at the Aetna Insurance Company and taking graduate courses in history at Trinity College in Hartford when John Farley arranged for him to meet Farley's uncle, the new Congressman for Hartford County. The first visit of the two began late at night—Dodd was three hours late getting home—and ran into the early hours of the morning. Boyd related in his memoir, *Above the Law: The Rise and Fall of Senator Thomas J. Dodd*,

> he made me feel immediately at home, entertained me with stories of my native Maine told in a flawless down-east accent,

---

36. Much of the most damaging information about Dodd in Boyd's memoir was attributed to Perian by name. This writer wrote Boyd asking whether anyone had contacted him after publication of the book to dispute the accuracy of what had been attributed to him or her, and he responded "no." As to Perian: "Carl Perian saw in advance all material about him and was pleased with it. Throughout he was a close, though hidden, ally in the matter. . . . How he survived with Dodd for more than two years after the book's publication is a mystery. I suspect, knowing both his and Dodd's love of intrigue, that he represented himself to Dodd as a kind of double agent able to keep Dodd up to date about me, and be a communication bridge between us, at the cost of seeming to be on my side."

Dodd seems to have surrounded himself with people who shared his "love of intrigue," including, in addition to Perian, Jay Sourwine from the Internal Security Subcommittee and, of course, Boyd himself.

related personal remembrances of Harry Truman, Sam Ray-
burn, Alben Barkley, and Adlai Stevenson. He drew from me
the story of my own life and background, my attitudes and
aspirations. However green and awkward I must have appeared, he seemed deeply interested in me. ... He took me
up to the mountaintop: We would work together, we would
lay plans "not for a year but for twenty years."

Boyd left the Dodd home at 2 a.m. "In a state of unutterable elation."
From then on he was a full-time partisan for Tom Dodd, sometimes as
a volunteer and for brief periods an employee.

When the new Senator went to Washington in January 1959, he
took James Boyd with him as "legislative assistant," soon to become
"administrative assistant."

It is obvious from Boyd's memoir that in the first years of his relationship with the Dodds, the Senator was a father figure to him, and
Boyd took comfort in his status as part of the Dodd family. In the
early pages of his book, Boyd's discussion of the Great Man in his life
is unashamedly loving; over the second half of the book hangs a cloud
of patricide.

In the foreword to *Above the Law,* Boyd accepts the characterization of himself as the Judas Iscariot, but rationalizes that he had been
confronted with a choice of loyalty to his chief and loyalty to integrity—"the choice between sentiment and justice." Also in play were
more temporal factors. There is implicit acknowledgment in *Above the
Law* (and Boyd has made clear elsewhere) that if Dodd had handled
him better, Boyd might never have brought about what fills most of
the rest of this book.

Many elements contributed to Boyd's disenchantment with his
hero.

Boyd had been aware that there was an imperious side to Dodd
even before he accompanied the Senator to Washington. Once during
a campaign Boyd had disagreed with one of Dodd's proposed suggestions, beginning "You can't do that ..." Dodd interjected, "Don't

ever tell me what I can't do!" Along with the increased importance of being a United States Senator, Dodd became increasingly tempestuous. He sometimes exploded at staff with petty complaints and was often abrupt or rude to underlings. The Dodd office had a tremendous turnover in help. An infrequent word of praise from the boss seemed forced, even mawkish.

Office morale problems were complicated by the heavy weight of dead wood on the staff—an ever-present symptom of the boss's corruption. In addition to his working staff Dodd always had as many or more political cronies and hangers-on on the payroll who were not expected to produce, which increased the quantum of work that the "working" staff had to handle. The staff included, at least on paper, many people to whom Dodd was obligated—some financially obligated and some politically obligated—who to a greater or lesser extent were receiving satisfaction of Dodd's obligation from the public purse. One of the first people hired by the new Senator was Sheldon Z. Kaplan, Dodd's former partner as representative of Guatemala. When Dodd cancelled the contract with Guatemala, he cost Kaplan a lot of money, which the new Senator made up to Kaplan by putting him on Dodd's official payroll until the scores were evened. His obligation to Kaplan was met by the general public. He owed Albert Morano $15,000, for which Morano received the no-show or semi-show position of "Special Assistant to Senator Dodd" from 1963 to 1969. He owed $23,000 to George Gildea, whose later testimony before the Senate Ethics Committee would be discounted on the theory that "He was an elderly gentleman and his memory was confused." Gildea landed a position with the Senate Juvenile Delinquency Subcommittee but was assigned to the Senator's office staff, where he did little productive work and wasn't expected to do more. Financial obligations—whether for interest or for principal—can be met in more ways than one.

All the non-productive or minimally productive people maintained on the office payroll ate up so much of the office's personnel budget that it was necessary for Dodd to appropriate to his own staff employees who were on the paid staffs of the Senatorial committees that he controlled: the Subcommittee on Internal Security and the Subcommittee on Juvenile Delinquency. This effectively increased the staff for Dodd's office while causing staff shortages on the Juvenile Delinquency and Internal Security Subcommittees, serving as a constant reminder of the systemic improprieties in the Senator's operations.

Dodd's insistence on delegating almost everything was also grating to a man like Boyd. The Senator tried to keep up the pretense that he was participating in the intellectual output of his office by rearranging paragraphs in articles or speeches—"I don't know if you boys will ever learn paragraphing!"—or moving a comma here or there, but such efforts merely invited derision. On one occasion he asked Boyd to critique an article that Dodd said he had written, and gave Boyd a 20-page document from which something on the opening page had been excised—physically cut out of the paper—immediately beneath the title of the article. Inside, Dodd had inadvertently neglected to expunge the "by David Martin" notation that had been removed from the cover page. In the eyes of his administrative assistant, pretense of this sort robbed Dodd of dignity. So did Dodd's increasing dependence on the narcotic of flattery.

According to Senate Clerk Francis Valeo, Dodd's positions on matters of public policy could be influenced by "effusive flattery, to which Dodd was highly susceptible." He was most comfortable with people who flattered him. Boyd reports in his memoir painful snatches of overheard conversations from the Senator's after-hours confabs with "the boys," typified by obsequiousness toward the Senator of the crudest form.

Presentation of a gift to the Senator was simply a way to flatter him; often gift and verbal flattery went together hand in hand: for example, a handwritten note on a social card accompanied a present from Metromedia's Florence Lowe to the Dodds of a portable TV set

(TVs were expensive in 1964) on the occasion of their thirtieth wedding anniversary. The salutation read: "To Two Wonderful People."

Dodd loved to receive gifts—a case of champagne, better still a lavish two-week vacation in California, being entertained by movie moguls. For a building contractor to lend Dodd a private airplane made things very convenient for the Senator, but it was also an act of deference toward Dodd, appropriate deference. It was the subtlest form of flattery.

Dodd apparently never noticed that most of the gifts and courtesies came from people who had some interest in his official acts. It would have been less than human for Boyd not to have felt a sense of superiority over an employer who manifested such personal insecurity.

Dodd's lack of engagement with the work of the Senate was also charged against the respect in which he was held by his aide. Boyd recently recalled,

> As the years passed, I never knew Dodd to study, even cursorily, a complicated issue; the briefest oral summary, sometimes seconds before a roll call vote, had to be enough. Nor did he respect legislative mastery in others. He would mock the latest tour de force of bill-piloting by John Pastore [D, RI]: "With those teeth of his he always looks like he is talking through a picket fence."[37] When Johnson pulled off another classic legislative legerdemain, Dodd would be derisive: "He will never be a great Senator, only a mechanic." On a decision day, Everett Dirksen would come to the Floor, to oppose or defend, armed only with the legislative text—the bill itself— creating his speech as he went along, rebuffing challenges by quoting the telling line from the text itself, never failing to find amid the morass the line he was looking for.

---

37. Dodd, at 5' 6", towered over Pastore, 5' 4." He privately referred to his colleague as "Toy Man."

These were the building blocks of significance in the Senate. And Dodd not only eschewed the detail work, the recruiting of supporters, the appeasing of opponents, the cajoling, the favor-swapping—but was, or feigned to be, contemptuous of it all.

Boyd could recall no instance in which another Senator would telephone or drop by to plot strategy to advance this or that scheme.

Outside the office Dodd would sometimes make belittling comments to service personnel, waitresses, or busboys. Boyd found it unpleasant to go out with him, and began manufacturing excuses about "being busy." Dodd didn't like to be told that somebody had plans other than those that revolved around himself. Ribicoff had by then moved from Kennedy's cabinet into a Senate seat; Dodd whined that Ribicoff's administrative assistant "is always with Ribicoff... But my administrative assistant is never with me any more. I guess he is not as interested in my welfare." His self-absorption was total, and it became his defining character trait.

By the end of his tenure, Boyd was receiving $22,900 as administrative assistant (the pay being set by Senate schedules), a very respectable sum in 1964, but, money aside, from his first day with Dodd in the Senate, working with the Senator became decreasingly rewarding: Boyd's early hero worship dissipated, then turned to disrespect and dislike. Meanwhile, Boyd became increasingly cognizant of Dodd's ethical shortcomings, and those shortcomings assumed greater significance to Boyd, proportionately, as the Senator's personal shortcomings became increasingly offensive. Which is to say: It is easy to explain away ethical shortcomings on the part of a person one likes and respects, but it is impossible to tolerate dishonesty in somebody that one has grown to dislike and to disrespect.

Complicating Boyd's balancing of the basic values involved was the influence of Mrs. Carpenter, who was much more to him than a co-conspirator against Dodd. Boyd, married with four children, and

Carpenter, married but without children, found themselves involved in a romantic relationship.

Carpenter was more outraged by Dodd's official conduct than was Boyd, more resolute in bringing him down. A good part of her attitude turned on the length and quality of her exposure to Dodd: Carpenter had never known the freshman Congressman who had won Boyd's admiration; she had known only the demanding Senator, hobbled by alcohol, who delegated everything. She felt no tug of lingering affection for Dodd because she had never felt that much affection for him to begin with. But there was more to it than that. In a 1984 interview for *The Whistleblowers,* by Myron Glazer, Carpenter (by then Mrs. James Boyd) said, "I was more enthusiastic about doing something than Jim. It was understandable. I was younger, less sophisticated, more naive. Maybe I was more outraged for that reason." Boyd, with a decade of bumping around on the Connecticut political scene, was tolerant of the cynical side of politics—he himself was tinged about the edges with at least a touch of the mentality that he ascribed to Ed Sullivan. The "naivete" of his girlfriend, her unfamiliarity with the way that the

Dodd's beloved personal secretary, Marjorie Carpenter, became "that Carpenter woman."

great game of politics was played—and her intolerance of the way that it was played—went a long way to nudging Boyd toward Carpenter's viewpoint.

Gerard Zeiller, who handled Dodd's constituent service, later testified at the Ethics Committee hearings that he thought both Boyd and Carpenter were very intelligent, but "I felt she was dominant in the pair, that she was the stronger willed of the two."

Dodd was always good at reading others, and quick to sense slights, real or imagined. He sensed the change in Boyd's attitude and began to be less open with him, perhaps began to resent him. Still, he seemed to long for a closeness with Boyd, for the closeness they had shared in the early days.

Boyd's family, his social and religious background, mirrored Dodd's, and both were consumed with politics, brilliant men with ready wit and rich vocabularies, similar diction and cadence. Both were good looking men, shorter than average, Boyd a couple of inches taller than Dodd. Boyd was 22 years younger. Boyd was the fifth son, the son Dodd would have wanted. On election night of 1964, the Senator invited only Boyd and Carpenter to join him in his inner sanctum at his hotel suite in the Hartford Hilton, to view the early returns with him alone, just the three of them. Only when it was clear that he had won an overwhelming victory were the doors opened to Grace, the children, the others.

By that time, the relationship was beyond repair. Boyd and Carpenter, with O'Hare and Golden and occasionally others on the staff, were regularly trading stories about their boss, principally focused on the financing of Dodd's lifestyle, which began fairly innocently but became increasingly unfriendly to him. Sooner or later talk like that was likely to get them in trouble with the boss. During the 1964 campaign for re-election, either Boyd or Carpenter or both may have spoken too loosely with Dodd loyalists: James O'Connor, a young lawyer related to Grace Dodd, part of Dodd's usual "in-state" retinue, who was then in charge of maintaining the campaign's official financial paperwork, or Bill Curry, or Curry's wife, Beverly. Beverly Curry was one of the many people Dodd put on the payroll of the federal government whose functions, if any, were unclear, or at least unclear to the Senator's administrative assistant. Either O'Connor or the Currys may have sounded an alert.

Immediately after the election, Carpenter began asking Ed Sullivan for records of contributions and copies of the official campaign finance reports, which she claimed were necessary to fill gaps in the files at Dodd's Washington office. Sullivan, who buried his own ego inside of Dodd's, is likely to have mentioned the request to the Senator. Dodd operated on a "need-to-know" basis. Why was this data important to "the Washington office"? Was it? When Sullivan did not respond to the request, Carpenter repeated it. At that point word almost certainly got back to Dodd. Putting together the various clues, Dodd realized that something potentially dangerous to himself was unfolding. At later hearings of the Ethics Committee, Dodd testified that Judge Blumenfeld—his old friend Joe Blumenfeld—was the first to tell him that "everybody in Connecticut seems to know about the disloyalty of some of your employees but you, and you had better know about it." Dodd was to learn that "I was surrounded by people who were betraying me."[38]

On December 7, 1964, Dodd fired Carpenter and Boyd. The explanation he gave to others as to why his two highest-ranking staff members were no longer with the office was: "I found Boyd and Carpenter playing house together. It got to be such a scandal I had to fire the both of them." When Dodd's situation became heated, rumors began to circulate (and still live—vibrantly—within the aging band

---

38. Dodd also told the Ethics Committee that Blumenfeld had told him of a visit the judge had received from Boyd's wife, Gloria, who had recited a tale of woe about her wayward husband. From Dodd's perspective, it could only help his position to remind the Committee how thoroughly a blackguard was this Boyd.

of Tom Dodd loyalists in Connecticut) that Boyd and Carpenter had been discovered in the office *in flagrante delicto.*

Almost immediately Dodd relented in part about firing Boyd. With all of his abilities—never mind whatever evidence he might already have assembled—Boyd had the potential to be extremely dangerous. Although Boyd was dismissed as administrative assistant, Dodd continued to give him out-of-the-office ghosting assignments as part of an effort, Boyd believed, to keep some control over the future behavior of himself and of Mrs. Carpenter. The divorce between Boyd and his wife was in process, and Boyd had substantial support obligations. Given Boyd's circumstances, Dodd might reasonably have considered that Boyd could be controlled by a paycheck. He kept Boyd under his thumb by blacklisting Boyd for employment anywhere else in governmental or political circles—the only arenas in which Boyd could expect to earn a respectable paycheck—while using the carrot in talking to Boyd, both directly and through intermediaries, about how Dodd wanted to bring him back to the office. Bad strategy. In 1984 Boyd told Myron Glazer, interviewing him for *The Whistleblowers,*

> I didn't come to the decision to really go at it, tooth and nail, until I saw him trying to keep me from getting a [new] job. I didn't want to go back with him. I was trying to get away from him for some time, but he tried to use the power to keep me from getting a job, and then, in a roundabout way, boasting to me what he was doing, toying with me as if I were some kind of a creature, instead of a partner as we had started out.

Boyd appreciated the fact that there would be no point to reporting Dodd's misconduct to the FBI. The FBI did not have the authority to investigate a Senator without the expressed approval of the Attorney General, and the FBI was unlikely to seek approval, or to conduct any meaningful investigation of Hoover's #1 cheerleader in the Senate.

Dodd had made a practice of publicly fawning over Hoover, inserting into the *Congressional Record* whatever might come along about Hoover that was adulatory, or proposing a Congressional gold medal for him. A phone call from Boyd to the FBI would mark the start of payback time: Instead of investigating Dodd, the FBI would tip him off and immediately relay to Dodd whatever information Boyd had proffered, thereby giving the Senator a chance to cover his tracks.

Nor would there be any point to presenting allegations to the recently formed Select Committee on Standards and Conduct of the Senate, commonly called the "Ethics Committee." Past Senate investigations demonstrated that the Senate had little interest in policing its members.

Boyd understood that if Dodd was going to be brought down, the spotlight of press publicity would first have to be focused on him. Then the Senate might be compelled by the overwhelming pressure of public opinion (if such should materialize) to do something. Boyd remembered that J. Parnell Thomas had been brought down because a secretary had leaked documents from Thomas's office to Drew

Pearson, documents that established the Congressman's corruption. At that juncture, a relationship began with Pearson's junior partner, Jack Anderson.

"Washington Merry-Go-Round," the newspaper column by Drew Pearson and Jack Anderson, was the most widely read political column

Jack Anderson was "the Serpent in the Garden of Eden," said Dodd's defender, Senator Russell Long.

in the country, carried in more than 600 newspapers nationwide. Everybody in the capital read the column in the *Washington Post*—and a whole lot of them worried about the possibility that some day Pearson's eye, powerful, insightful, and judgmental, might focus on themselves. Anderson was not yet his senior's equal in the world of American journalism, but he was coming from the same place as Pearson.

In its obituary of Anderson in 2005, the *New York Times* discussed Anderson's investigative technique: "He quietly cultivated dissatisfied and idealistic lower-level government workers, convincing them that the public's right to information trumped the bosses's personal interests. His stock and trade were the secret documents he persuaded sources to leak."

Anderson and Boyd were ripe for each other. Whether Boyd called Anderson or vice versa, they were drawn to each other. But Anderson made clear that he needed documentary evidence before proceeding. Documents. Boyd had already been thinking along these lines himself.

Boyd had expected that Michael O'Hare and Terry Golden, still on Dodd's staff, would take any necessary documentary evidence out of the office and make copies available for transmittal to Anderson. June 11, 1965, was settled on as the date for a major haul of materials, but at the last minute O'Hare felt that he could not morally participate in removal of documents from Dodd's office. This forced Boyd and Carpenter to a hard decision from which they did not recoil: Boyd and Carpenter—former employees barred from returning to Dodd's premises—would burgle the Dodd office to get the evidence that Anderson demanded as the price for his cooperation. Always security-minded, Dodd frequently had the office locks changed. This time he had good reason to be concerned. Immediately after firing Carpenter and Boyd he had the locks changed once more. But Judith Berling, a young secretary in the Dodd office (who had been secretary to Boyd), made a key to the new locks available to Carpenter.

On the afternoon of Saturday, June 11, 1965, Boyd and Carpenter, carrying two empty suitcases, committed the first of several break-ins at the office of Senator Thomas J. Dodd in the Senate Office Building. They timed their initial foray for late in the day, when they felt they would be least likely to be interrupted. By using different entrances and exits and maintaining outward nonchalance as best as possible, they minimized the chance that a doorkeeper would pay attention to them.

Once inside the building they went to a payphone and called the telephone numbers for the Senator's office, to be certain that no one was there. Then, using the key, they entered, locked the doors behind them, and got to work sorting through the file cabinets in search of the information damaging to Dodd. They knew pretty well which files might contain what they were seeking, but files led to related files. The work was time-consuming and had to stop before nightfall: If they had to turn on lights, the glow would be visible to people outside the building; the longer the lights were on, the greater the chance that they would attract unwelcome attention. As the skies darkened, Boyd and Carpenter casually exited the building, carrying the same two suitcases, now crammed with documents.

Anderson made arrangements for the photocopying of the materials (a daunting task in 1965), and after that was accomplished, Boyd re-entered the office and returned the originals to their proper file drawers. They returned the next day, Sunday, and then again the following weekend, and again the next, making off with some 7,000 pages of documents. Before they completed their work, they had made seven or eight surreptitious entrances to take or to return documents. The odds on them completing their trespasses without detection would seem to have been slim, but they never aroused suspicion. The account of their covert operations in *Above the Law* is as captivating as a thriller by Eric Ambler or Frederick Forsythe.

On a Friday early in October 1965 Terry Golden was fired. Dodd explained that Golden was too close to Carpenter and Boyd. O'Hare

"Traitor" is how Dodd described Michael O'Hare.

was given the task of dismissing his girlfriend from her job, which may have been the larger part of the reason O'Hare became more invested in the conspiracy against Dodd. Let us digress again, now for consideration of O'Hare's relationship with Dodd and the Dodds:

O'Hare's relationship with the Dodd family dated back no further than the spring of 1961. In May of that year O'Hare was a financially strapped student at Catholic University in Washington. He responded to a posting at the university's student employment agency seeking a part-time bookkeeper for Senator Dodd. The Senator himself interviewed O'Hare. Dodd later described the college boy as "a threadbare lad, a starveling."

O'Hare counted himself lucky to get the position, and started the part-time job at $20.00 a week. He very quickly progressed to full-time, then to de facto office manager, then to official office manager, meanwhile assuming more and more responsibility for the personal affairs of the Senator and of his family. He was office manager, factotum, majordomo, and frequently chauffeur, valet, butler. His contact with Dodd and with the Dodd family had been both more intense and of a more personal nature than was Boyd's. The following anecdote from a "Washington Merry-Go-Round" column hints that O'Hare felt considerable obligation and loyalty to Dodd, and perhaps genuine affection:

[Dodd] became intoxicated while dining out in Georgetown and insisted on going on to the Crazy Horse, a teenage rock 'n' roll joint then run by his friend Sanford Bomstein. O'Hare persuaded the Senator that he should go home instead of the Crazy Horse, but knowing Dodd well, O'Hare waited outside the Senator's house to observe what would happen. As expected, Dodd stumbled out of his home in the company of his secretary, Doreen Moloney, and attempted once again to go to the Crazy Horse. "No, you can't do that," O'Hare admonished. "You have to go back home." The Senator from Connecticut allowed himself to be led back into the house.

While O'Hare felt at home in his role with the Dodds, he idolized John F. Kennedy. Dodd's obvious satisfaction over the death of Kennedy was a shock to the young man that refused to dissipate; the Senator's cynicism weakened to breaking point the demands that personal loyalty might have made upon O'Hare. Meanwhile, in conversations with O'Hare, Boyd's friend Jack Anderson eloquently reinforced O'Hare's own feelings that the young man should act against what he believed to be corruption in government. O'Hare, like Boyd before him, was torn between the demands of loyalty and the demands of personal integrity. Then the dismissal of Terry Golden snapped the weakened ties of loyalty.[39]

One last factor that might have influenced O'Hare, the precise weight of which can never be measured, was brought to light by the Senator: Dodd later said that Boyd and Carpenter "had always exercised a kind of mesmeric influence over O'Hare." "Mesmeric" is

---

39. In *Above the Law* Boyd writes that Golden's dismissal merely brought home to O'Hare that his remaining days on Dodd's staff would be few in number, and that if he were to give his fullest cooperation it had to be immediate: that weekend. More than one motive may have been involved, but given the timing of O'Hare's decision, it is difficult to accept that spite played no role in it.

perhaps the wrong word as well as an overstatement, but it is probably true that Boyd, eight years older than O'Hare, handsome and dashing and self-confident, brilliant too, and (if the newspaper columns by Dodd's partisan, William F. Buckley, Jr., can be believed), very successful with women, was an older-brother figure for O'Hare.

The weekend immediately following the dismissal of Terry Golden, O'Hare the bookkeeper snuck the full set of the Senator's financial records for the preceding five years out of the office. There were checkbook records, campaign finance returns, income tax filings—the works. According to Drew Pearson, there were tears in O'Hare's eyes as he proceeded. He told Pearson: "I've been protecting this information with my life. Now I'm giving it for publication for the world to read."

It took seven hours to photocopy the records, after which the originals were returned to their rightful place. Anderson went to Carpenter's place with a big black bag and picked up the copies.

O'Hare had thought his own tenure with Dodd was about over, but as events turned out, it was not. Dodd—wholly unsuspecting of O'Hare—repeatedly refused to accept O'Hare's resignation, pleading that he stay with the Senator "just a few more weeks," while Boyd cajoled him into staying on as a mole, a spy. With his powerful and conventional sense of decency and morality, O'Hare was wholly unsuited for such a role. O'Hare did not finally separate himself from the Dodd office until January 30, 1966, 14 or 15 weeks after his removal of the financial records, and a week after Pearson and Anderson's opening salvos in their crusade to bring down the Senator. For almost four months, O'Hare had engaged in continuing acts of disloyalty to a man who was his employer but very much more. He left Dodd with no job to go to and little or nothing saved to fall back upon. He also knew that in very little time his role in the conspiracy against Dodd would become widely known, dimming his prospects for employment. But he felt as though a great weight had been lifted from his shoulders, and it had been. Or rather, with time, it might be.

Before the Ethics Committee Dodd recounted that when the Pearson and Anderson articles first appeared,

> I called [O'Hare] in and I said, "Somebody must be stealing or must have stolen documents out of this office. Do you have any idea who it is?" No, sir, he didn't have any idea. And it wasn't until later that I learned that he was one of those stealing them. But he always protested to me that he had no knowledge, knew nothing about it. . . . and this continued right up to January of this year, when he was taking documents out of my office day by day and he would come in and look me in the eye, and when I'd say to him, "Mike, I'm distressed about this, there must be somebody here stealing my property," he would lie through his teeth.

Although Dodd's statement was somewhat mixed up chronologically, the gravamen of his claim against O'Hare was essentially true, and O'Hare knew it. When O'Hare was about to testify before the Ethics Committee, he encountered Dodd's son Jeremy, aged 27 and then employed, or at least on the payroll, of the Senator's office staff. Jeremy called out to him: "Wait a minute, Mike." Jeremy poked O'Hare in the chest with a finger and warned: "I just want to tell you one thing. When this thing is all over I'm going to follow you to your fuckin' grave." O'Hare made a half-hearted rejoinder.[40] A contemplative and sensitive man, O'Hare was deeply conflicted about his role, and he punished himself with self-doubts. There was never any reason for Jeremy Dodd to follow him.

The materials collected by Boyd, Carpenter, and O'Hare constituted the documentary evidence required by Anderson. On January 24,

---

40. "I didn't know what to say, so I said 'That's OK with me.' "

1966, Pearson and Anderson began laying out the allegations against Dodd, backed up by extensive quotes from the papers in the Senator's files. They would devote over a hundred columns to Dodd. They began with an expose of Dodd's relationship with General Julius Klein, representative and lobbyist for various private and quasi-public West German entities.

Could the Senate Ethics Committee be prodded to investigate? Probably not. An article in *Washington Observer* reports that General Klein called his longtime friend, the Republican leader in the Senate, Everett Dirksen, to ask if he might be allowed to testify in defense of Dodd. "No, Julius," replied Dirksen: "There is not going to be any hearing on Tom Dodd."

CHAPTER SIX

The Investigation

DIRKSEN ALMOST CERTAINLY WOULD have been correct in telling General Klein that there would be no hearing on Dodd, but Dodd demanded one. Believing that a bold front was the appropriate stance for him to take, Dodd wrote to the Ethics Committee, offering up his files relevant to the general and inviting the committee to investigate the matter. He issued a press release about his offer. The next day the newspapers headlined "Dodd Calls for Probe."[41] Dodd more or less forced the Ethics Committee to proceed. He was taking a gamble, but given the Senate's past performance on such matters, he felt it was probably a safe one.

The Senate Ethics Committee had had a very short life span when Pearson and Anderson began their crusade against Dodd. It had been established largely for the sake of appearances after the Bobby Baker scandal in 1963 had clouded the Senate's image. Rob-

Mississippi Senator John C. Stennis was the southern Senator from Central Casting, however where Caucasian males were concerned, he had a sense of fairness and remarkable judicial temperament.

---

41. As part of his response, Dodd also instituted suit in federal court, *Thomas J. Dodd v. Drew Pearson and Jack Anderson,* based on libel and invasion of privacy. The libel count was dismissed fairly early in the litigation; the invasion count lingered but ultimately was also dismissed, and in 1969 the Supreme Court declined to accept the case for review.

ert G. Baker, known as "Bobby," had enjoyed the modest title "secretary to the majority of the Senate," but as Lyndon Johnson's protégé he came to wield enormous power throughout the federal government as a "can do" man. Dodd (who was never involved with him) was not alone in thinking Baker to be "the smartest man in Washington." Investigations into Baker's doings by the Senate Rules Committee, led by North Carolina Senator B. Everett Jordan (D), led to Baker's conviction and a jail sentence for bribe-taking and income tax evasion, and also to the establishment of the Ethics Committee.

In the Baker proceedings, however, evidence pointing at financial misconduct by particular members of the Senate was not followed up; Chairman Jordan expressly refused to allow inquiry into the possible improprieties of Senators. The overwhelmingly prevalent attitude—among Senators—was that a Senate committee had no business investigating particular Senators over claims of corruption. If allegations against Senators were to be pursued, who could know how many Senators might be unfairly stigmatized by misleading appearances? Who could know how much of the Senate's time and energy would be taken up considering scurrilous, politically inspired charges? No, a Senator had to be the judge of his own conduct. That much was for certain.

By invoking the Ethics Committee's examination, Dodd could feel fairly comfortable that he would emerge with a clean bill of moral health. Not only did tradition so dictate, but so many Senators had been involved with Klein that any adverse ruling about Dodd's relations with the general would have wide-ranging, bipartisan ripple effects. He could feel confident that no committee of the Senate would invite such a happening.

Senator John C. Stennis of Mississippi (D) was chairman of the committee. Like all Senators from the deep south (including the leading southern liberal, J. William Fulbright of Arkansas), Stennis voted the segregationist line. Some did so in the belief that doing so was an essential sop to an ignorant constituency; others were, like so many of their constituents, bred to be racists from the womb. Stennis's early history hints that he may have been the real thing.

Stennis first came to public attention at the age of 33 as the prosecutor in a trial arising out of the murder of Raymond Stewart, a white planter, on March 30, 1934. Three black sharecroppers were indicted, arrested, tried, convicted, and sentenced to death—all within seven days of the murder. Speedy justice, southern style. The only substantial evidence against the accused consisted of their confessions, and the confessions had been extracted by torture, recounted in horrifying particulars in the U.S. Supreme Court decision *Brown v. State of Mississippi,* 1936. Transcripts made clear that Stennis was fully aware of the tactics that had been used by the sheriffs in obtaining the confessions. The United States Supreme Court unanimously held that the confessions should have been excluded from evidence, and that the convictions violated the fifth and fourteenth amendment rights of the accuseds.

It is difficult to ascribe positive virtues to someone who actively participated in the most disgraceful aspects of America's past, yet Stennis appears otherwise to have been a man of integrity. When he ran for the Senate in 1947 he popularized what he called his personal motto—"I want to plow a straight furrow right down to the end of the row"—and he seems to have lived by his motto. During his years in the Senate he came to be highly respected by members from both parties, northerners as well as southerners. On a personal level he was no doubt as disgusted by Dodd's dealings with A. N. Spanel and David Dunbar as were Pearson and Anderson, but Stennis did not make big decisions on a personal basis.

It was Stennis's job to preside over the Ethics Committee. He had served for ten years as a judge in Mississippi, and he brought to the committee's proceedings a fine judicial temperament and a judge's instinct for limiting the issues as much as possible. Sitting by his side were five other Senators, all men of stature within the Senate: Vice Chairman Wallace F. Bennett (R, UT), Mike Monroney (D, OK), John

Sherman Cooper R, KY), Eugene J. McCarthy (D, MN), and James B. Pearson R, KA).

The committee never got around to investigating most of the allegations raised in the Pearson and Anderson columns, but in response to Dodd's letter to the committee and his press release, on June 22, 1966, it began public hearings on Dodd's relations with General Klein. The hearing room was packed with the Washington correspondents for all of the nation's major newspapers, the representatives of the wire services, and the press photographers.

What looked like a wise public relations move on Dodd's part turned out to be a tactical error.

In the language of the introduction to the committee's published transcript, the committee was particularly interested, at the outset, in evidence bearing on whether "Senator Dodd employed the official sanction of [a trip to Germany in April 1964] as a subterfuge for a scheme to improve the reputation which Julius Klein had in Germany."

General Julius Klein was a shameless self-promoter, a living and breathing Gary Trudeau creation, a public relations man who spent most of his career and the better part of his efforts publicizing General Julius Klein. At the Ethics Committee, Michael O'Hare related this charming anecdote:

> I believe it was the middle of 1963, the Senator traveled to Chicago to speak to a group at General Klein's request . . . they represented a group whose contract General Klein was trying to get.

> Following the Senator's return from Chicago he had several members of his staff, including me, at his home in Georgetown. At that time he imitated General Klein's thick German accent, and he told us an instance that happened at the dinner, or it was a luncheon, an afternoon luncheon.

General Julius Klein asked only that Dodd "say something nice about me, Tom."

The Senator said that he was speaking, he was in the middle of his speech. General Klein was sitting next to him. In the middle of the speech General Klein reached over and tugged at Senator Dodd's coat and in a whisper that was heard throughout the dining room, much to everybody's embarrassment, General Klein said: "Say something nice about me, Tom."

The general had somehow managed to bamboozle his way into seemingly close relationships with a good many very important people; said Senator Hubert Humphrey (D, MN) in 1962, the general had "more friends in the Senate and House of Representatives than any man I know." The general made certain that every important person in the Federal Republic of Germany received a copy of Humphrey's "testimonial." His friends included Republican Senators Everett Dirksen (IL), Jacob Javits (NY), and Styles Bridges (NH); Democratic Senators Stuart Symington (MO), and Wayne Morse (OR); House Speaker John McCormack (D, MA)—all of whom were saying something nice about the general. Dodd told the Ethics Committee that he "understood" that General Julius Klein had been with "Mr. Republican," Senator Robert Taft of Ohio, when Senator Taft died! True or not, Dodd was unquestionably in respectable company as part of the general's cheering squad.

The general's actual military history is unclear; much of it, like so much in the general's background, was myth fathered by himself. What is certain is that his elevated military rank arose from his service in the

Illinois National Guard and was principally attributable to political influence. He filled his staff with retired military men and decorated his offices with photos of himself with people like Generals Dwight D. Eisenhower and Douglas MacArthur. He liked to be known as General Klein; the "General" business was a very big part of his persona. One of the letterheads that he sometimes used for his public relations firm, "Julius Klein, Public Relations, Inc." (with offices in Frankfurt, Chicago, Los Angeles, New York, and Washington), was emblazoned with a flag in an upper corner, something like a heraldic device, along with two stars, signifying his military rank, *Major* General.[42] According to the sketch of Klein published in an early edition of *History of Chicago Jewry*, Klein was "Chicago's Foremost Jewish Soldier." He rose to the office of National Commander of the Jewish American Veterans, an organization he helped to found—although it seems certain that he never had any significant military experience. The "Jewish" angle made the general an especially desirable spokesman for German interests that might want to distance themselves from a Nazi legacy. He parlayed his quasi-bogus military status and his genuine political connections into a successful lobbying business on behalf of various German semi-public and commercial entities.

For years Dodd (along with other Congressmen) had been boosting Klein by inserting into the *Congressional Record* tributes to the general, which Klein would reprint and circulate among clients and prospective clients; by acting as host at Senate luncheons for Klein's visiting clients, thereby elevating the general's stature in the client's eye; and by promoting Klein for appointment to various government boards (along with other Congressmen).

---

42. Boyd wrote that the general's letterheads carried the military decoration, but none of the Klein letters seen by this author show it. This writer is proceeding on the assumption that the general had several letterheads, and that Boyd had seen one that did have the logo and mistakenly assumed they all did. In 2009 correspondence over this question, Boyd wrote this writer that he could still picture the letterhead "in my mind's eye."

Klein took disappointment poorly; when passed over for an appointment to the U.S. Advisory Commission on Information in favor of journalist John Siegenthaler, the general wrote Dodd, "You know, Tom, friendship is a two-way street. I don't blame you for what happened; what I am more disappointed in is that I didn't hear from you at all, either way. I am confident that had I been in your place and the roles had been reversed, I would have been in constant touch with you."

Why would a man like Dodd put up with such whining? Helen Batherson, who served for 11 years as the general's girl Friday, gave an explanation for the general's good reception at the Dodd office—indeed, for the general's good receptions all over Capitol Hill. She told Boyd and Carpenter that the general always carried large amounts of cash and "used to fix up double-sealed envelopes, one inside the other, which I would carry to the offices of friendly Congressmen, including Dodd." Perhaps Batherson exaggerated when she talked about envelopes delivered to Congress*men* (plural), but insofar as Dodd was concerned, her explanation is not inconsistent with what we otherwise know.

Much of the wind was taken out of the general's sails in 1963 when an investigation led by Senator William Fulbright before the Foreign Relations Committee into the activities of registered foreign agents revealed the general to be something of a pest around the capitol, causing Klein considerable personal embarrassment with his German clients. Fulbright pointed to Klein as one who "by exaggeration or misuse of his relationships with members of Congress can, for his own purposes, create for government officials and business interests a mistaken and sometimes unflattering picture of how our government institutions function." After that, Klein's clients began to cancel their contracts with him; his very existence in the public-relations business was threatened. By that point most of Klein's Senate pals had shaken him off, but not Dodd.

Dodd, though a member of the Foreign Relations Committee,

rarely attended its meetings, only partly because of the ill will between himself and Fulbright. He had taken no part in Fulbright's investigation, but he felt (or claimed to have felt) that Fulbright had savaged the general unfairly—and furthermore, that greater significance had been ascribed in Germany to Fulbright's hearings than was warranted.

The general was disappointed that Dodd had not participated and supported him during the Fulbright proceedings. Then Dodd followed up the hearings with a letter to Fulbright dated October 9, 1963, which appeared to be an effort on Dodd's part to distance himself from Klein. When Dodd's letter to Fulbright came to Klein's attention in late November, Klein was hurt and outraged, and wrote Dodd on November 29 complaining that the Senator had let him down:

> I asked you to be present at the executive session. You promised me the night before that you would attend—but you were not there. I wired you to be present at the public hearings—you were not there either. What are you afraid of? Do you consider friendship a one-way street? All I can say is I am ashamed of you . . . With this, Tom, I close the chapter for good.

But not quite yet.

The relationship was too beneficial for both of them to end on a sour note. Dodd "righted" the situation by again writing to Fulbright on December 9, saying in part

> I hope the record can also show that I have known General Klein for many years and I consider him to be a man of sterling character and of great competence. In addition, he is one of the most patriotic Americans I have met and he is dedicated and devoted to the best interests of our country. Over the years I have had a full and complete opportunity to know him and I can state without qualification that he is a man of unblemished honor and integrity.

(Fulbright wrote back that Dodd's letter had, regrettably, been received too late for inclusion in the committee's report.)

Thereafter the general began barraging Dodd with letters and telegrams and telephone calls from himself and from his higher-ranking staff members beseeching Dodd to assist the general in refurbishing his reputation within influential circles in Germany by personally going to Germany and pleading the general's case with key figures in the German government. From Klein's correspondence to Dodd it is clear that Klein thought Dodd had promised to make such a trip; that others such as Senator Stuart Symington had expressed some willingness to make such a trip; and that Klein had received assistance of that sort (or at least the general believed, and represented to Dodd, that he had received assistance of that sort) from Senator Jacob Javits. Klein's former secretary Helen Batherson testified at the Ethics Committee, "General Klein is a very persuasive type individual who calls repeatedly day and night to pressure someone to do something for him."

In February 1964, the general wrote Dodd from Germany, urging Dodd to come to Germany then and there, to join Klein and visit key people, presumably in Klein's presence, in an effort to staunch the disappearance of the Klein clientele. Dodd wrote back on February 14: "I have been trying and trying to get away to join you . . . " but the press of important legislation made it impossible for him to go just then; furthermore, "I have been thinking about this, and I believe that I might be more successful with the people in Germany if I talk to them alone. I don't think it is at all necessary for you to accompany me and there is a chance that it might be misunderstood. You know how anxious I am to help you and it is for this reason that I want to present your case in the best possible light." But Dodd told Boyd that because of the general's impatience he couldn't put off the trip any longer. Meanwhile, Dodd was in contact with Senator James Eastland (D, MS), nominal chairman of the Internal Security Subcommittee, seeking clearance on behalf of the subcommittee to undertake an official trip to Germany to interview Bogdan Stashynski. It was granted.

Stashynski, a Russian cloak-and-dagger operative, had defected to the West and confessed to having assassinated the legendary Ukranian patriot Stepan Bandera. Bandera was once believed to have led a fighting force of 200,000 *banderovsty* (as Bandera's followers were called in the Russian press), guerrillas dedicated to the cause of independence for the Ukraine. Bandera was found dead at the bottom of a flight of stairs in his secluded Munich home in 1959, and although the circumstances were mysterious, there was no evidence of foul play— not until the autopsy disclosed the presence of cyanide in the corpse. The death was reported at the time of its discovery in the *New York Times,* and two years later the *Times* reported the confession and the arrest of Bogdan Stashynski for the murder of Bandera. Bandera had been assassinated by poison dart!

Stashynski was convicted in the Federal Republic of Germany in 1961 of the murder and as of April 1964 was serving a lengthy prison sentence in Karlsruhe, Germany.

Senator Dodd testified before the Ethics Committee that he had long been preoccupied with the operation of the Soviet terror apparatus, of which assassins like Stashynski were an integral part, and that he wanted to interview Stashynski as part of an effort to publicize the terror apparatus and the role of common murder as an instrument of Soviet policy: "I was interested for a great many years in this apparatus. It was known to a great many people, and it has been a mighty tough job to convince the American public that it exists. And anyone who does so usually gets lambasted in one form or another."

Dodd, however, was prepared to risk lambasting in the interests of the greater good. He had been aching to interview Stashynski for a long time. So he went to Germany in April 1964 (purely coincidentally at a time when Klein was making a terrible ruckus about his disappearing clients), to interview the Red murderer. General Klein had nothing to do with his going. The members of the Ethics Committee, however, continued to be gnawed by their own question: Was the visit to Stashynski mere camouflage for a trip that was really undertaken as a public relations job for a public relations man?

Dodd left for Germany in April 1964, while the Senate was considering an important civil rights bill. He was to have been a floor leader for various parts of the bill. Every possible friendly vote might be needed to cut off a filibuster. According to Boyd, the general was making such a pain of himself that he had to be gotten off the Senator's back. According to Dodd, Stashynski beckoned.

Several days before departure, the general's Washington office delivered a fat briefing packet to the Dodd office, identifying six people Dodd was to visit, with background information on each, setting forth the talking points that Klein wanted made to each, arguments along the lines of

> Senator Javits visited you on behalf of the Republicans, and brought you the special message of support from my good friend, Senator Everett Dirksen, who comes from the State of Illinois—General Klein's home state. I am here on behalf of my Democratic colleagues . . . The wounds of the Hitler era have not healed and will never heal, as the present Auschwitz trials show [a reference to ongoing war-crimes trials then underway]. The Communists and left-wingers are taking advantage of this, and are using the trials and the Hitler period for propaganda in the United States. To offset this the help of General Klein and his organization has been of great assistance to us . . . He deserves not only our gratitude but yours and your continued support.

Also enclosed was a packet of endorsements of the general, nice things that others had said about him. It seems likely that the general did not send these along with the expectation that Dodd would pull them out for the eager attention of high-ranking German officials, as if at a sales conference; nor were they enclosed as a mere narcissistic act. They were probably provided with the hope that they might sedate whatever discomfort Dodd might have about performing the services Klein expected of him.

Dodd's high-ranking staff members David Martin and Gerard Zeiller both acknowledged at the Ethics Committee hearings that they had reviewed the packet and were disgusted by the presumptuousness inherent in the mere presentation of it to the Senator. Carpenter and Boyd were also disgusted by what it seemed to say about their boss: that the Senator, a man defined by self-importance, was being treated—and accepted treatment—by the general as if the Senator were no more than a shill. Carpenter testified that to her knowledge Dodd was familiar with the packet and had taken it with him on the German mission; Dodd repeatedly and categorically denied that he had ever seen the packet until his return from Germany.

Appointments were made to visit as many of the six names on Klein's list as were available. Dodd told the Ethics Committee that they were all people he wanted to visit, and that although none of them had any involvement with the Stashynski case, he always liked to visit high-up government people wherever he went. The overlap between the names of those he visited with those suggested by the general was purely coincidental. Upon arrival at the airport in Germany, the general's representatives met the Dodd party, but the Senator waved them away; they reappeared at Dodd's hotel, and again Dodd shooed them off.

Dodd did get to see four of the six names—plus Bogdan Stashynski—and the judge who had presided over the Stashynski trial.

Dodd told the Ethics Committee that he had spent two hours with the assassin. He underwent delicate but other-than-friendly examination on the matter from the committee's chairman, Senator Stennis, and its vice-chairman, Senator Bennett, both of whom kept harping on the fact that *Life* magazine, with a circulation of seven million, had written extensively about the Stashynski case two years earlier; what could Dodd conceivably hope to publicize that would augment *Life's* reportage? Answer:

I remember, for example, him telling me in detail how he murdered Bandera, which I had not known in detail, and how he followed him day by day, learned his habits, met him on the stairway of the apartment house, I believe it was, in which he lived, and shot this—I have forgotten what chemical it was, of some kind or another—at him, and killed him. I had suspected for a long time that this sort of thing was going off in the world, and so the questioning went on and on that afternoon.

Yes, I came away with a far better understanding of how it operated than I had previously . . . You do not learn it from *Life* magazine articles. And you do not learn it from judicial decisions. You learn it by looking a man in the eye . . .

Dodd had looked Stashynski in the eye. He had not, however, disseminated the information borne of his interview to any of the other members of the Internal Security Subcommittee or to the American public; what he learned from the visit was personal learning, unshared until about a year later, when the subcommittee published a 170-page report, which had minimal input from Dodd. Dodd signed a two-and-a-half page introduction to it; the rest of it consisted of 70 pages of testimony by Petr S. Deriabin, a Soviet defector, and David Martin of Dodd's staff, who had accompanied Dodd on the visit to Germany, plus another hundred pages of reprints of materials that had been languishing in the Senator's file cabinets for a long time. Chairman Stennis observed that not all of the two-and-a-half pages was directed at the Stashynski matter. [43] Bennett noted,

I think it is interesting that in this case we had a prior publication in a magazine with vast circulation of a story that came

---

43. Dodd: "If I could have done it in two and a half sentences I would have been satisfied. I do not think it is the amount of pages that is important here."

The only German leader with whom Dodd discussed the general
was Konrad Adenauer.

out two years or more before the Senate document, and if
there was any special information obtained as a result of your
trip it is apparently not included in the Senate document.

What, then, had been the urgency of the visit to Stashynski, at a
time when the civil rights bill was being debated? Answer: Thoughts
of the Russian killer were eating him up. And what, exactly, did he do
during the trip to further General Klein's interests?   Answer: Nothing, nothing at all.

As Dodd told the committee, the only official he had discussed
Klein with was Konrad Adenauer, recently retired as chancellor of
Germany but still an extremely powerful man, and then only when
Der Alte (the name by which the old man was commonly known) had
mentioned Klein's name:

I had a meeting with Chancellor Adenauer. He brought up
the subject actually. I didn't bring it up. He brought it up in
this fashion. He said, "What is the matter with Fulbright?" I
said, "Well I don't know . . . I don't believe he speaks for the
American people or for the administration."

Chancellor Adenauer was referring to a speech that Senator Fulbright had made a week or ten days before I visited
Germany. The title of it I believe was "Myths" or "Old Myths
and New Realities." He then asked me, "Well, What about
this?" As I recall it, What about this Klein business in this
Fulbright hearing? Or something of that sort. I don't remember the exact words. And I said "Klein has not been indicted
or convicted of any crime. This was an inquiry into the general subject of foreign agents registration." And that was about
the extent of the conversation.

That was the only mention that there had been of the general during the entire trip. If anyone had given Dodd an opening, he said,
he would have explained that the general had not been convicted of
any crime, because he felt that any implication of that sort was unfair
to the general ("I would have done the same for anyone"); however,
only Adenauer had given Dodd an opening, and so only Adenauer
had gotten any Klein-related input from Dodd. From their follow-up
questioning it was plain that Stennis and Bennett remained dubious.

The committee was also interested in a curious exchange of correspondence between Dodd and Dr. Ludgar Westrick, chief officer of
the German Chancellery serving Ludwig Erhard, Adenauer's successor, that took place some months after Dodd's visit to Germany. On
August 15, 1964, Klein sent Dodd the draft of a letter that he wanted
Dodd to send to Westrick, which said in part,

Incidentally, I saw General Klein recently, who, as you know,
works hand in hand with all of us. He has the confidence of

my Republican and Democratic colleagues and is especially
close to our leaders—like Senators Dirksen and Humphrey.
. . . General Klein has been rendering a great service not only
to our nation but also to your country. His advice has always
been most valuable to us Democrats—as it was and is to his
Republican friends.

The cover letter bore a hand-written notation: "Please destroy this
letter—I have made no copy."

Dodd wrote Westrick on September 11, in part,

Incidentally, I saw General Klein recently, who, as you know,
works hand in hand with all of us. He has the confidence of
my Republican and Democratic colleagues and is especially
close to our leaders—like Senators Dirksen and Humphrey.
. . . General Klein has been rendering a great service not only
to our nation but also to your country. His advice has always
been most valuable to us Democrats—as it was and is to his
Republican friends.

Westrick acknowledged the letter on October 17: "I was extremely interested in hearing your opinion on General Julius Klein and to
learn from your letter that the Speaker of the House Mr. McCormack
joins you fully in your opinion. Mr. Klein visited me recently, but we
have not yet reached a result that is to his satisfaction."

Dodd forwarded the note to Klein with a cover letter: "I was
pleased to receive the letter because it confirmed to me that our conversation had apparently made some impression, and I am hopeful
that the unspecified differences to which Dr. Westrick alluded can
somehow be overcome."[44]

---

44. The letter goes on: "I have asked David Martin to send you 100 copies of
the "Protocols of the Elders of Zion." A hundred copies?

This encouraged the general to try harder: After the presidential election that fall, he forwarded to the Senator a suggested follow-up letter for Westrick:

> I noted that you had a visit with General Klein, and all of us, of course, shall appreciate it if his problem, in the interest of both countries, is solved to a mutual satisfaction. . . . I don't have to repeat the high regard we have for the general and the great help he has been to us in the past, but most important we value his advice and counseling. I assure you that my and my colleagues' friendship and my desire to underline General Klein's value as advisor and counsel is a purely unselfish one and it is based on our feelings that he is an understanding bridge between our countries. These statements are not only shared with my Democratic and Republican colleagues, but also with our newly-elected vice President Hubert Humphrey, who recently stated how he will need the advice and counsel of his friend Julius Klein.

On December 11, 1964, Dodd prepared his further correspondence to Westrick:

> I noted that you had a visit with General Klein, and all of us, of course, shall appreciate it if his problem, in the interest of both countries, is solved to a mutual satisfaction. . . . I don't have to repeat the high regard we have for the general and the great help he has been to us in the past, but most important we value his advice and counseling. I assure you that my and my colleagues' friendship and my desire to underline General Klein's value as advisor and counsel is a purely unselfish one and it is based on our feelings that he is an understanding bridge between our countries. These statements are not only shared with my Democratic and Republican colleagues,

but also with our newly-elected vice President Hubert Humphrey, who recently stated how he will need the advice and counsel of his friend Julius Klein.

What did Dodd have to say about the letters? First, he was not certain that both letters had actually been sent, but as to the one that had been acknowledged by Westrick (and which was therefore undeniable),

> Ordinarily I would take a letter like that, if I thought it made sense and was truthful, and again in the public interest, and redraft it. My recollection is that I was probably hurried or harried, which was rather common and has been for all of my life in the Senate. But that letter seemed to me to fairly represent what I believed then and I believe now to be the truth about Klein . . . And so I sent that letter. There may have been another. I don't recall it. I am certain there were not several.

The Ethics Committee was also concerned that Dodd put up with a presumptive attitude on the part of the general, and that the general sometimes used demanding, disrespectful language in his dealings with a United States Senator. Senator Pearson: "What was the relationship between a Senator in the U.S. Senate and General Klein that would permit him to put pressure upon you, both in the Senate letter here and in regard to a trip to Germany, that would permit him to write to you the things he wrote to you in the correspondence?" Or, Senator Stennis: ". . . these more or less reprimands, as I interpret them, did you ever complain to him about it or reproach him about it?" Or, Senator Cooper: "What was it about this man, and was there anything about his association, which would permit him to use such language to you as is evidenced by this letter and several other letters? Did you ever tell him to take his business and go someplace else?" Dodd, it seems, was a tolerant man who could overlook the shortcomings in another human being. We all have our shortcomings. In his responses to the rehashed questions, he gave rehashed answers: "Some of his mannerisms perhaps I might not find comfortable, but I know a lot of people whose mannerisms I don't like, and I expect they don't like mine. But I thought well of Klein." Later, "Well, he is an aggressive person. Maybe it goes in that line of business [public relations], I don't know. I would just as soon say to him, I guess I have said on occasion, 'You push everything so hard.' All of these people [public relations people] do, but a lot of other people do too when they come to see me in the Senate. . . . I never found him to be a person who was obnoxious." And still later, "Well there are some people like this in the world, and he is one of them, and he is aggressive, as I have used the word repeatedly. I assume he probably writes other people in the same vein and tone. I know other people who conduct themselves in much the same way, but they have likeable qualities as well. I felt that he did." And again, "I know a lot of people who have manners and mannerisms that I don't particularly like, but there are many good qualities in them as well, and I have tolerated, and I think other human beings have bad mannerisms or the peculiarities of individuals because I thought that generally they were decent and worthwhile."

The short of it was: Dodd liked him. He said it several times during the course of the proceedings, "I liked him." The explanation seemed less than complete. Throw into the mix the admitted fact that the Dodds had enjoyed countless weekends at Klein's luxurious suite at the Essex House on Central Park South, Manhattan. ("I am not a rich man. I am not ashamed of it. I wish I were. And I was always glad to have a place to stay where I could, without cost.") That still did not seem to add up to a full story.

Marjorie Carpenter testified before the Ethics Committee that she had overheard David Martin, who had accompanied Dodd on the April 1964 mission to West Germany, speculating with Gerard Zeiller as to how much Klein must have paid Dodd for his services: "He must have paid at least $10,000." "Oh, easily." Dodd leaped to his feet as Carpenter spoke, his face inflamed, and demanded that Zeiller and Martin be called to the stand immediately to confirm or deny. Both men categorically denied the story.[45]

There were three possible reconciliations of the facts, but there were only two reasonable reconciliations: It is very hard to accept that Dodd had gone to Germany at the time of an important civil rights debate to interview a Russian thug who would be safely confined and available in a Karlsruhe prison for several more years, over a stale case that had already been well publicized. The other two possible reconciliations: 1) Dodd had gone to Germany to plead the general's cause, and he did plead the general's cause; or, 2) Dodd led the general to think that he was going to Germany in order to plead the general's cause, while actually giving the general the back of his hand. Helen Batherson's fuller thought, quoted in abbreviated form above, was

> General Klein is a very persuasive type person who calls re-peatedly day and night to pressure someone to do something for him, and perhaps it just got to the point of where the Sena-tor said, "Well I have to go to Germany anyway and I might as well say yes, I am going to do it," but I am not sure that he did.

---

45. Martin died in 1980 and received obituaries in the *New York Times* and the *Washington Post,* thereby making him a "historical personage." Zeiller was not.

Zeiller was a professional Senate employee, having served three Senators, and had worked for other federal entities. In an email to this writer Boyd wrote that Zeiller was "savvy, efficient, hardworking, and fun to work with. He also had a wide streak of cynicism/realism about his milieu. He did not fully believe, I'm sure, his private motto, 'all Senators are nutty,' but he did believe that most were similarly abnormal and at bottom self-dealers. When someone might complain of the Dodd incident of the day, he would counter with a similar but more perverse example by another Senator. Styles Bridges [whom Zeiller had served] was 'Dodd writ large.'

"Zeiller was therefore not disillusioned by Dodd and instead was good hu-moredly irreverent of him. But he was not a potential rebel. He believed in keeping his own conduct clean while skillfully trying to ride the establishment waves rather than throwing futile mudballs. A generally good man."

"I am not sure that he did"? Ms. Batherson was not sure that Dodd did "do something" for the general? Had Dodd "conned" the con man? Or had Dodd used the power and prestige of his office to further private interests? From an ethical standpoint, did it really matter which?

The public hearings on Klein lasted only a week, but after the last session, held at the end of June 1966, Pearson and Anderson continued their columns with further revelations (many of them reporting the same matter a second and even a third time), putting Dodd in a *Washington Post* headline at least once a week, frequently two or three times in the course of a week, and keeping the heat on Dodd—and on the Ethics Committee. Boyd had been correct: sufficient press publicity would prod the Senate to act.

Beginning on March 13, 1967, the Ethics Committee resumed its investigations, this time uninvited to do so by the Senator, this time delving into Dodd's financial affairs. Ultimately the committee focused on the claims that Dodd had siphoned off campaign contributions for his personal use and that he had intentionally "double-billed" numerous travel expenses.

After 14 months of constant hostile exposure, Dodd was showing the toll of the terrible stress. On occasions during the Klein hearings Dodd had become angry, had mishandled the committee, had personally attacked Committee Vice Chairman Bennett and Committee Counsel Benjamin Fern, had complained about noise outside the committee hearing room, as if the noise had been manufactured in order to prejudice his situation— "I hope this is not prearranged." He had exchanged unpleasant words with the venerable chairman, Senator Stennis. In the past year Dodd's face had become gaunt; Boyd wrote that "He had the look of a noble but ghostly old Indian, unable to comprehend the meaning of captivity."

The committee's counsel had broached to Dodd's counsel, John Sonnett, the possibility of stipulating as to many of the purely factual

LBJ came to Connecticut to rise money to re-elect Dodd to the Senate—or so he thought. Dodd had other ideas as well. To the right of Johnson: Congressman Emelio Q. "Mim" Daddario, Lady Bird Johnson, Dodd, and Governor John Dempsey

matters that would be involved in the second round of hearings. Sonnett had rejected the suggestion; then, two days before resumption of the hearings, the Dodd side agreed to stipulate to virtually all of the facts in dispute, probably to spare Dodd the physical and emotional drain that prolonged hearings on factual matters would involve for the Senator.[46] The stipulations provided the basic framework for the committee's conclusions.

Between November 20, 1961, and March 6, 1965, seven fundraising events, most of them $100-a-plate sit-down dinners, were held for Dodd. At five of them the principal speaker was Vice-President Johnson.

---

46. The interpretation set forth in *Above the Law* is that Dodd's side entered into the stipulation for strategic reasons—to prevent prolonged airing of the details in the press.

Vice-President Hubert Humphrey was the speaker at another of them. While each of these events had nominal chairmen and treasurers, all of them had been organized and directed by Dodd's staff, with all monies handled by the Dodd staff. All of the chairmen and all of the treasurers were kept in the dark as to the financial details, and those of them who testified at the Ethics Committee essentially acknowledged that they were figureheads. The events raised impressive amounts, of which the committee found "at least $116,083" was used to pay personal as opposed to campaign expenses, or to pay off personal debts as opposed to campaign debts; another $45,233 was found to be for expenses that were not clearly political and not clearly personal. Those figures represented as much as the documentary record might reveal of what Dodd had pocketed from the fundraising events over the prior several years. In the nature of things, no effort could be made to factor in those greenbacks given by Spanel (the would-be ambassador), by Mite Corporation's Blinken, and by however many others there might have been, whose "contributions" simply disappeared from sight.

Dodd explained: He had never been able to keep up with his campaign expenses, which caused him to go into personal debt. His personal financial problems left him near desperate, yet he struggled continually to do the honorable thing. Discussing before the Senate Ethics Committee, for example, a $5,000 loan to him from his old friend from Nuremberg days, Howard Brundage, he said:

> My recollection is that in 1960, I think that is the date, yes, 1960, again because of all this accumulation of difficulty and debts, battles for the nominations, the prior cost of the 1956 election, I was still in the hole. I remember it because actually, it is also true of the Kelley loan, I believe, I didn't ask Howard Brundage. He volunteered. It doesn't make any difference really for the purpose of this committee, but he knew I was having grave trouble.

Incidentally, he didn't want the loan paid back. I found
out after he died, from his family, that he had told his son that
he never wanted that loan paid back. I paid it back, as I did
some others here, particularly some widows.[47]

In order to help relieve Dodd's financial pressures, his then attorney, M. Joseph Blumenfeld, had suggested that they hold "testimonial" events in order to raise money to help Dodd out with his
personal financial problems. Blumenfeld, the committee was told,
would be appearing on Dodd's behalf to testify to that extent, and to
testify that as Dodd's attorney, he had counseled Dodd that it would
be legitimate for Dodd to proceed in this manner.

According to Dodd, there was nothing unusual about what he
had done: "In my home state of Connecticut testimonials are exceed-
ingly commonplace affairs, and it is universally known by those who
are in the habit of attending political functions that the proceeds of
testimonials are intended as personal gifts."

Whether the proceeds that Dodd used for himself had been intended for him personally, or had been intended for political use, had
very important implications: At least since 1954, the Internal Revenue
Service had maintained a crystallized policy: "The portion of a politi-

---

47. It was wholly irrelevant that Brundage's law firm, Brundage & Short, uti-
lized Dodd's influence in getting the firm's insurance-company client, Bankers Life
& Casualty, licensed to do business in the State of Connecticut.   In a letter to Short
of June 21, 1962, Dodd wrote: "I am enclosing a copy of the letter which I wrote
to Commissioner Premo [Connecticut's Insurance Commissioner] and a copy of
the answer which I received from him. I shall continue to follow this up and I wish
you would let me have your comments on the Commissioner's letter to me." That's
"constituent" service!   The Insurance Department conveyed the acceptance of the
Bankers Life application through Senator Dodd. Two days later the law firm of
Brundage & Short sent Dodd a check for $5,000, which, Mr. Short later explained
to Pearson and Anderson, was a loan from his late partner, Howard Brundage, to
Senator Dodd.

Probably all the members of the Committee knew the fuller story of the Brundage "loan": Pearson and Anderson had previously reported the story. But the committee members allowed Dodd's account to go unchallenged.

cal contribution received by a political organization or a candidate for political office which is diverted from political campaign purposes to the personal use of the candidate or other individual constitutes taxable income to such candidate or other individual." Funds so diverted had to be declared as personal income for tax purposes, with taxes paid on the amounts so diverted.   Failure to do so constituted income tax fraud.   Former Governor William Stratton of Illinois, a Republican, was prosecuted for tax fraud in 1965 under facts with some parallels to those in the Dodd case, and although Stratton was found "not guilty," he had to live through stress hell.

Dodd had neither declared receipt of the money nor paid income tax on it, so if it were established that he'd diverted political funds for his own use, he had to expect that he would face the same ordeal as had Stratton. Thus he had to maintain that the dinners were personal, not political, affairs, and that the proceeds of the dinners were intended by those who bought tickets to be gifts to himself within the meaning of the law. Gifts are not taxable income to the recipient of the gift—which explains why Dodd had never declared the proceeds on his tax returns, and why he had paid no income taxes on the money.[48]

---

48. Senator John Williams of Delaware, a conservative Republican who was favorably disposed to Dodd, related to Holmes Alexander, a conservative columnist who vigorously defended Dodd, that Williams had been visited by a "high official" of the IRS who suggested—with a wink—that the relevant IRS statutes were unclear and required clarification to make crystal clear that diversion of political funds for personal use would result in taxable income to the diverter. The IRS man asked Williams to introduce an amendment to the tax code to that effect. Williams recognized that the official was hoping to take Dodd off the hook by laying the groundwork for an argument by Dodd that the law had not clearly proscribed his conduct. A "clarifying" amendment to the tax code would almost certainly head off or defeat any prosecution that might be launched against Dodd. Williams, sometimes known as "Honest John Williams," refused to go along. To head off such a suggestion from other Senators, during the Senate debate on the censure Williams delivered a heavily documented speech showing that the tax code was not fuzzy, and that there was no honorable justification for plugging a non-existent loophole. He also told Holmes Alexander about it, who—notwithstanding his otherwise enthusiastic support for Dodd—reported it in his syndicated column.

All of the dinner chairmen and treasurers who testified swore that the purpose of each function had been to help Dodd with his personal financial situation: personal gifts. It required the explaining away of some documentary materials. Here is what four good soldiers had to say:

Art Powers, Selectman (mayor-equivalent) of Berlin, Connecticut, and treasurer of a dinner for Dodd held in November 1961, was asked to comment on this report about that dinner published in the *New Britain Herald:* "Selectman Arthur B. Powers, treasurer of the committee, said that the money will help Senator Dodd meet his campaign deficit [from the 1958 election]." Powers denied: "I know the man who put that in there, Mr. Covini from the *New Britain Herald,* and I think he was just filling in space. I don't recall ever saying that it was to be used for a campaign deficit." And, indeed, that had never been the purpose of the dinner: "It was a dinner in his honor, the funds of which could be given to Senator Dodd for his use as he saw fit." Or, "He could use the funds any way he saw fit."

Sanford Bomstein had been a key man in a reception for Dodd held on September 15, 1963, in the capital, sponsored by an ad hoc committee with the name "DC Committee for Dodd." The ostensible chairman was JFK's retired Postmaster General, J. Edward Day, but the strongmen of the committee were Bomstein and James Gartland, a staff member from Dodd's office. At a meeting of the committee—attended only by Bomstein and Gartland—motion was made and unanimously adopted (by Bomstein and Gartland) that the proceeds from the reception were to be used for "all bills pertinent to the activities of Senator Dodd for printing, travel, food and lodging [and] public relations for Senator Dodd, such as radio or television time." That certainly sounds as though the money had been intended for campaigny kinds of expenses.

At the Senate Ethics Committee hearings, Bomstein explained that "words are a funny thing and I am not very adept at words, and perhaps in my mind what I intended was not put down correctly." The intent of the resolution, he explained, was that the money could be used "for any purpose that [Dodd] so desired," or, put a different way, "the funds could be used for any purpose that he saw fit," which is to say, "the intent of it was that the funds could be used for any purposes Senator Dodd saw fit to use them for."

Paul McNamara, chairman of Dodd's 1958 campaign for the Senate, was deeply involved in raising money for "Dodd Day," October 26, 1963, when Vice-President Johnson came to Connecticut to raise money for the Senator at a series of events. McNamara began his widely circulated form letter seeking contributions:

> In 1964 our friend, Sen. Thomas J. Dodd, will campaign for re-election to the United States Senate. It does not seem necessary for me to stress the heavy financial burden his campaign will involve. For this reason, it is necessary for those of us who respect and admire Senator Dodd to lend whatever aid we can to assist him in presenting a vigorous campaign.

In his more personal solicitations, McNamara wrote, "I will be calling you in a few days about whether or not you are willing to make a contribution to Tom Dodd's campaign." His written solicitations were not quite the full story. Actually, McNamara said, the goal was "to get this man straightened out financially so he could start the campaign of 1964 with his head above water and with his not being the nervous wreck that he had become [because of his personal debts]. That is exactly what I considered [the purpose] to be." That's what Dodd Day had been all about—helping Dodd out of his personal financial bind.

Arthur Barbieri, New Haven Democratic Town Chairman and chairman of a find-raising dinner held in February 1965, had written prospective attendees that in Dodd's successful run for re-election in 1964, "a considerable deficit was incurred and must now be met."

Barbieri testified that he had believed at the time of his letter that there was a deficit of between $4,000 and $6,000 ("considerable"?), but no matter: "Actually, the intent was not just to make up the $4,000-$6,000 deficit at all. Had that been the intent, I would not have asked the committee to engage a large ballroom like the Statler-Hilton that holds 1,000 to 1,200 people, and to sell a $100 ticket to everyone." At the first meeting of his dinner committee, Barbieri testified,

> I specifically explained to them that it was the intent of the committee that I wanted to find out whether the committee would agree that we would raise this money for the Senator to do as he saw fit with it, because we were aware that over the years, without knowing all of his personal financial statistical background, that he was not a rich man, even though a great Senator, and I specifically mentioned this at my very first committee meeting, to all of the people present.

They agreed that the Senator should be able to do with the money as he saw fit. Indeed, said Barbieri, "the committee was expanded from 20 or 25 up to 75 or 100 or maybe more, and they were all aware of the purpose of the dinner, and they were all in complete agreement that it was to be given to the Senator to do with as he saw fit."

In support of his position, Dodd presented to the committee some 410 affidavits, each on a printed form that had a blank left for insertion of the signer's name—from subscribers to the various events held in his honor between 1961 and 1965. Each affiant swore that he or she had bought the ticket out of admiration for the Senator, and that their participation in the dinner was not tied to a campaign purpose. Their money had been "personal" money—a gift. In a 1972 doctoral dissertation on the censure proceedings, scholar Paul Edwin Wenger wrote that "the affidavits were less a sign of past intent than of present allegiance." Out of more than a thousand subscribers to the various events, there were 410 good soldiers.

The problem with Dodd's position was simply that much (not all, but much) of the materials promoting the functions, either "invitations" or press releases, explicitly linked the functions to past or prospective campaign finance needs, not personal financial problems, and no mailing or press release hinted in any way that the functions were being held to raise money for the Senator's personal use. McNamara's solicitation letters were typical.

Dodd said that he had had no hand in sending out invitations and should not be held responsible for the content of them:

> I did not see these letters, by the way. I did not draw up the program or the tickets. I wish I had now. I would sure have had in there more specific language. I think it would be pretty easy to write. But I think in those days nobody was thinking this way. And if you can understand the climate of our community, with these testimonial affairs all the time going on, I suppose that is how they came to be somewhat, I think now, sloppily written . . .
>
> I believe in my soul that no one was flim-flammed, and that is why I have said if anybody feels that he was, I do not have much, but whatever it is, I'll hock or sell or give them back their money.

When Vice-President Johnson confirmed that he would come to Connecticut for a day of fund-raising, Dodd wrote thanking him for "your generous offer to assist me in my forthcoming campaign. . . . How much it will assist us in getting my campaign drive under way . . . " Dodd explained that he had not been party to the drafting or mailing of that particular letter, although he did not dispute that he had signed it.

The visit took place on October 26, 1963, with the Vice-President

The Dodd family enters the hearing room: Tom, Grace, daughters Martha and Carolyn. At left is Dodd's chief lawyer, John Sonnett.

making four fund-raising appearances on the Senator's behalf. The day after the visit Zaiman reported in the *Courant* that "Throughout the trip, Senator Dodd expressed his gratitude to the Vice-President and Mrs. Johnson for coming to the state to help him build up a campaign war chest for 1964." Dodd later insisted that the *Courant* account was erroneous, but when Senator Charles H. Percy solicited Zaiman for confirmation, the reporter wrote back:

> In response to your inquiry about the story I wrote in 1963 during a visit by [now] President Johnson to help Senator Dodd raise campaign funds, which appears on pages 920-921 of the committee report, I stand by the story and the quotation I attributed to Senator Dodd. This quotation has never, up to this moment, been questioned by anyone, including Senator Dodd, nor has any other story I wrote about Senator Dodd's campaign dinners either before, during or after the

Boyd testfies while Dodd confers with one of Sonnett's assistants.

dinners. . . . I wrote a story that until this day, has never been challenged.

Well . . . Dodd challenged it: he dismissed Zaiman as a Bailey mouthpiece. Bailey did nothing to dispel that contention when he publically commented that he had never been aware of such events being used by political people to raise money for their personal use.[49]

---

49. Guess Bailey didn't know everything. Dodd was overstating in his claim that "it is universally known by those who are in the habit of attending political functions that the proceeds of testimonials are intended as personal gifts," but he was clearly not alone. Right after the Dodd scandal broke, New Haven Congressman Bob Giamo, for whom the city's Robert Giamo Federal Building is named, proved how smart he was by fessing up and putting the best face on things, before claims of cover-up could be added to claims of corruption. Yes, he had personally benefitted from such dinners and had accepted the proceeds as "gifts" within the meaning of the tax code (which is to say, he did not declare any proceeds on his income tax return). Just the week before, he said, he had hosted a cocktail party for himself to raise money to help cover those of his personal expenses that were of a quasi-political nature—"I sent a boy a check for his Bar Mitzvah [sic]."

President Johnson promptly said that he had never knowingly attended a dinner or fund-raiser for anybody in order to help them raise money for their personal use. Gloria Schaffer, later to become a major player in Connecticut Democratic affairs, who had hosted one of Johnson's appearances on Dodd's behalf at her luxurious home in Woodbridge, Connecticut, said: "I understood the funds were being raised for political purposes. I've never known them to be raised for any other purpose." Judge Blumenfeld said nothing: His promised appearance to testify for Dodd before the committee did not materialize.[50]

Dodd was quite definitely not alone in failing to keep his personal expenses within control or for failing to keep his political money crisply separated from his personal money. It was certainly true in the early 1960s that office seekers poorly understood the ethical reasons why the two should be separately maintained. The typical elected public servant saw little reason to be hypersensitive about maintaining walls in the keeping of books, and when it came to parceling out monies from the left pocket and monies from the right pocket, many if not most political people were ambidextrous. Politicians were much less fussy about things of this sort 40 years ago than they are now (or at least we hope so), and, in any case, Dodd was not alone.

Intentional double-billing—seeking reimbursement for the same expense from more than one source—was a different matter. It could not be rationalized as "culturally acceptable." It was unarguably dishonest. Frequently Dodd's schedulers would make dates for official U.S. Senate business that might coincide in time and location with Dodd's

---

50. One of the best accounts of the censure proceedings is Ferdinand Mount, "Dodd and Mammon" in the *National Review,* July 11, 1967. In recapitulating the evidence in Dodd's favor, Mount references an affidavit from Blumenfeld. That was error. No Blumenfeld affidavit is referenced in any other materials seen by this writer.

private business, thereby enabling the same expenses to be billed to the government or billed to a different entity (or maybe, accidentally, to both). For example:

Dodd accepted an invitation to address the National Council of Juvenile Court Judges in San Francisco, held on June 30, 1961. The invitation, channeled through Carl Perian at the Juvenile Delinquency Subcommittee," said

> As you know, our organization has little money, but on the other hand we do not want to appear on the cheap side, but we do feel that we would like to offer Senator Dodd an honorarium of at least $100. Furthermore, we do not know whether or not he intends to travel on subcommittee funds or whether our organization should provide for his transportation? We, or course, will reimburse him for the transportation if necessary.

The answer was "Both."

Dodd shaved his usual honorarium from his customary $500 or $750 (and occasionally as much as $2,000, when addressing a well-healed group like the American Medical Association) to $100, but he asked that that sum, plus travel expenses, be paid in advance, and prior to the engagement, on June 19, 1961, Dodd received $376.86 from the National Council for his travel expenses, plus the $100 honorarium (in addition to which the Council picked up his hotel bill at the Sir Francis Drake, the city's most elegant hotel). That was private business.

While he was in San Francisco, Dodd did some investigating incidental to his work as chairman of the Judiciary Committee's Juvenile Delinquency Subcommittee: In the words of the report in the *San Francisco Chronicle*, Dodd "interrogated" a dozen "problem" teenagers about gang mystique in the city by the Bay. Public business. A big article in the *Chronicle's* issue of July 5, 1961, features a photo of a distinguished looking white-haired gentleman in suit and tie, chatting with seven young men from the 'hood. According to the *Chronicle* piece, the interrogatees disclosed no substantive information whatsoever.

The *Chronicle's* reporter was Donovan Bess, a veteran of United Press and Reuters, with 20 years experience at the journalist's trade. He felt sufficient unease about Dodd's visit with the gang members that he sent his article to Drew Pearson the next day with a note: "Attached for your information is an article about how Senator Thomas Dodd fared during a two-hour 'investigation' of juvenile delinquency here last week. The Youth for Service officials were pretty dismayed at his performance. Citizens here have complained his tour was superficial, particularly since he only looked at Negroes."

No matter: When the chairman of the Juvenile Delinquency Subcommittee studies the behavior of "problem" teenagers in San Francisco—however unproductive his studies might be—at the least he should be reimbursed for his travel expenses. Dodd submitted a bill to the Senate and was reimbursed $397.27 for airplane fare from Washington to San Francisco and returning to Providence, R.I. (the airport that serves Dodd's then-residence in North Stonington, Connecticut). Dodd had already received payment for his travel expenses from the Juvenile Court judges. He got paid twice for the same expenses, one of the two reimbursement checks being a net profit for Dodd's personal checkbook.

At the time of Dodd's trip to Sacramento on behalf of developer Tom Frouge (page 131-3), Dodd stopped over in Los Angeles and spent a half-hour discussing Juvenile Delinquency with Mayor Sam Yorty (public business), and he addressed the Los Angeles Junior Chamber of Commerce, which gave him an honorarium (private business). He billed his expenses to the Senate Juvenile Delinquence Subcommittee, to the Los Angeles Junior Chamber of Commerce—and much of the expenses, again, to Frouge. A trifecta.

In *Above the Law* Boyd writes that Dodd regularly manufactured "official" business by stuffing hastily arranged interviews and the like into his itinerary on travels that were vacation trips, or which were otherwise not Congressional business, so as to give a color of public purpose to a trip that would have had none, in order to "legitimize" the submission of a bill to the Senate for his travel expenses.

The written stipulation entered into between Dodd's lawyer and the counsel for the Ethics Committee noted ten "overlaps" of official and non-official business on travels between 1961 and 1965. In seven of the ten situations, Dodd submitted bills for travel expenses, and accepted reimbursement, from both the Senate and from private organizations for the same expenses. In another six instances, Dodd had billed his re-election campaign committee for travel expenses and an outside organization for the same trip expenses. The dollar amounts involved were trivial, $300 or $400 here and there, yet for some reason, Dodd was one to pay attention to trivial amounts: His daily minutes usually included notations of small disbursements, such as "Tolls from LaGuardia to New Haven, $1.00"; or "went to lunch [with so-and-so], paid check $24.19," or "went to the gym. Paid Johnny $1.00 tip." $300 or $400 represented a year's tips for Johnny. (Although Dodd kept a close watch on the pennies, when he was in an expansive mood, he could be extraordinarily generous.)

The regularity with which the double-billing occurred was troubling to the committee.

Dodd's bookkeeper—O'Hare—testified that the Senator had expressly directed him to "double bill." Dodd's rejoinder was blunt and to the point: "Mr. O'Hare is a liar. It is as simple as that. He is a liar. That is exactly the proper language. That is exactly what he is. And I don't know any better term." Dodd acknowledged that the double-billings had occurred, but insisted that there was no intent on his part to defraud anyone, all innocent slip-ups resulting from the incompetence of Michael O'Hare, "one of the most inefficient and sloppy bookkeepers who ever lived." O'Hare had gotten him into this mess.

Whom to believe?

The committee believed O'Hare. Or, as Drew Pearson put it in a radio talk, "that committee, after weeks of listening to the arguments of a mighty Senator and his Wall Street lawyers and accountants on the one side, and a penniless young bookkeeper on the other, decided unanimously, without a dissent, that Mike O'Hare was telling the truth and that Senator Dodd was lying." Two of the instances of double-billing had taken place prior to O'Hare's employment by Dodd, a matter which must have influenced the committee's decision.

The committee also found against Dodd on the matter of the diversion of campaign funds for personal purposes. As to these two matters the committee recommended that the Senate censure Dodd for conduct which was "contrary to accepted morals, derogates from the public trust expected of a Senator, and tends to bring the Senate into dishonor and disrepute."

In the matter of the general, the committee's conclusion was more-nearly favorable to Dodd:

> Evidence was also introduced that Julius Klein provided to Senator Dodd certain favors, but the Committee could not establish their validity with the exception of the repeated use of the Klein suite in the Essex House Hotel in New York City . . .

> After drawing its conclusions, the Committee was of the opinion that the relationship of Senator Dodd with Julius Klein was indiscreet and beyond the responsibilities of a Senator to any citizen, but that there was not sufficient evidence of wrongdoing to warrant recommendation of disciplinary action by the Senate.

General Klein publicly protested that the committee's conclusion "leaves a cloud of doubt over my relationship with Senator Dodd and more significantly over the sworn testimonies of Senator Dodd and myself." He was right. It did leave a cloud of doubt. Committee recommendation or not, the odor of Dodd's dealings with Klein permeated the United States Senate, lingered, and prejudiced Dodd's situation, although it is not possible to gauge the extent of its effect.

CHAPTER SEVEN

The Censure

ON JUNE 13, 1967, THE SENATE opened debate on a proposed censure resolution:

> Resolved that it is the judgment of the Senate that the Senator from Connecticut, Thomas J. Dodd, for having engaged in a course of conduct over a period of five years from 1961 to 1965 of exercising the influence and power of his office as a United States Senator, as shown by the conclusions in the Investigation by the Select Committee on Standards and Conduct,
>
> a) to obtain and use for his personal benefit, funds from the public through political testimonials and a political campaign, and
>
> b) to request and accept reimbursements for expenses from both the Senate and private organizations for the same travel, deserves the censure of the Senate; and he is so censured for his conduct, which is contrary to accepted morals,

Dodd's only emotional support among the Senators came from Louisiana Senator Russell B. Long, a brilliant and flamboyant man who also had a touch of buffoon about him. Long's antics during the censure proceedings were wearying for all of the Senators—perhaps most of all for Dodd.

derogates from the public trust expected of a Senator, and tends to bring the Senate into dishonor and disrepute.

The galleries overhanging the Senate floor were packed with spectators. Grace, three of the Dodd children, and other relatives were among the observers. Senatorial wives customarily flocked to "headline" sessions of the Senate, but they were noticeably absent that day, thereby sparing themselves as well as their well-liked sister, Grace Dodd, the embarrassment of personal contact.[51]

Stennis began his presentation about "a pattern of financial misconduct." All of Dodd's testimonial monies had been gathered "under all the banners and trappings" of a political campaign and with the clear implication that the money was to be used to pay past and future political obligations. But they were not. Dodd's was a course of conduct "wrong on its face," which the Senate could not afford to ignore. He spoke for two hours, expressing compassion for Dodd, but insisted that the facts—and the duty of the Senate—were clear.

Dodd was in the midst of his opening statement when Senator Russell B. Long of Louisiana demanded a quorum call, which revealed that only 72 Senators were in attendance. He insisted that the proceedings should be adjourned until the next morning, so that the full Senate could hear Dodd. With that, the proceedings were adjourned.[52]

Long injected himself—wholly uninvited—as Dodd's Senate champion and "lawyer," and was to dominate the proceedings on the

---

51. Among the spectators, however, was "Mikey" Moore, a chubby teenager in a baseball cap, hailing from the suburbs of Flint, Michigan, who would later become well known as Michael Moore, the maker of polemical documentary films.

52. Scholar Paul Edwin Wenger has tabulated that in the nine days of debate, "the average number answering roll calls was just over 95 out of a total of 100." Inasmuch as Senators Daniel Inouye of Hawaii and B. Everett Jordan of North Carolina were ill and did not attend any of the censure debate, Wenger points out, "attendance lapses by the remaining 98 were almost nonexistent."

floor of the Senate, which ran nine days and filled over 300 pages in the *Congressional Record*. His biographer, Robert Mann, says that Long was brought to Dodd's side by his "instinctive affection for lost causes."

At 7:48 a.m. the next morning, the President took a telephone call from Senator Long. The conversation, recorded on "Dictabelt," began with the Senator reminding the President how long ago Dodd had confided to Johnson about his financial situation, about his debts arising from the 1956 and 1958 campaigns, and how the President had said "you'd be glad to help him get out of debt." The President stopped Long right there: Much as he liked Dodd, and would like to help Dodd, the President said that he had never heard anything about '56 or '58, and that he and Dodd had never discussed Dodd's personal debts—"I never heard about any debts, Russell"—and he had never offered to help Dodd get out of debt. He also had never heard the word "testimonial," in the political context, to mean that the honoree was free to use the monies for whatever he wanted.

Long persisted. So did the President. Johnson insisted that it would hurt Dodd's position for the President to get involved, and would hurt his own position as well. "You just leave me out of it, Russell; I don't know why you want to give me any more problems than I got, pardner."

Long pleaded that after the President heard Dodd's speech on the censure—as well as Long's own—the President would feel differently about it, and that at that point perhaps Johnson might quietly pass the word on Dodd's behalf. If the President preferred, Johnson could pass the word through an aide, and only to the President's very closest and most discreet Senatorial allies. Johnson responded that he had never known a Senator who could keep a secret, "not in my life, not one." The less Long tried to involve Johnson, the better it would be for all of them.

Later that morning Dodd began his opening statement. In an impassioned appeal he asked, "May the vengeance of God strike me if I'm telling you a lie." As reported in the *Washington Post:*

Dodd dramatically raised his right hand. As his voice boomed across the hushed chamber, the Senator said, "I swear to you now and I will swear forever, I am telling the truth. If I had to face my Maker in a minute, I'm telling you the truth. . . . Have any of you known me to lie, to cheat you, or to do any dishonorable thing? Get up and say so now!"

The Senate was still. . . .

"I'd rather be dead than dishonored. . . . I do not ask for mercy. I ask for justice."

Dodd concluded with a scathing attack on the four conspirators, focusing on O'Hare, "a thief, a liar, a perjurer, and a traitor." "In this hour of truth and humiliation, it's really very simple. Either you believe me or you believe O'Hare." He spoke for an hour and 40 minutes, delivering what to some was a stirring, classic appeal. Mary McGrory of the *Washington Star,* later a Pulitzer Prize-winning journalist, did not view it that way; she reported that Dodd had "shrouded his case in sentimentality, vituperation, self-pity."

Russell Billiu Long was the son of "Kingfish" Huey Long, who had dominated Louisiana politics until his assassination in 1935. The son, sometimes identified in the press as "the Princefish," was a brilliant and flamboyant man (who also had a serious drinking problem, later conquered), then serving as Democratic "whip" in the Senate, and he was commonly believed to be destined for much higher leadership roles. Long's personal style was appealing to the electorate of rural Louisiana but it was ill-suited to formal proceedings of great weight. Ferdinand Mount, covering the censure for the conservative *National Review,* described Long in action as an "extraordinary demonic force of nature":

Chubby, bulb-nosed, jabbing gestures with his spectacles or an unlit cigar, embracing two Senators at once, rising to ask for a quorum call or a parliamentary enquiry, or tell some tale

of Louisiana in the days of Huey Long ("my old daddy"), cas-
tigating columnist Jack Anderson as the serpent in the garden
of Eden, raising incredibly tedious legal niceties, repeating
himself, quoting John F. Kennedy on Daniel Webster, grin-
ning at jokes at his own expense, wandering up and down
the gangways of the Senate like some incessantly mumbling
soothsayer in Caesar's Rome.

During much of the debate, Dodd sat helplessly while Long went on
and on; sometimes Dodd visibly winced at Long's antics, or buried
his face while Long commanded the attention of the Senate and of the
press. Long was the only Senator who gave Dodd emotional support;
perhaps Dodd would have been better off with none. After it was all
over, Dodd publically thanked Long for having helped "in his own
way."

The most interesting of the arguments presented by Dodd and
by his supporters during the debate was that there was no clear rule
proscribing his use of testimonial proceeds for personal use, and that
to proceed against him on that basis would be to hold him to ex post
facto standards. It was precisely the same argument that many honorable people, including Senator Robert Taft of Ohio, had raised in
1945 against prosecuting Nazis for ill-defined "crimes against humanity." In the Dodd case, Senator Mike Monroney from the Ethics
Committee, while conceding that no formal rule proscribed Dodd's
conduct, insisted that there was a "higher standard of conduct, nebu-
lous though it may be"—a response that must have had a familiar ring
to it in the ear of the Nuremberg prosecutor.

As debate continued over the nine days, Dodd became increasingly drained physically, and obviously so. The arguments presented
by Dodd, Long, and their occasional supporters were destroyed by
Senators from the Ethics Committee, Monroney, James Pearson, and
principally Wallace Bennett, the Robespierre of the Committee, a
straight-laced Mormon who also wrote hymns. *He* didn't entertain
his constituents at country clubs; a man could be a successful Senator

without joining a country club. *He* had never treated his staff to an outing at a race track, yet his staff was still loyal. Eugene McCarthy stated that he would resign from the Ethics Committee if the Senate failed to vote for censure.

Dodd's comments on the Senate floor were tragically desperate, the sadness inherent in them undiminished by the fact that they were also very much strategic: "How many times do you want to hang me? You want to do it? Do it— Be done with me! Do away with me! In the twilight of my life! And that will be the end of me!"

Three efforts by Long, joined by Senator John Tower of Texas, to soften the verbiage of the censure resolution in this way or that way, were overwhelmingly rejected, 18 votes being the most that could be rounded up in favor of wording that was less damning. Then, after considerable parliamentary maneuvering, it was decided to vote separately on the two "counts" presented by the Ethics Committee: the first issue (first in the order set forth in the committee's formulation of the issues) involving the diversion of political funds for personal use and the second, whether Dodd was guilty of intentional double-billing of his expenses.

Long and Dodd pushed hard for a vote on the "double-billing" prior to the vote on the "first" issue. They argued that the double-billing matter involved a clear allegation of criminal wrongdoing and was therefore the more serious of the two charges: determination of that matter was all that really mattered. Tactically, they had other thoughts:

The second count was the weaker of the two. Its determination turned entirely on the word of Michael O'Hare, a man whom Dodd painted as duplicitous and deceitful—witness his dealings with his loving employer. Other Senators might have regarded Dodd's characterization of O'Hare as correct. Would you believe such a man over the word of your fellow Senator?

If Dodd could prevail on the double-billing issue, then an opening might arise for significant delay, during which the whole proceeding might be derailed. Dodd was emotional in urging an immediate vote, an immediate vote, that is, on the matter of the double-billing. Again, quoting from the *Washington Post:*

> "Give me a night's rest, either in sorrow or relief," he be-
> seeched his colleagues. "Don't drag me through any more,"
> Dodd implored, his voice rising to a shout. "If you want to
> make me a thief, do it today, before the sun goes down and I
> will slink away . . . unable to look you in the eye tomorrow."

To no avail: The vote proceeded immediately, but on the first matter first, the claim that Dodd had siphoned off campaign monies for his own use. Dodd lost the vote on that issue decisively, after which the second issue didn't really matter.

Dodd's fellow Connecticut Senator, Abe Ribicoff, gave him support— such as it was—as to both counts. Ribicoff voted against the censure but made clear that he did so out of compassion for Dodd. He told the press that he had asked himself, "How much suffering must a man endure?" This position skirted the merits of the committee's recom- mendation, and it would allow Ribicoff to get on as well as possible with that segment of the Connecticut electorate that liked Ribicoff the least.

Dodd's sincere support came from Long and from South Caro- lina Senator Strom Thurmond, the Dixiecrat presidential candidate who was about to be married to a beauty-contest winner of grand- daughter vintage. Dodd was also backed by Senator Tower, a man of some *gravitas* who nonetheless was widely known to consume more bourbon than was good for the country. Two good 'ole boys and a drunk.[53]

---

53. And even they had misgivings about Dodd's conduct. In his only speech during the debate, Thurmond said "Without question, the Senator from Connecti- cut acted improvidently and unwisely . . ." Tower said: "My own conscience . . . balks at the idea of censuring a man for conduct . . . however much I disapprove of it personally . . . in the absence of any specific law or code. . ." Both, therefore, viewed Dodd's conduct in an unfavorable light.

Arrayed against them on the first count were the other Senators, among them some of the most honorable men in America and at least as many who were not: George Aiken, Birch Bayh, Clifford Case, Frank Church, Joseph Clark, Everett Dirksen, Jacob Javits, Henry "Scoop" Jackson, Mike Mansfield, Eugene McCarthy, Walter Mondale, two Byrds, two Kennedys, two Williamses. Mrs. Dodd shook her head in despair to think—with considerable justification—that the censure (she later commented) had "opened my children's eyes to hypocrisy."

The tally on the first count was 92 to 5, Dodd himself being the fifth "no" vote. He had been deserted by his colleagues in a way, and to an extent, that Senator Joe McCarthy had never been. Mrs. Dodd told herself and others, with somewhat less justification, that the Senators had been cowed by fear of Drew Pearson.

Next came the vote on whether Dodd should be censured, as well, for having intentionally double-billed his travel expenses. (Technically, the vote was on whether to delete from the censure resolution the clause pertaining to double-billing). Here was a tougher question. Although the committee had accepted O'Hare's claims, that was no reason that a jury of 100 Senators had to rubber-stamp the conclusion of a committee of six Senators. Certainly, a United States Senator was entitled to have a matter of credibility resolved in his favor by a jury of other Senators—at least as against the word of an "outsider," and a treacherous outsider at that. Abe Ribicoff's question began to make sense to others: "How much suffering must a man endure?"

Dodd's groveling may have had some impact, at least now that the honor of the Senate had been redeemed by the censure vote on the first count. Some Senators may have asked themselves whether there might not be some examples of double-billing hidden in their own books. By a vote of 51 to 45, Dodd was exonerated from the claim pertaining to double-billing.

The senior Senator from Connecticut was then recognized. The *Washington Post* reported:

His voice cracked and there were tears in his eyes as he continued to speak: "I think a grave mistake has been made. And I'm the one who has to bear the scars of that for the rest of my life." . . . His voice faltered once more and he seemed to be weeping softly when he said: "Without the wonderful support of my wife, I don't think I could have carried on for the last 18 months. . . . In here (clutching his fist against his heart) I don't have any feeling of wrongdoing. If I did, I would resign tomorrow. I love the Senate and I like all of you and I hope you'll find it within your power to do toward me as I would do toward you."

Dodd grasped the rails of his desk and swayed slightly. "I hope my honor is not diminished in your eyes. And so I bid you all farewell for today."

As he was escorted out of the hall, the *New York Times* reporter noticed that tears crept down his cheek.

Dodd's speech was sincere. In his heart he knew that he had done nothing wrong. Not really wrong. He could proudly assert that nobody had ever bribed him. The mere thought was inconceivable to him. So what if thus-and such or this-and-that? Why was that any different from what everybody else did? Was that not all part of the game, the rules for which, unwritten but nonetheless well-established, had been determined long before he had come to the Senate? Did his claimed transgressions not comport with traditionally accepted conduct? Why should the Senate, for the first time in its history, turn a skeptical eye toward the financial dealings of one of its own; why should it turn a skeptical eye on *his* financial dealings? Why should the Senators now ignore the Senate's centuries-old tradition of courtesy and accommodation for one of its members?

I am telling you the truth, he had implored, and at least 45 of his colleagues had turned a deaf ear. He would rather be dead than dishonored, but he had not been given the option.

Other factors contributed to his tears:

The image that he had constructed for himself as the lord of an impressive manor had been destroyed by his pleas in his unsuccessful defense, by revelation of his well-hidden but now-confessed poverty. He had accepted Dunbar's cars because he could not afford to buy a new car; he had accepted the use of the general's suite because a man in his position could not afford to pass up a free bed; he had raised money for campaign expenses and used it instead for bread because he was poor, and dependent on the charity of others (if charity is what it had been); and, if anybody had felt "flim-flammed" over the price of a dinner ticket, he would make it up to whomever— although he did not have much with which to do so.

He had to expect that he was likely to be prosecuted, if only so that the Johnson administration could maintain that it had not chosen the Republican Stratton for prosecution out of partisan considerations. If the Senate's 92-to-5 vote had predictive value, he was likely to face conviction for income tax fraud.

He had to expect that his constituents would repudiate him when he came up for re-election in 1970.

Perhaps most painful was the realization that he had been betrayed by people he could reasonably have regarded as more nearly family than as mere employees, by people whom—in his own way—Dodd had loved. Perhaps he asked himself, What must he have done to poison against himself his staff, led by the three who knew him the best and who owed him the most? He knew that all of the other Senators were asking that question.

There were many layers to his sadness and to his humiliation.

Part of the reason for the overwhelming vote against Dodd is that he was not well-liked by his peers. Some Senators were turned off by a pompously self-righteous aura about him, and wanted to see him humbled; others were pleased to see discredit heaped on a professional anti-communist. Although Senators as individuals are almost invariably self-promoters—and probably always have been—as a body they disapprove of too-obvious grandstanding. Dodd was regarded as a grandstander. Senators respect and admire competence in the art and craft of legislating. Dodd didn't care to compete in the legislative arena. He had never shown much interest in the doings or accomplishments of his Senate peers, and when his career was hanging in the balance, almost none of his peers showed much interest in him.

Others who voted against him may have been bowing to consideration of "public opinion" (whether correctly or incorrectly gauged). The fact that the Senate was considering Dodd's transgressions at the same time that the House was considering high-living and payroll-padding by the flashy black New York City Congressman Adam Clayton Powell, Jr., certainly had a prejudicial effect on Dodd's situation: It was necessary for Congressmen to make clear that deviant white officials were held to the same standards as deviant black officials.[54]

It is impossible to know whether Long's antics cost Dodd some votes and, if so, how many.

Some Senators may even have been put off by Dodd's actual conduct, but the number of Senators who were genuinely scandalized was probably a small fraction of 92. In a memo to LBJ in April 1966, Johnson's aide Harry McPherson reported on a private conversation between himself, NBC correspondent Ray Scherer, and Senator Harrison "Pete" Williams (D, NJ), in which Scherer had asked Williams "if all of you fellows couldn't be destroyed by staffs making your files available." Williams had agreed, but added that "Tom seems to have

---

54. If anything the outcome of the two cases made clear that blacks and whites were not held to the same standards, or at least were not punished by the same standards. Powell, whose offenses were minor compared to Dodd's, was expelled from the House (the Supreme Court later ruled improperly so) while Dodd was censured but no effort was made to deny him his seat in the Senate, and he continued with his seniority intact.

gone pretty far; he's made some mistakes." Dodd's real sin was the sin of excess.[55]

An important significance of the outcome was fully appreciated by few: The basis on which Dodd was censured was not one with great implications for the Senate at large. The committee declined to come to grips with influence peddling: the use of senatorial influence in the awarding of contracts and appointments; acceptance of contributions, gifts, or favors from people that a Senator might be investigating; or the propriety of a Senator taking cash from those dealing with the government—or not dealing with the government. To the eyes of Pearson and Anderson, the Ethics Committee had swept under the carpet the most significant of the allegations against Dodd, limiting itself to easy issues that did not get to the root of the ethical problems characterized by reform-oriented critics as "the culture of corruption" in Congress. Boyd sent the committee a lengthy and detailed letter reminding it of all the neglected issues, gracefully challenging the committee to take up the remaining matters. But no. What to Pearson and Anderson (and Boyd) constituted the culture of corruption in Congress could— and did—survive the Dodd proceedings virtually unscathed.

Stennis no doubt saw things differently. Unless one accepts the suggestion that he simply wanted to get the proceedings over as quickly as possible, one must reconstruct his thinking based on his personality and character—which involves considerable speculation inasmuch as Stennis never articulated his opinions on the underlying policy issues of the Dodd proceedings.

He probably believed that any effort to police the minds and motives of his fellow Senators in their official conduct would open a pandora's box, so his committee focused on matters of garden-vari-

---

55. Williams himself seems to have gone pretty far and made some mistakes: He was convicted in 1981 of taking bribes after having been entrapped in an FBI "sting" (known as the ABSCAM sting), for which he served time in prison, and he was later to suffer further degradation and humiliation: He was *denied* a pardon by President Bill Clinton.

ety dishonesty, only tangentially related to Dodd's responsibilities as a Senator.

Funneling off money raised for campaign expenses for the candidate's personal use was such a matter. Although nobody used the phrase in debate, an experienced lawyer or judge would certainly have recognized the fact pattern as presenting an "Obtaining Money Under False Pretenses" case, a crime in Anglo-American law at least since an Act of Parliament of 1757. Double-billing was also a matter not peculiar to Senators; it was a matter of simple dishonesty rather than malfeasance in one's role as a Senator.

Although the committee touched on possible influence peddling on behalf of the general, Spanel, and Dunbar, those matters involved Dodd's judgments and work as a Senator—territory into which Stennis was unwilling to venture. The committee "got rid" of those issues. However reluctantly, it gave Dodd a "pass" with regard to his relations with the general, and it referred the Spanel and Dunbar matters to the Justice Department for its consideration. Blinken's cash was not addressed.

Stennis, whose life revolved around the Senate, was also deeply concerned about upholding the honor of the institution. He secured the "conviction" of Dodd—albeit for one of Dodd's lesser offenses— but that was sufficient to bleach the taint from the Senate, from Stennis's Senate. If the work of his committee and the outcome of the vote should discourage "the boys" from putting both feet in the trough, so much the better. The image of the Senate could survive Dodd's doings intact—right alongside the culture of corruption.

Michael O'Hare, rather than Boyd, took the brunt of Dodd's counterattack during the proceedings, and he was badly rattled by the experience. After everything was over, he went to Ireland to get his head back together. He returned to the United States emotionally composed but without employment prospects. Drew Pearson got him a job with the Southern Railway, but that didn't work out, and Pearson

then found him a position with Big Brothers in Washington, an organization with which Pearson had powerful ties. O'Hare worked there
from 1969 to 1972, and then his situation began to pick up. He retained not only gratitude toward Pearson but also tremendous respect
and admiration for him: A handwritten note in Pearson's files from
O'Hare asks Pearson for an autographed photo and adds that O'Hare
had never asked Senator Dodd for a photo.

In 1972, after Dodd's death, O'Hare began a ten-year tenure as
comptroller of the Overseas Development Council, a Washington-
based, non-governmental policy institution concerned with global
problems of development. From there he went to the Carnegie Endowment for International Peace, also based in Washington, as finance
director and secretary of the board. After 16 years with the Carnegie
Endowment, in 1998 he became executive administrator of the Naval Medical Research Center's malaria program—his first government
position after separating from Senator Dodd. He retired in 2004 and
relocated to the Chapel Hill, North Carolina, area.

O'Hare had been deeply involved with Terry Golden, but in the
different times that were the 1960s the differences between O'Hare,
a Catholic, and Golden, a Protestant, seemed insuperable, and they
never married. She went on to a different life in Hawaii, and this
author has been unable to track her down. O'Hare married, had a
daughter, divorced, and then married a second time, to Kathleen Hurt
O'Hare, by whom he had two children. He died in Chapel Hill in
April 2009 at the age of 73 from complications after a stroke.

Over the intervening four decades, Boyd had maintained occasional affectionate contact with his one-time protégé, and continues, as
of this writing, to have some friendly contact with Kathleen O'Hare.

Boyd and Marjorie Carpenter disentangled themselves from their
other domestic commitments and were married in 1967. (Both Mr.
Carpenter and the first Mrs. Boyd promptly remarried.) Boyd worked
in journalism for several years, had a number of articles in the *New
York Times Magazine* (including a piece in 1970 on Richard Nixon's

"Southern strategy" that has influenced later writings on the subject), and other pieces published in *Washington Monthly* and *The Nation*. He had a very large hand in the writing of Pearson and Anderson's big seller, *The Case Against Congress* (1968), and was credited as co-author of Jack Anderson's memoirs, *Confessions of a Muckraker* (1979), and, with Anderson, of *Fiasco* (1983), a study of the oil crisis of the early 1980s. He was the executive director of the Fund for Investigative Journalism and of a related entity, the Project for Investigative Reporting on Money in Politics. A sharp, agile, and plucky guy, Jim Boyd also had well-honed survivor instincts.

While the Dodd hearings were going on, Marjorie Carpenter Boyd held a responsible position with a civil rights organization; later she worked with the organizations headed by Boyd, wrote some articles for *Washington Monthly*, established a successful real estate agency in the Virginia horse country, and raised the Boyds' daughter and son. She retired from real estate in 2002, at which time the Boyds moved to the western part of Virginia, not far from their daughter.

Boyd, 81 as of late 2009, and Marjorie Carpenter Boyd, then in her later 60s (give or take), gave this writer a five-hour interview in November 2009. They are forthright people, and their discussion of the man who had played such an important part in their lives was remarkably free from bile. Boyd manifested the relaxed self-confidence of an honest man. He regretted that the course he had determined to take inevitably led to his separation from people he'd felt close to: "I was disheartened but not surprised or judgmental when many that I continue to remember fondly—Gerry Zeiller, Bill Curry, Paul McNamara, Art Powers, San Bomstein—lined up with Dodd in the crunch. After all, I had put them all on the spot and enmeshed them in a mess they'd as lief hide from but one where tradition and practicality called on them to be good soldiers."

Otherwise ... Boyd has no regrets.

CHAPTER EIGHT

The End

DURING THE CENSURE PROCEEDINGS, Dodd's hypertension condition became so alarming that he required massive doses of blood pressure medication. This in turn led to severe potassium deficiency, with the result that he had to be fed intravenously. At least that's what he told journalist Leslie H. Whitten. Whitten, at the time a reporter for the Hearst papers, had excellent relations with Dodd's office and was not unsympathetic to the Senator. In a luncheon interview, Dodd laid bare his soul. It's odd that no journalist other than Whitten, either from the Connecticut press or from the Associated Press or United Press, no left-wing or right-wing columnist, was admitted to this confidence. The explanation is that it probably wasn't true.[56]

Dodd had a tendency to hypochondria, would sometimes manifest the symptoms of sick people in his circle, and would exaggerate those illnesses from which he might actually suffer. He was not above claiming illness, severe illness, or even morbid illness, in a plea for favored treatment. According to Boyd in *Above the Law,* Dodd also had

---

56. This writer ran into Whitten in September 2010 and reminded Whitten of the article in which he had reported, 43 years earlier, that Dodd had had to be fed intravenously. Whitten did not recall the piece, but was curious about it, and asked: "Was that *true?*"

what might be called "hypochondria by proxy" (not Boyd's phrase). Boyd cites examples in which Dodd asked for consideration because of grave illnesses from which, he claimed, his wife, his son Christopher, or his key staff member, Ed Sullivan, were supposedly suffering. It seems likely, however, that the stress of the censure proceedings actually did aggravate his hypertension.

After the censure vote, Dodd struggled along for several months, and then, in October 1967, signed himself into the little known South County Hospital in Wakefield, Rhode Island, removed from the eyes that would have followed him if he had gone to the Walter Reed Hospital or to the National Institutes of Health, where a Senator ordinarily was treated. His doctor, S. John Turco, a family friend as well as a physician, wrote Dodd's lawyer, John Sonnett (a copy of which made its way into Drew Pearson's private files, now at the LBJ Library): "He was admitted because of extreme nervous and physical exhaustion and has been under sedation."

It was early 1968 before Dodd resumed an active role in Congress, making his first splash in the newspapers when his press secretary, Robert R. Siegrist, quit after a mere seven-week tenure, publicly explaining that the Senator had exploded at him, accusing Siegrist of working in league with newsmen to harass him. In March 1968 a rumor that the Justice Department was gearing up to bring criminal charges against Dodd brought a call from the Senator to Mike Manatos at the White House, who noted: "This has completely unnerved Dodd who told me that if such a thing happened he intends to tell some things he knows." Then, in June of that year, after the Washington chapter of "Big Brothers" held a dinner in honor of Drew Pearson, Dodd took to the floor of the Senate to denounce "the Rasputin of our society": "Drew Pearson is a liar. He is a monster. Those associated with him are thieves, liars and monsters. . . . His business is lying. He is a devil. It appalled me that he was honored as a Big Brother: a molester of children who had the records of his arrest destroyed"—this last being a reference to an innocuous charge discredited in 1914 that was later resurrected periodically by Pearson's enemies.

Legislatively, Dodd devoted considerable effort to making it a federal offense to (as Dodd summarized it on the Senate floor) "unlawfully enter a federal office or without authorization knowingly and wilfully remove any document from such office, or to make unauthorized copies of documents either inside the office or at any other place, or to receive such documents or copies of such documents." Yes . . . "this, of course includes the office of a member of the U.S. Senate or the U.S. House of Representatives."   Dodd was not thinking only of himself; the same thing, after all, had happened to J. Parnell Thomas, the HUAC chairman who had been brought down when his secretary had surreptitiously removed damaging documents from Thomas's office and given them to Drew Pearson.

With time, though, Dodd recovered his equilibrium. Much of the financial pressure on him was relieved when he sold the Stonington estate in 1968 and moved into a more modest house, a recent-vintage "colonial" on the edge of the historic district of Old Lyme, Connecticut. It was still a proper residence for a public servant, if not for a United States Senator, and it freed Dodd from the never-ending financial drain that went along with keeping grander premises at Laurel Glen.

He also recovered a good part of his popularity. The tremendous publicity surrounding Dodd's ethics was only a national story, not a Connecticut one. Only six Connecticut newspapers carried Pearson and Anderson: two dailies, the *Waterbury Republican* and the *Willimantic Chronicle,* plus four weeklies. The *Chronicle,* not an "important" paper in the state, failed to print many of the columns about Dodd, and two of the weeklies also dropped some of the columns. "Washington Merry-Go-Round" had no subscribing newspapers in Hartford, New Haven, Bridgeport, Stamford, or New Britain, and the press in most of the state largely ignored the revelations about Connecticut's senior U.S. Senator as the exposures emerged. There was no effort on the part of any Connecticut newspaper to follow up the inside-page coverage that might have been given to the Dodd case, with "local-angle" articles.[57]

While anti-Dodd coverage had been slight, pro-Dodd coverage by William F. Buckley, Jr., John Chamberlain, George Sokolsky, and other right-wing political commentators was impressive. The principal burden of the right-wing message was that Dodd had been targeted by left-liberals out to discredit an anti-communist. Dodd, too, would make this argument whenever he had an opening before an appropriate audience, and to right-of-center voters it had a ring of truth to it. Dodd did not really believe it himself, though. At a small dinner party at Senator Birch Bayh's house in April 1966, attended by the Dodds, NBC's White House correspondent Ray Scherer, Senator Harrison "Pete" Williams of New Jersey, and White House Aide Harry McPherson, Dodd said that he thought that Pearson was out to get him "because I would not oppose Bress"—that is, because Dodd, as a member of the Senate Judiciary Committee, had sided with David Bress, Johnson's nominee for U.S. Attorney in the District of Columbia, rather than with the other candidate, Tyler Abell, who just happened to be Pearson's stepson. There was no talk about his "anti-communism."

The actual censure, of course, had to be carried prominently in the newspapers, but of the two dozen allegations documented in the Pearson and Anderson columns, the vast majority of Connecticut voters were unaware of all but a couple of them. Few knew about Spanel

---

57. The explanation for the seeming lack of interest in Dodd among Connecticut editors is (for the most part) less sinister than might appear at first blush: the explanation is not corruption, but rather, afganistanism. Afganistanism is a word that long predates the Taliban; in the journalists' world it refers to the practice of gun-shy editors to ignore scandals involving powerful local citizens, or burying them on inside pages, while devoting their front pages to happenings on the other side of the globe.

or Dave Dunbar's Oldsmobiles, and if they had heard about General Klein or about the double-billing, well . . . Dodd had been cleared of those matters. The only thing for which Dodd had been "convicted" was the use of testimonial funds for non-campaign purposes, and those people with pre-existing good will for Dodd could easily rationalize that in terms such as "so he used some of the money to pay for flowers for wakes"—an actual example cited to this writer by the son of a straight-laced Irish judge of the period. As one Republican legislator was quoted in the *New York Times* at the time, "Most of the public doesn't give a damn about testimonial dinners." Under the circumstances, the half-life of the censure vote was much shorter than it might otherwise have been.

The assassinations of Martin Luther King, Jr. and Robert Kennedy in 1968 enabled Dodd, the most consistently outspoken Congressional proponent of gun control, to draw favorable press attention to himself.

As early as 1963—before the assassination of John F. Kennedy—Dodd was introducing gun-control legislation prepared by the staff of the Senate's Juvenile Delinquency Subcommittee. The assassination of the President propelled him into the spotlight. Dodd's focus was principally against the sale of cheap "mail-order" guns, a largely foreign-import business. In the assassination of President Kennedy, Lee Harvey Oswald had used an Italian military rifle, not a Colt (made in Hartford) or a Winchester (made in New Haven), and Oswald bought it mail order for $19.95. Dodd's positions were helpful, rather than threatening, to domestic arms producers, many of whom were Connecticut based, and to the proprietors of retail gun shops who had to compete against mail-order outlets. Executives of the gun companies continued to respond to pleas for contributions, including many who were longtime stalwarts in Republican Party fund-raising. Dodd's characteristically splendid orations rarely failed to invoke memories of "the death of a beloved President," but despite pleas to the memory of JFK, Dodd's earliest proposals failed to get off the ground.

In 1965 Dodd was the Senate sponsor for a Johnson administration gun-control proposal that met persistent, spirited, and ultimately fatal opposition from the National Rifle Association.

After the King and Robert Kennedy assassinations in 1968, the Johnson administration threw intensified effort behind gun control legislation, for which Dodd was again the most vociferous Senate spokesman, attacking the NRA for its tactics of "blackmail, intimidation and unscrupulous propaganda." Out of it came the Gun Control Act of 1968, which, though falling very far short of the wishes of gun-control proponents, was the first significant federal legislation on the subject in over 30 years.

In *The Saturday Night Special* (1973), published two years after Dodd's death, the prolific investigative journalist Robert Sherrill insists that Dodd was never personally invested in the fate of the gun-control bills that bore Dodd's sponsorship. He depicts Dodd's role in the battle for gun control as opportunistic, devious, and frequently duplicitous, asserting (apparently on the authority of Carl Perian, with whom Sherrill spoke) that Dodd sometimes intentionally took steps that threatened the legislation he purported to be promoting, as, for example, demanding that the votes be rounded up of subcommittee members likely to vote against letting a gun-control bill get out of the committee. According to Sherrill, Dodd was producing mock drama for the purpose of generating incandescent headlines. No matter the sincerity of his crusade, it did bring the headlines.

The more virulent the attacks on him by "the gun nuts" (as Dodd referred to his opponents on the issue), the stronger he became politically. The Gun Control Act of 1968 left so much to be done (and as of 2011, still so much to be done) that there was room for Dodd to make many more speeches on the subject—and to engender many more helpful attacks upon him by the gun nuts.

According to press reports, the Internal Revenue Service was recommending that criminal charges be brought against Dodd, but decisions of that sort were made by the Department of Justice, not by

Dodd's enemies believed that he behaved himself with the Nixon administration so as to ward off prosecution for tax evasion.

the IRS. The Justice Department did not operate in a political vacuum, certainly not during the Nixon administration and it was easily influenced by hints from the White House. No one could doubt that Dodd would trade sympathetic consideration of the administration's positions in exchange for being left alone. On December 23, 1969, the Justice Department finally announced that there would be no tax prosecution. Was the Nixon administration paying Dodd back for his non-partisan approaches to appointments and legislation of interest to the administration? It is equally likely that the actual litigators at the Justice Department were still feeling the sting of the government's loss in the Governor Stratton case of four years earlier, and could foresee a Dodd prosecution as leading to the same outcome: acquittal.

The Department's announcement was a Christmas present surpassing all others. Dodd happily and regularly cited the decision as "proof" of his innocence and pointed to himself as one of the few political people whose honor had been conclusively established. It seems certain that the IRS also abandoned any civil claim for back taxes—otherwise, Dodd would have been thrown into bankruptcy and quite publicly so. He had dodged the bullet. Both bullets—the criminal bullet and the civil bullet.

Within a year after the censure, Dodd's political picture had brightened. A *New York Times* article reported that his renomination and re-election in 1970 were genuine possibilities. Senators stopped shunning him; Senator Cooper, a member of the Senate Ethics Committee, praised him on the Senate floor. Joe Blumenfeld forwarded to Dodd a clipping by Joseph Alsop—the same Joseph Alsop who had predicted a Democratic landslide in 1958—this time predicting that there was little likelihood that Dodd would be turned out of office.

Re-election wouldn't be easy. It wasn't just that Dodd had been censured for financial irregularities; it was that Dodd, as always, refused to mend fences, to build bridges, or to have any relationship with other pols except on his own terms. In the Connecticut election season of 1966, as the Dodd scandal got underway, Dodd passed up an opportunity to bank some good will for the future, taking no part in helping to elect the Democratic "ticket." His good friend from West Hartford, E. Clayton Gengras, a rich man who, like Dodd, had an overriding identification with the Catholic faith, was the Republican candidate for Governor. Rumblings appeared in Zaiman's columns that "somebody" might challenge Dodd for re-nomination the next time around.

During the next election cycle, in 1968, in the midst of the highly charged confrontation between party regulars and anti-war activists at the Democratic National Convention in Chicago, Abe Ribicoff, running for re-election to the Senate, denounced the police over the "Gestapo tactics in the streets of Chicago." Instantly Ribicoff became the white knight of every idealistic young person in America. Dodd might have sat on his hands, but no: he just had to rise to the defense of the Chicago police, thereby echoing (at least in Ribicoff's ears) the response that Chicago Mayor Daley had shouted at Ribicoff from the convention floor— "Go fuck yourself."[58] Little wonder that

---

58. Sometimes reported as "Go fuck yourself, you Jew bastard."

Ribicoff's uncharacteristic outburst at the convention came as a shock not only to Daley but also to every political person in the State of Connecticut, maybe even to Abe Ribicoff himself.

as the Connecticut Democratic State Convention of 1970 approached
to consider nomination of someone for Dodd's Senate seat, Ribicoff
came out for Dodd's challenger, Joseph Duffy, an ordained Protestant
minister who was then national president of Americans for Democratic Action. Duffy opposed the war in Vietnam as passionately as Dodd
favored it.

Other candidates came forward too, notably Stamford businessman Alphonse J. Donahue, Jr., a titan of the sewing-notions industry
(that is correct), a Fourth Degree member of the Knights of Columbus,
a Knight of Malta, a Papal Knight of St. Gregory, and with 12 children, twice the Catholic that Dodd was. Among his political credits,
Donahue had been toastmaster at a dinner for Tom Dodd in 1963, at
which Vice-President Lyndon B. Johnson had appeared as the main
speaker, and in 1964 he had served as finance chairman for various
re-elect Dodd entities. He and Dodd had been good friends for many
years (or so it might have seemed). Donahue brought in as his political "brains" a big-league player from Washington, Mike Monroney, Jr.,
son of Senator Mike Monroney. The younger Monroney had been a
key man in Humphrey's unsuccessful presidential campaign of two
years earlier. Donahue pleaded ignorance as to whether he was John
Bailey's horse in the race, but everybody knew he was, especially after his announcement of candidacy was attended by 200 Democratic Party dignitaries. The list of those in attendance included some
names from the political graveyard: ". . . and former Stamford Mayor
Thomas Quigley"—the same Mayor Thomas Quigley whom Dodd
had unsuccessfully campaigned against in a local Democratic primary
13 years earlier. What went around came around.

Despite some shortcomings in the charisma department, Donahue could at least finance his own campaign, and once he was elected, "organization" leaders could count Donahue as "dependable."
Dodd, on the other hand, for a quarter of a century had been going
out of his way to stick his finger in Bailey's eye. Bailey did know about
Tommy.

Also in the race was State Senator Edward Marcus, a bright, handsome, and dynamic young lawyer from New Haven, reminiscent of a younger Abe Ribicoff, who was (to borrow Chester Bowles's phrase) very much on the make. Like Dodd, Marcus had stuck his finger in Bailey's eye more than once. He was backed by New Haven Democratic Town Committee Chairman Arthur T. Barbieri, the same Arthur T. Barbieri who had lent his name as chairman of one of the more important and successful Dodd fund-raising dinners. Marcus was Barbieri's home-town candidate; what else could Barbieri do but support the home-town candidate?

In those days, Senate nominees were designated by the party's state convention with the delegates to the state convention being selected by the local Democratic town committees. The town committee's delegate choices could be challenged in a local primary. The Dodd forces determined to challenge the Stamford Democratic Town Committee's slate of state-convention delegates pledged to the city's favorite son, Donahue. In a period when ethnic and religious considerations dominated strategic evaluation, Dodd almost certainly thought that getting the other Irishman out of the race was essential; otherwise, he and Donahue would split the Catholic vote. If Donahue lost his own town, however, he would be all done, leaving Dodd as the sole surviving Catholic contender, competing against Duffy, a Protestant clergyman, and Marcus, a Jewish lawyer. Duffy and Marcus would divvy up the vote of the non-Catholics, leaving Dodd the big winner. Dodd decided to bet the bank on the Stamford primary, but the ball fell red, and the Donahue forces swamped the Dodd slate three to one. It was not Donahue who was forced out.

The magnitude of Dodd's defeat at the hands of the unprepossessing Donahue made clear that the scandal had hurt Dodd much more than polls and pundits had envisioned, spelling the death knell of Dodd's campaign. Nine days later the press reported that Dodd had suffered a minor heart attack. In discussion with a White House physician inquiring on behalf of President Nixon, Dodd's cardiologist described it as "a mild coronary occlusion with minimal changes in his EKG," and projected a hospital stay of a couple of weeks followed by another month of recuperation. The following month Dodd announced that he would cease his efforts to win his party's nomination for re-election. In the primary between the three remaining contenders, Donahue, Duffy, and Marcus, Duffy the anti-war candidate from the ADA—Dodd's last choice for Senator—came out on top.

Dodd ran for the seat as an Independent, with his son Christopher, a likable young man recently returned from Peace Corps duty in the Dominican Republic, and newly married to one of the Senator's staffers, as his ostensible campaign manager. If Dodd should prove no more than a spoiler for the Democratic Party nominee, Duffy, that would be all right too. Dodd had always kind of liked the Republican candidate, Congressman Lowell Weicker.

In three-way debates during the couple of months before election day, there could be no question about the "winner." Even as a young lawyer, when it might have seemed inappropriate, there was a stentorian quality to Dodd; now, after 12 years in the Senate, his performance as "The Senator" was unrivaled on screen or stage, and certainly not if the other two people on the stage were high-school debaters like Weicker and Duffy. Marcus (who became chairman of the State Democratic Party in the 1990s), turned his back on the party's official candidate and publicly endorsed Dodd. Bailey was afraid that Dodd's presence on the ballot as a third-party candidate might prompt Irish defections from the Democrats and drain votes away from the party's gubernatorial candidate, Emelio Q. Daddario. Hoping to counteract that, Bailey brought in big Irish names from "outside," Ted Kennedy and Larry O'Brien, to campaign for the party endorsees, Daddario, whose victory or loss would determine Bailey's continued control of Connecticut patronage, and Duffy, in whom Bailey had neither stake nor interest.

Bailey's strategy did not work: Both Duffy and Daddario were soundly defeated, Duffy by Weicker and Daddario by Republican Congressman Thomas Meskill.

If one starts off with the assumption that 100% of voters were for Dodd, and subtracts those voters who religiously voted for whomever the Republican or Democratic candidate might be, and then subtracts all of those who were passionately opposed to the war in Vietnam (by 1970, a sizable number in Connecticut), and then subtracts those who believed that a censured Senator, regardless of the merits of the censure, might not be an effective advocate for Connecticut—and last, subtracts those who actually believed that Dodd had misused his public office for personal gain or had otherwise done something that was dishonest, it would be surprising if the resulting figure was as high as 25%. Yet Dodd garnered 25% of the vote, running third to the winner, Republican Lowell Weicker (41%), and Democrat Joseph Duffy (34%). He carried both of the home towns of his youth, Norwich and West Haven, as well as two important smaller cities, New London and East Hartford, and in lots of other places he either ran ahead of Weicker or ran ahead of Duffy. He might have spun the outcome as a victory for himself, an exoneration of sorts, a moral victory. But he didn't. After Tom Dodd's many years on the political battlefields, the fight had been leached out of him.

Dodd didn't show up at his state-wide campaign headquarters for the tallying of the vote. Nor did he deliver the expected statement by the vanquished, with the usual thank yous to the people who still believed in him. There was no gracious exit. Christopher drove him from the family's "private" election-day headquarters in Wethersfield back to the house in Old Lyme, where "Daddy," as Chris called his father, poured himself a glass of Dewars Scotch and thanked his son for all that he had done. Then Christopher went to the official headquarters in Hartford, where he told the press, "He isn't feeling really bad or really happy," adding a private plea to the *Courant's* reporter, "I hope you guys will leave him alone for a few days."

Seven months after his election-day defeat, Thomas J. Dodd was dead of a heart attack, at the age of 64. "He had a good death, didn't he," Grace's sister, Helen Farley, commented more to herself than to the oral history interviewer. "Grace called me when he died. I went right over to Old Lyme. He was still sitting in a chair. It reminded me that Grace and I would be talking in the room and Tom would be sleeping or dozing and he'd say, 'Keep talking, girls. I like to hear the sound of your voices . . .'"

Abraham A. Ribicoff, then the senior Senator from Connecticut, delivered a eulogy to him in the Senate; such is the game of politics. The Senate floor was virtually empty at the time of the tribute.

Grace had been a wife from an earlier era: She had built her own life out of idolizing, promoting, and, at the end, insulating and protecting Tom, as best she could, from others and from himself. She had supported him best at the moments when he had needed her the most. He always referred to her as "Mother." Now her job was done. She joined Tom 19 months later.

CHAPTER NINE

Epilogue

TOM DODD KNEW WHAT A GOOD father was, and he wanted to be one, tried as best he could. His correspondence files at the University of Connecticut include several lengthy and affectionate letters dated in the 1960s to his son Jeremy, then a student in Central America. Still, his paternal instincts were outweighed by his near-total self-absorption. He consumed all of the oxygen in his surroundings, leaving relatively little for others, including his children.

In her oral history interview, Helen Farley recalled that Tom would sometimes fly off the handle, and his scoldings of the children would become orations, after which he would be terribly remorseful. In *Above the Law,* Boyd wrote that Dodd would sometimes upbraid his sons fiercely in the presence of the staff. During the 1964 re-election campaign, the key people from Dodd's Washington office—Boyd, Carpenter, O'Hare, David Martin, and Doreen Moloney, the stenographer who took the Senator's personal dictation—were all moved into the same rented house in West Hartford that the Dodd family had taken, in the interests of easy coordination of the re-election campaign. According to Boyd, the Senator would give his sons

Senator Christopher Dodd welcomes a friend at the dedication of the Thomas J. Dodd Research Center on October 15, 1995. On that date Tom Dodd was symbolically inducted into the ranks of great men.

menial tasks like handing out campaign literature, and would openly belittle them to the office staff living with them under the same roof. Whenever possible, the sons were part of the retinue that followed the Senator everywhere.

Dodd made up for his shortcomings in the parenting department by giving his children extravagant presents, financial support that extended well into adulthood, and for daughter Martha an elaborate high-society wedding at a time when he appeared to his staff to have been desperately broke. He could be as protective of his children as a mother hen. As much as possible the prerogatives of a United States Senator were extended to the children: assistance for Tom, Junior, on his academic papers, rendered by researchers on the staff of the Library of Congress; employment for Jeremy from insurance-industry people beholden to the Senator; lengthy long-distance telephone calls

Early 1960s. From left: Christopher, Martha, Tom, Jerry, Nicky (in front), Grace, Tom, Jr. (partially obscured), and Carolyn.

placed from Christopher's dorm room at Providence College to girls all over the country, charged to the United States Senate. Many of the "charter" airplane flights that Dodd glommed from businesses doing business with the federal government were used to shuttle the children here and there.

Those of the Dodd children whose lives we know about, however, have evidenced as adults none of the sense of entitlement that might be expected of people who were raised in the over-privileged environment of their childhood.[59]

Tom Dodd, Jr. (who long ago ceased to use the "Junior") served as U.S. ambassador in Uruguay and Costa Rica during the Clinton administration, but most of his career has been as a faculty member at Georgetown University's School of Foreign Service. The "write-ups" about him on the website "ratemyprofessors.com" are embarrassingly positive: "A very straightforward guy who genuinely cares about his students"; another says, "Professor Dodd is such a nice guy—make the effort to get to know him"; a third, "one of the sweetest men you'll meet on campus."

Martha Dodd Buonanno died of cancer at the early age of 68 in 2009. Married to prominent Providence, RI, lawyer Bernard V. Buonanno, Jr., mother of five, she was an active mentor/volunteer in the Providence public schools and was involved in other decent causes.

Carolyn Dodd's adult life has been defined by her work as a Montessori-trained teacher. Over the years legions of educators and prospective educators have come to visit her Hartford classroom, with few knowing that the unassuming, consummate professional they were observing was the sister of their United States Senator.

Christopher Dodd is remarkably unrapacious for a man who has spent almost all of his adult life in Congress. He is a patient, non-confrontational man, who has gotten along very well largely by going

---

59. Nicholas Dodd has led a completely private life, as has Jeremy since the 1960s.

along. He is universally liked by his peers not only because of his easy personal style, but also because he is truly considerate of others.

The children, of course, had a mother as well as a father. In her oral history, Helen Farley reported an occasion on which "I was in Washington with Grace, and we were going to church one day and we had to pass the house where Drew Pearson lived. As we passed Drew Pearson's house, Grace said to me, 'I have forgiven him.'"

The most successful of Dodd's sons by conventional standards is Christopher Dodd. As Dodd's next-to-last child in a brood of six, Christopher may have been somewhat insulated from the costs borne by the son of an egocentric father. He was to become Connecticut's longest-serving United States Senator.

Tom and Christopher Dodd were poles apart in personality and personal style, temperament, world view, and policy orientation. Other than DNA, they had little in common. Notwithstanding their many and important differences, however, Christopher's loyalty to and admiration for his father are legendary. Christopher has often commented on the fact that he was in the Peace Corps in the Dominican Republic during 1966-1967, when his father was under constant attack, and that the rest of the family largely shielded him from the pain that their father and the other children were going through. His repeated references to this fact suggests that he felt some variety of survivor guilt.

Christopher's comments to journalists show unashamed affection for his father: "We were very close, particularly in the later years. He was not good with children. Even though he had six kids, he wasn't the kind of guy to go fishing, or to whack a baseball. Where my father began to get really wonderful was as you got older. He was well-read, he loved poetry, he loved to debate. It was wonderful getting older." He attributes the undeniable fact that his father diverted political funds to personal use by pointing out that Tom "didn't separate and distinguish his political and his personal life."

After the Peace Corps, Christopher joined the National Guard, which at the time involved a few months of active training followed by several years in "readiness," with occasional drill weekends. Membership in the National Guard was a virtual guarantee that one would not be deployed to Vietnam. In a 1995 interview with David Lightman, then the *Courant's* Washington correspondent, Christopher acknowledged that he had joined the Guard to avoid being sent to Vietnam—because, Christopher said, by 1968 he had become opposed to the war in Vietnam. Very few who avoided military service in Vietnam ever ascribed their failure to serve to anything other than a deep-seated opposition to that war. Still, Chris Dodd is one of the few public figures to openly admit that he joined the National Guard for "cover." (His affiliation with the Guard would ultimately pay an unexpected dividend: Three decades later it enabled him to tout himself in the Iowa presidential primary of 2007 as the only presidential contender "with military experience.")

He also worked for the *Northern Virginia Sun,* a now defunct Arlington, Virginia, daily that was distinguished principally for local coverage. He attended law school. His prior academic record was such that his law school choices were limited to places like the University of Louisville, now part of the State of Kentucky's university system, but at that time a municipal university of the city of Louisville, from which he graduated in 1972. In 1970, during the "independent" phase of his father's last campaign, Chris Dodd married Susan Mooney, a staff member from the Senator's Washington office. His father's election defeat later that year was followed by the death of the Senator in May 1971 and of Grace Dodd in January 1973. That spring Christopher Dodd was sworn in as a lawyer in Connecticut. He immediately discounted reports that he would run for office. He had no political ambitions or interest in elective office; he just wanted to be "lawyer Dodd" with the firm of Suisman, Shapiro, Wolf and Brennan, then (as now) the most-nearly white-shod law firm in New London, Connecticut. His law practice was never of sufficient significance that his name entered the *New London City Directory,* which lists all lawyers practicing in the city.

He and Susan bought a house in North Stonington, the town where the senior Dodds had lived during their happiest period, within Connecticut's Second Congressional District, the district covering most of the state to the east of the Connecticut River. One year later the district's incumbent Republican Congressman gave up the seat to run for higher office, leaving it open. Tom Dodd loyalists, notably Alvin Goodin, who had been with Tom Dodd at least since 1958, maybe earlier, prodded Chris to go for it. Chris did not need much prodding. The rest is political science.[60] After three terms in the House, Chris succeeded Ribicoff in the Senate in 1980, and he was thereafter reelected to the Senate five times, always with runaway victories. Early in 2010, Christopher Dodd announced that he would not seek reelection to his seventh term in the United States Senate.

An important item on Christopher Dodd's personal agenda has been righting the wrongs he believes to have been visited on his father. The caption to an Elizabeth Bumiller human-interest piece in the *New York Times* on the publication of *Letters from Nuremberg* reads, "Dodd's Other Campaign: Restoring Dad's Reputation." Bill Curry, Jr., former counselor to President Bill Clinton and twice the Democratic Party nominee for Governor of Connecticut—who is the son of Tom Dodd loyalists Bill and Beverly Curry—told *Newsweek* in 2009 that "much of [Chris's] life has been a kind of reclamation project for his father's reputation."

Prisons are full of convicts whose families insist with unquestionable sincerity on the innocence of their sons or fathers, notwithstanding the weight of contrary evidence, and they cannot be faulted for efforts to overturn convictions or to obtain pardons for their kin. Except when DNA tests lead to miracles, they do not succeed. Christopher

---

60. Goodin served as Chris's campaign manager in that first campaign. He was later a partner in the real estate syndicate that provided necessary office space for Congressman/Senator Christopher Dodd. From up above, Ed Sullivan nodded approval.

Dodd has performed miracles. He embarked—perhaps unwittingly, and without a thought-through battle plan—on what was essentially a political campaign, intended to elect his father to a place of honor in history. As in all political campaigns, connections and access to funding often trump other considerations.

The principal vehicles to restoring Tom Dodd's reputation have been the construction and the presence on the campus of the University of Connecticut of the Thomas J. Dodd Research Center, and the bi-annual award of the Thomas J. Dodd Prize in International Justice and Human Rights, spawned by the Dodd Research Center. Through the center and the prize (as well as publication of *Letters from Nuremberg*), Christopher Dodd has largely succeeded in reframing the memory of his father, from Connecticut's corrupt Senator into the ardent crusader against tyranny in Nazi Germany and the Stalinist world.

The Dodd Center is the repository not only of Tom Dodd's papers, and the certain repository of the Christopher Dodd papers, but also of the collections of personal papers of hundreds of other donors.[61] Federal tax law encourages the gift to educational institutions of the papers of significant and arguably significant people by their heirs by allowing, under certain circumstances, a charitable deduction for the supposed economic worth of the collection being donated. Though difficult to price, the papers of a significant United States Senator, someone of Fulbright caliber, have considerable financial value. How about the papers of an insignificant United States Senator, a William Purtell? Who is to say who is which? What criteria distinguish one set of papers from another? These are clearly subjective matters. When children donate their father's papers to an educational institution, however, they may be in a position to claim a tax deduction

---

61. Prescott Bush donated his papers to the University of Connecticut before there was any Dodd Center. Had he known of their ultimate resting place, he would almost certainly have given them instead to his own alma mater, Yale.

for whatever figure an appraiser of historical documents can convince an IRS examiner to accept (if, that is, the IRS should inquire into the basis of the appraiser's opinion).

The net result is that a lot of "historical" documents, many wholly devoid of even sentimental significance, get archived and protected as if of genuine value, and universities must have suitable repositories for their collections, repositories that architecturally shed appropriate light on the importance, or the pretended importance, of the holdings within, of those who created the holdings, and frequently, of the progeny of the creators of the holdings. Archival repositories must be constructed for the preservation of paper over centuries, must be climate-controlled at all times, and must be staffed by trained archivists. They are expensive to construct, and then they are very expensive to keep in operation. The expense of organizing and cataloguing and then preserving and servicing 36 years of the official papers of Congressman/Senator Christopher Dodd, likely to arrive at UConn in the next few years, will come to a truly staggering number.

Still, every state university has and must have a facility such as the Dodd Research Center, almost as much as a top-flight university needs a top-flight basketball team.

UConn had been planning for the construction of a major new building to house the collections of important papers given to it (and that might be given to it, if it had an impressive repository), along with the university's own archives, at least since the mid-1980s. From the outset, college administrators posited that the university would be seeking maybe a million dollars in private funding for the project to supplement appropriation from the state budget, thereby sugar-coating a very expensive pill for the responsible officials in the Governor's office and the state legislature. "Naming rights" were for sale.

Enter Christopher Dodd, circa 1990. University officials and Christopher undertook numerous preliminary talks about UConn's proposed new archives building, its scope, location, and design, the possibility of naming it for Tom Dodd—and about whether Chris would bring in the million dollars in private funding. Internal university memoranda make clear that university officials wanted to be absolutely certain that the piper would be paid. No problem, no problem, Chris reassured the university officials.

One thing the university tried to parry was Christopher's repeated wish to have a room in the building, a public room, visible, not too large, not too small (no, an administrator's or scholar's office would not be what he had in mind), within which to replicate his father's Senate office, containing Tom Dodd's desk, some of his favorite furniture, the huge oil portrait of him. It was to be a re-creation similar to "the rath of Dodd," which his father had dreamed of creating.

Christopher did not want the room actually set up until after his own retirement from the Senate (much of the memorabilia was in use in Christopher's Senate office) and college spokesmen tried to postpone such determinations until Chris's retirement, which an administrator joshed (presciently, as it happened) might be in about 18 years. (Spoken in 1992, making further discussion of Dodd's rath due in 2010.) A note by a college representative after a meeting with Chris says, "This issue is not going to go away."

By 1991 the basic outline of an understanding had been worked out, which was formalized by Christopher Dodd's letter of December 18, 1991, to UConn President Harry J. Hartley, asking on behalf of himself and his siblings that the new building be named in honor of their father, and committing himself to the raising of one million dollars in private funds toward the cost.

Dodd told UConn officials that he had already received pledges for about half a million—and he had pledges of at least that much (and probably for the whole million) from Tom Dodd's old friend Bill Mc-Cue, whose McCue Mortgage Company was perhaps the largest mortgage-brokerage firm in Connecticut, doing the lion's share of federally subsidized and federally guaranteed mortgage loans; from Chris's own friend, Edward J. Downe, Jr., an investment banker who was about to plead guilty to insider-trading violations; and mostly, from John W.

Kluge—the same John W. Kluge who had headed Metromedia back in the 1960s, in the days when Thomas Dodd was quashing investigations into violence on the TV.

Intervening years had been kind to Kluge: In 1986 he sold Metromedia to Australian media czar Rupert Murdock at a price variously reported as two billion or four billion dollars (Metromedia became the nucleus for Murdoch's Fox network), after which for several years he battled it out nip and tuck with Sam Walton of Wal-Mart for the title of Richest Man in America. Kluge had already given over 100 million dollars to Columbia University by the time Chris Dodd needed a couple of peppercorns for the Thomas J. Dodd Research Center.

Mr. Kluge never forgot a good turn. And who knew but that a man whose thumb was in a pie-cart-full of baked goods might indeed want some more good turns in the future.[62] However, Kluge's generosity was not motivated principally by payback promises; his generosity was motivated by reciprocal good will between America's sometime-richest man and the Senators Dodd, father and son—a good will that carries with it broader implications for the polity than a relationship baldly based on quid pro quos.

Later, major corporations—United Aircraft and U.S. Tobacco—decided that the Thomas J. Dodd Research Center was precisely the kind of project that they, too, wanted to get behind! It is not hard for a United States Senator to raise tax-deductible contributions of one million dollars, not for a good cause. The Dodd million tumbled out of the air.

The total cost for the Thomas J. Dodd Research Center came to ten million dollars. The state appropriated the necessary public money during the administration of Governor William O'Neill (D),

---

62. A front-page article in the *New York Times* of August 6, 2010, discusses how big-money interests seduce Senators by making university endowments in the Senator's name. The *Times* followed up on September 5 and 7, 2010, with discussion of how big contributions to a politician's favorite charity (sometimes bearing the politician's name) accomplish the same thing.

who as a youngster had studied Latin as a pupil of schoolteacher Mary Dodd Dwyer, Tom Dodd's sister. Construction began in October 1993, during the administration of Governor Lowell Weicker. By that time Weicker had left the Republican Party and had been elected Governor as a third-party candidate, but whatever his party registration, Weicker always enjoyed excellent personal relations with Chris Dodd. At the time of its opening and formal dedication on October 15, 1995, the Governor was John Rowland, a Republican who served three terms in the House of Representatives in the 1980s, while Chris Dodd served in the Senate. For much of the time the chairman of the UConn Board of Trustees was Lewis B. Rome, a longtime power in state Republican politics but who, like virtually everybody in the political game, liked Chris Dodd personally. Republicans like Rome, Rowland, and the lapsed Weicker were pleased to defer to Chris on a matter of no real significance to anybody other than Chris and his siblings. Why not? If rationalization be needed, they could always point to the million dollars as an explanation for the selection of the name for the building. Those of UConn's innumerable committees that might resist the naming of the building in honor of a disgraced Senator were skirted so as to avoid possible embarrassment.

The Thomas J. Dodd Research Center is a truly beautiful building that is not simply a "research center," a library adjunct and resting place for rarely consulted documents. The center is in constant demand for academic and public events of all kinds. Its meeting halls and Konover Auditorium (named for Mr. and Mrs. Simon Konover, who had been very significant contributors to the university for many years) bring students and off-campus visitors into the building on a regular basis to attend a conference or see a film or go to a concert in the auditorium. It stands next to UConn's main library, the Homer D. Babbidge Library, and the complex formed by the two stands at the academic core of UConn's main campus. Every day hundreds, sometimes thousands, of young people pass its impressive facade. The facade is largely glass, but heavily tinted glass, so one has to enter the door to see, to the left, the impressive bronze bust of Thomas J.

Dodd, a great work of art by Connecticut sculptor Norman Legassie. The bust shows a man of senatorial bearing, a strong man, strong in intellect and strong in character. The Thomas J. Dodd Research Center and the bust of Dodd stand as permanent reminders of the enduring message of Thomas J. Dodd, and as a character reference for

(one can only assume) one of Connecticut's greatest statesmen. Why else would it have been named the Thomas J. Dodd Research Center?

A throng of rock-concert size attended the dedication of the Thomas J. Dodd Research Center on October 15, 1995, including every Connecticut political figure of significance or pretense, with many dignitaries attending from outside the state, as well. Among them were some who genuinely came to pay homage to the honoree, including South Carolina's ancient Senator Strom Thurmond, then 92 years old, and conservative political columnist William F. Buckley, Jr., who had spearheaded a "Justice for Dodd" group in 1966-67 (and who became a member of the Dodd Center's "national advisory board"). President Bill Clinton was the featured speaker, with a few others horning into the program to pay tribute to the honoree, the inspiring fighter against oppression.

The most appropriate of the speakers, however, was Senator Joe Lieberman, who said that the day was one "to witness Chris Dodd's devotion to his father's memory": "What we are all here to celebrate

and admire is the love of a son for his father, the dedication of a son to the memory of his father." That was the truth of the matter.

According to the Dodd Center's website, the ceremony dedicating the Dodd Center

> inaugurated "The Dodd Year," a year-long series of special events, speakers, exhibits, and colloquia. Devoted to the theme of human rights, The Dodd Year recalled Thomas Dodd's participation as a senior prosecutor in the International Military Tribunal, the first of the Nuremberg War Crimes Trials. The Dodd Year program brought an array of world figures to campus, including Madeleine Albright, Elie Wiesel, and Oscar Arias [1987 Nobel Peace Prize winner] and concluded in the fall of 1996 with an address by Mikhail Gorbachev.

The Dodd Year was just the beginning.

The website of the Thomas J. Dodd Prize in International Justice and Human Rights says, "Thanks to the continuing efforts of Senator Christopher J. Dodd and members of his family, in 2003 the University of Connecticut established a new endowment entitled the Thomas J. Dodd Prize in International Justice and Human Rights." The family's

Thomas J. Dodd, Jr., former ambassador to Uruguay and to Costa Rica, addresses a "Dodd Year" gathering.

continuing efforts may have helped *establish* the prize, but the family did not *fund* it. The website goes on: "The Dodd Prize would not be possible without the generous support of philanthropist and businessman John W. Kluge.[63]

The Dodd Prize, awarded bi-annually, is a purse of $75,000 accompanied by a commemorative replica of the bronze bust of Dodd—much as the Nobel Prize is a purse accompanied by a gold medal bearing the likeness of Alfred Nobel. Over the years, the Dodd Prize generally has been divided between two recipients, among the better known of them being former British Prime Minister Tony Blair and Bertie Ahern, the Taoiseach (prime minister equivalent) of Ireland, who shared the award; South African jurist Richard J. Goldstone, chief prosecutor at U.N.-sponsored criminal trials involving Serbian and Rwandan genocides, and in the news in 2010 for his investigation of human rights violations in Gaza; and author Marianne Pearl, widow of *Wall Street Journal* reporter Daniel Pearl, who was assassinated by al Qaeda.

One is reminded of Alfred Nobel, the inventor of dynamite, who converted an iron and steel mill into a munitions factory and became one of the world's leading makers of armaments, amassing a staggering fortune in the process. An obituary was headlined "The merchant of death is dead," and began, "Dr. Alfred Nobel, who became rich by finding ways to kill more people faster than ever before, died yesterday." Actually, the newspaper had made a mistake: The fellow who had passed away was Alfred's brother Ludvig. But Alfred read "his" obituary, and, according to legend, it brought home to him how he would be remembered in history, prompting him to take stock of his moral cupboard. He was profoundly disturbed by its cruel empti-

---

63. Kluge died in September 2010 at the age of 95. His obituary noted that by then financial reverses had reduced his fortune to $6.5 billion, placing him far down on the list of the wealthiest. According to the *Times* obituary, Kluge was frank to admit that he had always been ruled by financial ambitions, and that he held to a simple maxim: make money and minimize taxes.

ness. No no, he did not cease to manufacture armaments, but he did rewrite his will. In the new will he established the Nobel Prizes, including the coveted Nobel Peace Prize. Today the association of Nobel's name with the names of Albert Schweitzer, Nelson Mandela, the Dalai Lama has given a sheen of pacifism to the name of Alfred Nobel and obscured the fact that he was no Gandhi. He was the merchant of death.

Similarly, association of the name of Thomas J. Dodd with the names of Justice Goldstone and the other award recipients, and with the participants in the Dodd Year, lends some of their aura to the memory of Thomas J. Dodd and begins to obscure the fact that on June 23, 1967, the United States Senate had voted that Dodd's continuing conduct over a period of several years had been "contrary to accepted morals, derogates from the public trust expected of a Senator, and tends to bring the Senate into dishonor and disrepute." The only Senators who had stood by Dodd on that crucial vote were the other Senator from his own state, Ribicoff, a "captive" supporter, joined by Strom Thurmond and Russell Long, two good 'ole boys from the Deep South, and one more, John Tower, who, like Tom Dodd, was widely known to have a serious alcohol problem. All of the other Senators joined in condemning his conduct.

With the passage of decades, the Senate vote could begin to be reevaluated. At the official opening of the Dodd Center, while filing out of the building, Bill Buckley privately observed to Hadassah Lieberman, wife of the Senator, "all [Tom Dodd] needed was a traffic cop to tell him these funds go here and those go there." While this infraction led to catastrophic consequences for Dodd, to Buckley's thinking, at its root it was merely a rules-of-the-road violation. From the other side of the political spectrum, progressive politician Bill Curry, Jr., pointed out to readers of *Newsweek* in 2009 that Tom Dodd had "had a testimonial and he grabbed a few grand to pay a couple of mortgage payments. It was just somebody trying to keep his head above water. It wasn't somebody out on a yacht or out with a lobbyist or living a life that remotely approached luxury."

A pencil drawing of an idealized, almost ethereal Senator Thomas J. Dodd adorns the published material of the Thomas J. Dodd Prize in International Justice and Human Rights, and the large heraldic banners that flank the stage at the bi-annual presentation of its award. It is hard to believe that the contemplative, saintly visage shown in the drawing is the same Tom Dodd who as a Senator had celebrated the death of John F. Kennedy, who was among the less conscientious of his peers, the Tom Dodd who had described Americans opposed to continuation of the war in Vietnam as "hippies looking for a piece of the action."

Perhaps none of that had ever happened.

Notes on Sources

Above the Law and James Boyd

As is apparent from the text, in my interview with him James Boyd passed the tests of credibility. In one of his several 1966-1967 *New Republic* columns hostile to Dodd, Robert Yoakum reports that Boyd corrected Yoakum's assumptions about some details unfavorable to Dodd, assumptions Boyd thought unfounded. I had the same experience: In my discussions and correspondence with Boyd, and Mrs. Boyd, they corrected previously published mis-information about the Senator that was unfriendly to him. I was also impressed that Boyd parried my requests that he elaborate on passages in his book that pointed to salacious relationships in the Dodd circle, declining to be drawn into talk that might prove emabarrassing to people who ought to be left alone. Notwithstanding his elephantine memory, he pleaded no knowledge as to the identity of the "mole" referred to on p. 96 herein and in *Above the Law* on p. 78. All of which leads to the conclusion that Boyd is a class act—as well as credible.

Nevertheless, *Above the Law* shouldn't be read as gospel. Among the matters discussed in his book is the to-the-death campaign that Dodd mounted against Boyd, Carpenter, O'Hare, and Golden, in an effort both to punish them for their disloyalty and to discredit the evidence against himself by discrediting the reporters. Dodd, attacked

by dogs (as he must have viewed the four), used his tremendous official and personal influence to deprive them of employment and to
subject them to harassment by the FBI and a team of private investiga-
tors hired by Dodd. At the Ethics Committee hearings, when Carpenter related how Dodd had hounded her out of subsequent employment, the Senator nodded vigorously in agreement.

Boyd responded to Dodd's campaign against himself and his circle. His continuing personal investment in bringing down Tom Dodd
is made clear from Boyd's numerous memoranda to Jack Anderson,
contained in Anderson's personal files (discussed below), intended to
assist Anderson in marshaling the evidence against their joint prey.

Above the Law was written during this period of turmoil. I believe that Boyd attempted in the book to avoid exaggeration of Dodd's
faults—not so much because any sense of fairness outweighed an instinct for the survival of himself and his co-conspirators, but because
Boyd understood that if he were caught in exaggerations it would
detract from his credibility. Nonetheless, some of his recollections
and interpretations were clouded by the emotions stirred up in that
whirlwind in 1966-1968, which must have helped shape the views of
both Dodd and Boyd as to "facts" and also as to what was and was not
"fair." For example:

In May 1963, Robert Lucas, editor of the *Hartford Times,* wrote
Dodd complimenting him on the quality of his speeches and asking him about the role of ghostwriters in their preparation. Dodd's
response (probably drafted by Boyd) is dated May 24, 1964, and is
preserved in Dodd's official files. He replied to Lucas, "It is not infrequent that I make three or four separate statements in a single day
and I follow them up with a formal speech at night. It is, therefore,
obvious that I, or anyone else in my position, must have some help."
As for two particular speeches Lucas asked about, Dodd wrote, "All
of my statements of personal policy or political philosophy such as the
two you mention are my own work."

I did not find a copy of this letter in "Boyd's collection" in the Jack

Anderson papers discussed below; Boyd apparently did not have that letter photocopied, and thus he did not have it before him when he discussed ghostwriting in *Above the Law*. There, presumably working from memory, he wrote that when Lucas asked about the role of ghosts in speech drafting, "I was assigned the task of ghosting a letter from Dodd to Lucas which denied that Dodd ever used ghosts. The Senator did contribute one editorial change, striking the word 'almost' from a line that originally read 'Therefore, the writing is almost always entirely my own.'" The account in *Above the Law* is demeaning to Dodd to an extent unwarranted by the actual correspondence—not a matter of intellectual dishonesty on Boyd's part, but simply evidence that the mind plays tricks in times of war.

Or see the matter of General Klein's letterheads, p. 174.

When I say, "According to Boyd. . ." or "Boyd wrote. . ." I am referring to *Above the Law*. Quotes introduced with words such as "Boyd recently recalled . . ." refer to materials taken from one of several lengthy emails that Boyd sent me responding to specific queries.

I apologize for those instances in which I may have borrowed from Boyd without proper credit—apologies both to Mr. Boyd and to those readers who might view information tracing to Boyd more critically than information that comes from other sources.

Although Boyd's book was the departure point for my own, my work is principally based on the hundreds of passing references to Dodd in books about other public figures or historical events of Dodd's times, on newspaper articles, occasional magazine pieces (Dodd generated surprisingly little magazine coverage), and on manuscript sources.

Thomas J. Dodd Papers

The Dodd papers at the Dodd Center, of course, constitute the most voluminous of the relevant manuscript collections. One gets into the Dodd material via a very thorough finding aid available on the

Internet, which will give the reader a detailed view of the scope and contents of the collection. In the series of boxes related to the Nuremberg trial I found the copy of the Kempka transcript referred to on pp. 30-32. The sketch that "Hitler's chauffeur gave Tom Dodd," however, was not re-gifted to UConn, nor was the collection of Dodd's correspondence to his wife. (Dodd himself believed that Boyd and his group had stolen all of that material from his office files and had never returned it, but the Nuremberg letters were not in the office at the time of Boyd's raids.)

All of Dodd's speeches and press releases from his Senatorial period are also at the Dodd Center; they are more easily accessed there than in the *Congressional Record* or in other sources.

The Dodd collection has been sanitized by removal of those materials obviously related to Dodd's downfall. The long series of files grouped as "Personal Correspondence, 1955-1970," contains no files captioned Dunbar, Frouge, Klein, Kluge, or Spanel (although copies of scattered correspondence sent by Dodd to each can be found elsewhere in the collection).

According to the report of the Ethics Committee to the Senate, the committee turned over to Dodd a set of the materials the committee had received from Pearson and Anderson, and that material is also not to be found at the Dodd Center.

The Dodd heirs bowed to a misguided sense of propriety. The family either destroyed the material not placed in the center or retained it themselves or gave it to UConn with the understanding that it be closed to the public until some date or happening in the future, in an effort to protect their father's reputation from what they thought to be unfair inferences.

The collection's finding aid says that in box 436 is a copy of the "Certificate of Merit" discussed on pages 39-40. The aid seems to be in error: What is to be found in box 436 would appear to be the original of the certificate. The collection also includes, in box 421, file 9493, two well-worn pocket-sized prayer books, *Rosary Novenas to Our Lady* (1925) and *Devotion of the Precious Blood* (1937).

Jack Anderson Papers

Jack Anderson died in 2005 and left his papers to George Washington University in Washington, D.C., and the Anderson collection was opened to researchers at GWU's Gelman Library in June 2010. The Anderson collection includes 13 boxes of material containing the several thousand sheets of confidential materials surreptitiously borrowed by Boyd and his associates, then photocopied, with the originals surreptitiously returned to the Dodd files. That is: George Washington University has a set of most if not all of the material expurgated from the official Dodd archive at UConn. At the Gelman Library can be found the correspondence and documents that support the 100-plus "Washington Merry-Go-Round" columns that focused on Dodd, including the lengthy handwritten letters sent to him by Ed Sullivan, which should have been marked "Burn this letter" (p. 128-131). Along with the correspondence are hundreds of sheets of telephone records (with names of call recipients), ledger pages, income tax returns, Dodd's typed daily schedules, many of Dodd's personally dictated daily minutes—apparently the entire set of the material that brought down Tom Dodd. Some of the files in the Anderson collection retain the original subject headings given to them by Anderson or his staff in the mid-1960s: "Dodd's pampered family," "Dodd's gift shop," "Petty chiseling," "Dodd's bag men."

Still more documents about Dodd are likely to come to light.

On August 20, 2010, I spoke with a Freedom-of-Information officer at the FBI, who advised me that my long-standing FOI request for its files on Dodd was still awaiting processing. The FBI has three lines for the processing of FOI requests—those that the bureau can accommodate without too much difficulty and that are processed reasonably promptly; those that will be somewhat more time-consuming to process, which get handled on a less-urgent basis; finally, the monster requests, which are handled on downtime. Satisfying my request, the officer said, would involve the duplication of 4,600 pages of documents, for which reason the request was going into the queue for monsters, and it was likely to be "another year or two" before the FBI could get to it. When the FBI's carton of documents materializes, I will give it to the Dodd Center.

The Ethics Committee's files will be opened to the public 50 years after the close of its hearings, or 2017. The committee's files will almost certainly contain still another set of the materials photocopied by the Boyd group, plus information that came to the committee from sources other than Anderson—information that may have been unknown to either Boyd or to Anderson.

LBJ Presidential Library and other manuscript repositories

In addition to the Dodd Center and the Gelman Library, I also visited the LBJ Presidential Library at the University of Texas, which has all of the official papers of Johnson and his numerous aides. The papers of Drew Pearson are also at the Johnson Library and contain Dodd material that for the most part does not overlap with that in the Jack Anderson collection at the Gelman Library.

I dipped into the collections of other repositories with the help of their on-staff archivists. The staff at the Truman, Eisenhower, and Nixon Presidential Libraries, all administered by the National Archives, and at the Senate Historian's Office helped me via emails and correspondence, as did the people at the University of Virginia, which has the papers of Homer S. Cummings. There are no Dodd materials of note in the FDR Library, and other than oral history transcripts, none of significance at the Kennedy Library.

In the "manuscripts" class, one should not overlook the oral history collections maintained by Columbia University, the Johnson Library, the Kennedy Library, and the Dodd Center. For my purposes, the most useful of the oral history transcripts were those of interviews with Chester Bowles and Prescott Bush, at Columbia, and Helen Farley and Mary Dodd Dwyer, at the Dodd Center.

Newspapers

I have also relied on contemporary newspaper articles. Dodd's own clipping collection, available at the Dodd Center, was principally culled from Connecticut newspapers by a contracted "clipping service," and it contains numerous duplications of the same AP or UP wires, along with a few stray out-of-state items. The clippings were mounted into unwieldy scrapbooks with Scotch tape that has deteriorated, allowing some clips to come free from their mounts and causing some pages to stick together, and many of the older clips have faded and crumbled, making Dodd's clipping collection somewhat difficult to use.

The archives of the *Hartford Courant,* the *New York Times,* and the *Washington Post* are all available and "searchable"—with "advanced search" tools—on the Internet for a fee. They are particularly useful for "zeroing in" on specific matters. Anyone wanting to undertake newspaper research about Dodd might begin with his obituaries in the *Courant, Times,* and *Post,* all lengthy and very interesting.

Pearson and Anderson's "Washington Merry-Go-Round"

The Pearson and Anderson staff maintained a card file indexing all of the name references in their columns, with dates of publication and a summation of the substance of each reference. The index indicates that the column referenced "Dodd, Thomas J.," 217 times. I am giving to the Thomas J. Dodd Research Center my own set of the index cards listing the Dodd citations, and the final typescripts for 202 of the 217 columns; the Gelman staff is unable to locate 15 of the typescripts. For those 15, I relied on photocopies of the *Washington Post* printout of the columns for the missing dates. Most of the columns published between January 1966 and July 1967 were reproduced in the *Congressional Record* for 1967, pp. 8682-8722, although the columns as published in the newspapers frequently varied somewhat from the typescripts wired by Pearson and Anderson to their subscribers.

While I read all of the columns, I did so only after digesting the raw materials on which they were based, so that for the most part my reportage of the more controversial aspects of Dodd's career is based on the primary sources themselves, rather than on Pearson and Anderson's reconstruction of them.

Most of the "Washington Merry-Go-Round" columns about Dodd track the documentary evidence. Pearson and Anderson did some editing of the primary sources, not made clear in their reports but not in a manner that tampers with the meaning or intent of the originals. As to some of the other columns that are not clearly based on documentary evidence familiar to me, I suspect that Anderson may have become taken up in the chase and may have unintentionally—or even, perhaps, intentionally—made the story "better." A couple of examples:

The "Washington-Merry-Go Round" column of January 7, 1967, reporting Carpenter's trip to Connecticut to deliver Blinken's cash contribution (p. 138) makes it out to be more sinister than Mrs. Boyd reports it to have been in her correspondence with me. Another "Merry-Go-Round" column, of January 25, 1967, reports that on the occasion of Kennedy's death, Dodd stood in front of a TV, air-conducting the funereal music being played on the television. This delicious detail was repeated in Oliver Pilat's well-regarded biography of Drew Pearson. But when I called on them in November 2009, neither of the Boyds, who had been present on the occasion, recalled that particular detail—a detail one would think to have been unforgettable. Could Anderson have been embellishing the story? I included the "conducting" in early drafts of my manuscript but ultimately scratched it from my text.

One of the last columns mentioning Dodd, published June 22, 1972, after Dodd's death, reports that on the day of the censure vote Dodd commandeered a pistol from the cache of gun exhibits kept by the Juvenile Delinquency Subcommittee and carried it onto the floor of the Senate, tucked inside his jacket pocket. I included this dramatic story right up to the last draft of the manuscript, then removed it from the final copy because of my doubts about it.

Congressional Record

One last matter, about the *Congressional Record:* For other than formal speeches, the *Congressional Record* is less reliable than contemporary newspaper accounts because of the willingness of its producers to tamper with the facts of the matter. I have checked the *Record* only to note the discrepancies between its account as to what happened on the Senate floor with what the *New York Times* or the *Washington Post* reported as having happened. When dealing with a Senator as adroit (and crafty) as Tom Dodd, the *Congressional Record* comes pretty close to useless as a research tool.

Bibliography

I HAVE TAKEN SOME LIBERTIES FROM standard bibliographical form in what follows, listing most books by the last name of the author, grouping other books under the name of their subject, and inserting random commentary, but I expect that interested readers will be able to follow it. The list includes only the most useful of the many books and magazine articles I consulted, and it omits all but a few of the thousands of newspaper articles that I read (or at least that passed through my hands).

Bowles, Chester, *Promises to Keep: My Years in Public Life, 1949-1969.* New York: Harper & Row, 1971.

Boyd, James, *Above the Law: The Rise and Fall of Senator Thomas J. Dodd.* New York: New American Library, 1968.

Bumiller, Elizabeth, "Dodd's Other Campaign: Restoring Dad's Reputation." *New York Times,* September 24, 2007.

Burrough, Bryan, *Public Enemies: America's Greatest Crime Wave and the Birth of the FBI, 1933-1934.* New York: Penguin, 2004.

Cone, Stacey, "Democratic Morality and the Freedom Academy Debate: A Conflict About Institutionalizing Propaganda in America, 1954-1968." *American Journalism,* 21(4), 13-38, Fall, 2004.

DeConde, Alexander, *Gun Violence in America: The Struggle for Control.* Boston: Northeastern, 2001. ("Some writers have depicted [Dodd] as a gun-control crusader whereas others have portrayed him as an opportunist . . . " Lets the reader decide which, but gives some hints.)

DeLong, Thomas A., *John David Lodge: A Life in 3 Acts*. Fairfield, CT: Sacred Heart University Press, 1999.

Deming, Barbara, "The Ordeal of SANE." *The Nation*, March 11, 1961. (Memo, David Martin to Dodd, March 11, 1961: "There is a very interesting article on "The Ordeal of SANE in *The Nation* of March 11, 1961. I believe this entire situation is shaping up much as we had hoped it would.")

Dodd, Thomas J., *Freedom and Foreign Policy*. New York: Bookmail, 1962. (Consisting of strung-together speeches ghosted by David Martin and James Boyd, and edited by Martin and Boyd, who also handled the dealings with the publisher. Even Dodd may never have read *Freedom and Foreign Policy*. Dodd retained an outside ghost writer, Ed Lockett, a well-regarded Washington ghost, to prepare a sequel, but nothing ever came of it.)

_____, ed. Christopher J. Dodd and Lary Bloom, *Letters from Nuremberg*. New York: Crown, 2007.

Donner, Frank J., "Is There an Ethic in the House?" *The Nation*, September 23, 1968.

Feldstein, Mark, *Poisoning the Press: Richard Nixon, Jack Anderson and the Rise of Washington's Scandal Culture*. New York: Farrar, Straus and Giroux, 2010. (Dual warts-and-all portraits of two dermatologically challenged adversaries, Richard Nixon and Jack Anderson, not directly useful for information on Dodd but essential reading for anyone appraising Jack Anderson's writings.)

FULBRIGHT, Senator J. WILLIAM: Fulbright has had a good number of biographers, principal among them being Tristam Coffin, *Senator Fulbright: Portrait of a Public Philosopher*. New York: Dutton, 1966; Haynes Johnson, and Bernard M. Gwertzman, *Fulbright the Dissenter*. Garden City, NY: Doubleday, 1968; Lee Riley Powell, *J. William Fulbright and His Time*. Memphis, TN: Guild Bindery Press,1996; and Randall Bennett Woods, *Fulbright: A Biography*. New York: Cambridge University Press, 1995. They all reference pretty much the same material set forth in the text.

Garment, Suzanne, *Scandal: The Culture of Mistrust in American Politics.* New York: Times Books, 1991.

Gentry, Curt, J., *Edgar Hoover: The Man and the Secrets.* New York: W. W. Norton & Company, 1991.

Glazer, Myron Perez and Glazer, Penina Migdal, *The Whistleblowers: Exposing Corruption in Government and Industry.* New York: Basic Books, 1989. (Reports interviews with Boyd and Carpenter done in 1984, 17 years after the censure and 25 years before my visit with Mr. and Mrs. Boyd.)

Gleisser, Marcus, *The World of Cyrus Eaton.* New York: A. S. Barnes, 1955.

Goertzel, Ted, et al, *Linus Pauling: A Life in Science and Politics.* New York: Basic Books, 1995.

Harwood, Richard, "Julius Klein PR Inc: The Image Builder Was Always His Own Best Client." *Washington Post,* July 17, 1966, p.A1. (Harwood, a now-legendary *Washington Post* journalist sometimes known as "Black Death Harwood" because of the fear he engendered in the political community, wrote the fullest sketch of the background of the colorful General Klein.)

Hutchinson, John, *The Imperfect Union: A History of Corruption in American Trade Unions.* New York: Dutton, 1970.

Hyman, Sidney, *The Lives of William Benton.* Chicago: University of Chicago Press, 1970.

JACKSON, ROBERT H.: The biographies of Justice Jackson do not focus on Nuremberg, and lack any significant information about Dodd. The only published items that particularly focus on the relationship between Justice Jackson and Dodd are two overlapping articles by Professor John Q. Barrett of St. Johns University, Jackson's official biographer: "From Justice Jackson to Thomas J. Dodd to Nuremberg," XXVI *Supreme Court Historical Society Quarterly,* I, 6-8- (2005); and "Tom Dodd's Nuremberg," available on the Internet via www.roberthjackson.org.

JOHNSON, LYNDON B.: All of the principal Johnson biographies have references to Dodd, especially references to the selection of the Vice-Presidential candidate in 1964, less about foreign policy issues, and only occasionally about the censure proceedings. For the record, they are: the Johnson trilogy by Robert A. Caro; another three-volume set by Robert Dallek; and Doris Kearns Goodwin, *Lyndon Johnson and the American Dream*. Presidential scholar Michael Beschloss also has two volumes based on Johnson's recorded conversations.

Katz, Milton S., *Ban the Bomb: A History of SANE, The Committee for a Sane Nuclear Policy, 1957-1985*. Westport, CT: Greenwood Press, 1986.

Krosney, Herbert, "Senator Dodd: Portrait in Contrasts." *The Nation,* June 23, 1962. (Probably the most useful of the magazine articles about Tom Dodd.)

Lieberman, Joseph I., *The Legacy, Connecticut Politics, 1930-1980*. Hartford, CT: Spoonwood Press, 1981.

_____, *The Power Broker: A Biography of John M. Bailey, Modern Political Boss*. Boston: Houghton Mifflin, 1966.
(Joe Lieberman's two books of Connecticut history constitute wonderful political reportage.)

Lyford, Joseph P., *Candidate*. New York: Holt, 1959.

Mann, Robert, *Legacy to Power: Senator Russell Long of Louisiana*. New York: Paragon House, 1992.

MANSFIELD, Senator MIKE: David Broder once called Mansfield "the greatest living American," which begins to explain why Mansfield, a dull guy from Montana, has inspired many biographies. I believe that I checked all of the Mansfield books, but the most useful for my purposes were Louis Baldwin, *Hon. Politician: Mike Mansfield of Montana,* Missoula, MT: Mountain Press, 1979; Francis R. Valeo, *Mike Mansfield: Majority Leader,* Armonk, NY: M. E. Sharpe, 1999; and Don Oberdorfer, *Senator Mansfield,* Washington, D.C.: Smithsonian, 2003.

Molzahn, Kurt Emil Bruno, *Prisoner of War*. Philadelphia: Muhlenberg
    Press, 1962.

Mount, Ferdinand, "Dodd and Mammon." *National Review,* July 11,
    1967. (Well-considered analysis of the censure proceedings,
    sympathetic to Dodd.)

National Review, Obituary of Dodd, June 15, 1971. (In Dodd's opinion,
    the *National Review* was the best magazine on the market.)

New Republic (See Yoakum, below)

North American Congress on Latin America, *Guatemala*. Berkeley, CA:
    North American Congress on Latin America, 1974, 1979.

NUREMBERG TRIAL: There is a mountain of Nuremberg literature
    out there. Most useful for my purposes were Telford Taylor, *The
    Anatomy of the Nuremberg Trials: A Personal Memoir,* New York:
    Knopf, 1992 (Taylor, a distinguished civil libertarian, didn't like
    Dodd, whom he regarded as a grandstander, and suspected Dodd
    of allowing his political ambitions to influence his professional judg-
    ments at the trial; Dodd probably didn't like Taylor either); Ann and
    John Tusa, *The Nuremberg Trial,* New York: Atheneum, 1983; Nor-
    bert Ehrenfreund, *The Nuremberg Legacy,* New York: Palgrave
    Macmillan, 2007; Leon Goldensohn, *The Nuremberg Interviews,*
    ed. Robert Gellately, New York: Knopf, 2004; Stave Palmer, et
    al, *Witnesses to Nuremberg: An Oral history of the Nuremburg
    Trials,* New York: Twayne Publishers, 1998; and, of course, Dodd's
    Letters from Nuremberg. Though she does not mention Thomas
    Dodd, anybody interested in the Nuremberg trials should begin with
    Rebecca West's contemporary reportage of the trial done in 1946
    for *The New Yorker,* but more accessible in both of two Rebecca
    West anthologies, *A Train of Powder,* New York: Viking Press, 1955,
    and Rebecca West: *A Celebration,* New York: Viking Press, 1977.

Von PAPEN, FRANZ: Von Papen has generated a lot of literature, includ-
    ing a biography with a wonderful title, *The Sorcerer's Apprentice,* by
    Richard W. Rolfs, Lanham, MD: University Press of America,
    1996. I checked all of them, but the most useful was Von Papen's

own *Memoirs,* New York: E. P. Dutton, 1953; Henry M. and Robin K. Adams, *Rebel Patriot: A Biography of Franz von Papen,* Santa Barbara, CA: McNally & Loftin, 1987, and *The Sorcerer's Apprentice.*

Rovere, Richard H., *Senator Joe McCarthy.* New York: Harcourt Brace, 1959.

"Scrapbook," "The Dodd-Father." *Weekly Standard,* October 8, 2007.

Shelton, Isabelle, interview with Grace Dodd. *Washington Evening Star,* December 22, 1961, p. B-7. (Shelton relays Grace Dodd's exciting first hand account of the assault on the U.N. representatives at the Dodd dinner in Katanga in 1961, regrettably not quoted in the text, and as the account might otherwise be lost to researchers, I am citing it to be certain that others are aware of it.)

Sherrill, Robert, *The Saturday Night Special.* New York: Charterhouse, 1973. (A history of Congressional efforts at gun control by a well-known muckraking journalist, highly critical of Dodd's role.)

Speer, Albert, *Inside the Third Reich: Memoirs.* New York: MacMillan, 1970.

Summers, Anthony, *Official and Confidential: The Secret Life of J. Edgar Hoover.* New York: G. P. Putnam's Sons, 1993.

Tynan, Kenneth, "Command Performance," *Harper's,* October 1960; *see also* "The Easy Chair," being Dodd's rejoinder, and Tynan's re-rejoinder, both in *Harper's,* January 1961.

United States Senate, Hearings Before the Select Committee on Standards and Conduct, United States Senate, Eighty-Ninth Congress, Second Session, on the order of the Select Committee to Investigate Certain Charges Relating to Senator Thomas J. Dodd, Part I, Relationship with Julius Klein. U.S. Government Printing Office, 1966.

_____, Hearings Before the Select Committee on Standards and Conduct, United States Senate, Ninetieth Congress, First Session, on the Order of the Select Committee to Investigate Certain Charges Relating to Senator Thomas J. Dodd, Part 2, Political and Official Finances. U.S. Government Printing Office, 1967.

(The two volumes of transcripts of the Ethics Committee hearings provided the basis for my discussions of Spanel's "ambassadorship," Dunbar's cars, General Klein, the use of testimonial dinner proceeds and the propriety of same, and "double-billing." Much of the crucial evidence was in a long stipulation contained in the second of the two volumes. UConn does not have a set of these two volumes, essential to understanding the namesake of the Thomas J. Dodd Research Center, so I am offering my set to the Dodd Research Center.)

_____, Murder International, Inc.: Murder and Kidnaping as an Instrument of Soviet Policy (Hearing before the Subcommittee to Investigate the Administration of the Internal Security Act and other Internal Security Laws of the Committee on the Judiciary, United States Senate, Eighty-Ninth Congress, First Session, March 26, 1965). U.S. Government Printing Office, 1965. (Dodd's report about Stashynski, p. 181.)

_____, Report of the Select Committee on Standards and Conduct, United States Senate, on the Investigation of Senator Thomas J. Dodd of Connecticut To Accompany S. Res. 112, U.S. Government Printing Office, April 27, 1967. (Reprinted as Appendix Two in Boyd's *Above the Law.*)

Waldman, Steven, "Governing Under the Influence." *Washington Monthly,* January 1988. (According to the colorful Georgia Senator Herman Talmadge, who knew of what he spoke, "Alcoholism is as much an occupational disease among politicians as black lung is among coal miners." Read all about it in this fascinating 1988 piece.)

Wenger, Paul Edwin, *A study of legislative discourse in the censure debate concerning Senator Thomas J. Dodd.* Ph.D. thesis, University of Iowa, 1972, available through University Microfilms. (An academic analysis of the rhetoric and strategies of spokesmen for the Ethics Committee, of Dodd/Long, and also of the "non-antagonist" Senators during the floor debate on the censure motion. I am giving my copy of this scarce but insightful document to the Dodd Center.)

Yoakum, Robert H., "Testifying for Dodd." *New Republic,* March 18, 1967.

————, "The Dodd that Failed." *New Republic,* April 1, 1967.

————, "For Dodd and Yale." *New Republic,* June 3, 1967.

————, "What Hath Dodd Wrought." *New Republic,* July 8, 1967.

————, "Alive and Well in Washington." *New Republic,* February 10, 1968.

> Yoakum also had two lengthy pieces in the *Columbia Journalism Review* in 1966 or 1967, detailing the press coverage in Connecticut of the Dodd scandal, which tell you a lot about the press in general, as well as about Dodd. Unfortunately, I have misplaced the titles and dates of them, and (believe this) the *Columbia Journalism Review* can't provide them!

Zaiman, Jack. Zaiman's columns of classic political reportage are all available by searching the *Hartford Courant* archives on the Internet. Unfortunately, there is no easy way to retrieve the reportage of other perceptive Connecticut political reporters of the period, notably Alan H. Olmstead and Eric Sandahl.

Zelizer, Julian E. *On Capitol Hill: The Struggle to Reform Congress and Its Consequences, 1948-2000.* New York: Cambridge University Press, 2004.

Photo Credits

Virtually all of the photographs in this book were adjusted for contrast, sharpened for printing, or otherwise received plastic surgery from James Luft of Luft/Leone Design, Madison, Connecticut, whose assistance is gratefully acknowledged.

Most of the pictures come from Thomas J. Dodd's personal photo collection housed at the Thomas J. Dodd Research Center, University of Connecticut, Storrs, Connecticut, stored in boxes 424-430, including those shown on pp, xii, 9, 21, 25, 27, 29, 36, 40, 63, 72, 75, 80, 84, 85, 90, 95, 101, 103, 104, 115, 117, 119, 122, 124, 128, 182, 190, 222, 229, and 238. The photo on page 27 showing Dodd and Justice Jackson is from box 371. Virtually all of these photos are unidentified as to source or photographer.

Those taken on October 15 and 17, 1995, shown pp. 236, 249, and 250, are from the University of Connecticut archives (not from Tom Dodd's personal collection), and most of those were taken by the university's on-staff photographer, Peter Morenus, who arrived at UConn just in time for the opening of the Dodd Center, and who still serves at the university. The photo of the interior of the Dodd Center, p. 248, also comes from the university archives, photographer unknown.

Photographs taken at the hearings of the Senate Ethics Committee, pp. 148, 160, 168, 173, 198, 199, and 206, are from the files of the *U.S. News and World Reports,* donated to the photo archives of the Library of Congress and all were taken by its staff photographer, Marion S. Trikosko. Photographs of Norman Legassie's bust of Dodd, frontispiece, of the exterior of the Dodd Center, p. 248, and of the Dodd home piece, of the exterior of the Dodd Center, p. 248, and of the Dodd home in West Hartford, p.49, are by Charlie Croom, photo editor of the *Yale Daily News*. The Dodd homes in West Haven, p.6 and in Lebanon, p. 14, were photographed by the author; the photograph of the Norwich house, p. 3, is by Carl Abissi of Norwich.

The photos of Michael O'Hare, p. 163, and of Dodd with Marjorie Carpenter, p.156, were provided by Marjorie Carpenter Boyd, photographer unknown.

The photograph of Reverend Molzahn on p. 17 comes from the dust jacket of his book *Prisoner of War,* photographer not identified.

The sketch that "Hitler's chauffeur gave to Tom Dodd, " p. 31, is by Erich Kempka, who died in 1975.

The photo of Wilhelm Keitel, p. 27, was taken from the Internet, wiki-media.com.

Index

Bold-faced entries immediately following a person's name refer to the page location of one or more photographs showing that person.

The sublistings under each name are not alphabetized, but are presented in the order in which the subject (insofar as it might involve the main entry in the index listing) first appears in the text.

This index is intentionally rather comprehensive as to names other than Dodd, Thomas J., to compensate for the fact that there is no index reference to the subject of this book.

ABOUT THIS TYPE

Bulmer is the name of transitional serif typeface originally designed by William Martin (1757–1830) in 1792 for
the Shakespeare Press. The fonts used in this book are a
contemporary digital revival supervised by Robin Nicholas at Monotype Imaging, based on a 1928 revival by
Morris Fuller Benton of the American Type Founders.